Jane Pilcher 1990

For RICHER,
For POOR

Contents

Preface

This book is dedicated to my parents, Lore and Wally, who helped me through my own transitions.

The title is taken from an article by Ray Pahl published in *New Society* in 1978. In this he described how he had asked school leavers to write essays imagining that they were sixty-five and looking back on their lives. This marked the beginning of a much larger research project on the Isle of Sheppey in which I was involved first as a post-graduate student and later as a Research Fellow. I am especially grateful to Ray Pahl for his intellectual guidance and support during that stage. My research also owed much to the stimulation and encouragement offered by other friends in Canterbury, particularly Lorraine Hewitt.

Furthermore, I would like to acknowledge the support of Vlastimil Malinek, who patiently taught me word processing and helped to print the final manuscript. Also, Ruth Collinson, Maureen Taylor, and Mary Evans who read the final draft and gave me valuable advice and encouragement. The final version is, however, entirely my responsibility.

However, my greatest debt is to all the respondents and others on Sheppey who allowed me into their lives and about whom it is my privilege to write. In particular, the teachers at Sheppey School – Richard Barson, Ian Gliddon, Jane Washford, and many others. Also the staff at the Careers Centre – Rosemary Gallagher, Eileen Spiers, Derek Bignall, and Tony Turner. To Dennis Grover and his family for looking after me and to Chris Zammit and her family, Joe and Anita, who taught me about life on Sheppey.

Finally, I am grateful to the ESRC and the Joseph Rowntree Memorial Trust for financial support whilst the data was being collected and to the Department of Social and Political Studies at Plymouth Polytechnic for administrative and technical support including access to a micro-computer.

1
Introduction

One of the founding principles of British society between 1945 and the 1970s has been that of 'full employment'. During this period it was thought that employment was available to everyone who wanted it, and this view served to fashion the way in which people left school, started work, and began families. Employment has traditionally been one of the determinants of adult status and citizenship, and it also serves to determine social identities in other respects – which class an individual belongs to, their lifestyles and their status as 'men' or 'women' are all determined by the kinds of jobs they find.

During the 1970s, mass unemployment became recognized as an enduring structural feature of the labour market. This has had particularly serious repercussions for young people's jobs, so that leaving school no longer leads automatically to starting work. For many people, their social status, their role in the community, and their role within the family have had to be reconstructed and this has important implications for young people who are encountering these problems for the first time in the post-war period.

I have described 'full employment' as a 'principle' since it was never universal and it applied mainly to men's experience of work. At the same time that men's employment was decreasing, women's was increasing, and the long-term changes that have taken place are better characterized as part of an on-going process of restructuring in employment. Hence, part-time work and home working are actually on the increase. Whilst traditional manufacturing industries have suffered during the economic recession, other industries have been established, resulting in a shift of employment between sectors and between regions (Gregory and Urry 1984). There has been a consequent collapse in traditional training places for young people and increasing intervention by the state in the transition from school to work through the Youth Training Scheme and other schemes designed to equip them for the new world of employment that no longer seems to want them. Despite the unevenness of these changes, and the fact that 'full employment' was never a possibility for everyone, it is possible to say that young people leaving school now are facing a very different set of employment prospects to those who left ten years ago. Sociological models of 'youth' need to be recast as a result.

In this book I examine the effects of employment and unemployment upon young people leaving school, entering new relationships, and growing up. This can be seen as a *process*, a series of events taking place between leaving school and entering early adulthood. Here it is traced by following a cross-section of young people over a five-year period from when they were sixteen and (in most cases) leaving school until they were twenty-one.

'Youth' and 'young people' are in many respects social categories that are actually defined by employment. The age at which a young person can become a young worker has been set at sixteen since the raising of the school-leaving age in 1972. From this age onwards they are potentially able to start families, although the age at which they do this in practice varies according to class and gender. Hence, the way in which family formation takes place is in many ways dependent upon the labour market situation of different social groups, the different training, pay, and conditions of boys and girls, skilled and unskilled manual workers, clerical workers, professional and managerial workers (Wallace 1987). To give a stark example, a working-class girl may be earning a living at sixteen and engaged to be married or expecting a baby at the same time. She perceives herself as an adult. A middle-class man at twenty-two will probably still be studying and may be financially dependent upon his parents. He perceives himself as in a transitional stage between childhood and full adult status. In this way the various 'transitions' into adulthood are determined not just by legal age thresholds but also by social and economic contexts. Furthermore, whatever the 'official' definitions of transition, these are in fact perceived and experienced in different ways by different groups of young people. Indeed, the 'official' definitions are themselves in a state of flux at present with young workers (or potential workers) being defined as 'trainees' on lesser incomes until the age of eighteen, and the age of dependency being defined upwards to twenty-five by the new social security regulations. Although the minimum school-leaving age is fixed at sixteen, the precise age at which young people make these other transitions is variable and I have followed them until they are twenty-one – by which time they are in a variety of situations.

The main theoretical context within which this study is set, is that of social and cultural reproduction.[1] Growing up – whether in or out of work – is not just a question of getting older. It is a question of becoming fully socialized young men and women who are able to take up their respective roles in society. Leaving school, leaving home, and forming a new household represent critical moments in this process, for these are the stages at which a person actually enters new sets of relationships. The way in which cultural and social reproduction takes place through the transition from school to work has been extensively discussed and documented (Jenkins 1983; Willis 1977). The main argument is that leaving school and starting work is not a traumatic experience for young people because they have already been socialized into the appropriate roles at different levels of the class structure. They are thus 'reproduced' as workers. The different emphasis placed upon economic or ideological determination in this process varies with the different contributors to the debate (for example Bowles and Gintis [1976] are examples of the former and Bourdieu and Passeron [1977] of the latter approach). Similarly, the emphasis given to parents or peer groups as mediums of reproduction likewise varies (see for example Carter's approach in 1961 compared to Willis's in 1977). However, what all the studies of cultural reproduction with respect to young people have in common is a focus upon the articulation of the education system with the economy – the 'economy' meaning the masculine world of full-time employment – the very world embodied in the ideology of 'full employment'. A whole number of studies have argued that the world of work has entered young people long before they have entered the world of work (see

Roberts [1984] for an overview). Nevertheless, the *point* of reproduction is the transition from school to work and this has been
the subject of a range of studies over the post-war period, as well
as a topic of some wider concern (see Clarke [1978] for a review of
these).

However, most of this discussion took place before the advent
of mass unemployment. I begin with the proposition that rising
unemployment and the restructuring of the labour market have
led to a potential 'fracture' in the process of social and cultural
reproduction. The roles into which young men and women have
been socialized by school, family, and normative social expectations are no longer available for everybody. What are the consequences of this? From this general research problem there spring
four more hypotheses which the study addresses.

First, it is evident that social and cultural reproduction imply
primarily the reproduction of employment roles. Young men and
women come to accept the jobs available to them and might even
look forward to doing those jobs. Expectations transmitted by
parents and peers are futher reinforced at school and this takes
place in different ways at different levels of the education system
and the labour market (Bourdieu and Passeron 1977; Bowles and
Gintis 1976; Jenkins 1983). In this way the work-force is reproduced. However, the collapse of jobs in the traditional manufacturing sector and the disappearance of many types of industrial
training means that many of the jobs young people traditionally
entered are no longer there; they may well have to enter new
kinds of work. The first hypothesis, then, is that there is likely to
be a 'fracture' in the reproduction of work roles.

Secondly, employment roles have implications for the reproduction of leisure styles and youth cultures. Popular conceptions
of 'youth' and sociological studies of youth have often focused
upon distinctive youth culture and youth leisure styles that have
been at least partly determined by the level of young people's
wages and spending power (Hall and Jefferson 1976; Mungham
and Pearson 1976). The post-war explosion of youth culture was
based to some extent upon their position as an 'affluent' group in
the labour market serving to supply and create commercial markets (Abrams 1961). It was also based upon young people's relatively privileged position as supported dependents within the
family so that to some extent other financial responsibilities were

removed. Thus they were able to spend their money on clothes, records, and magazines. This pattern too is threatened by mass unemployment and the combined effects of the Youth Training Scheme and other schemes – such as the Young Workers' Scheme – in depressing young people's wages. Some studies have described a resultant 'culture of unemployment' replacing one of affluence (Roberts, Duggan, and Noble 1982a). Here we can draw upon social psychological studies of unemployed young people that have sought to demonstrate exactly how and why young people suffer from unemployment. Is this reflected in their subcultural responses? The second hypothesis, therefore, is that there is likely to be a 'fracture' in the reproduction of youth cultures and leisure styles.

Third, the restructuring of the labour market has implications for the reproduction of gender roles. Gender identities – often inherent in work roles and in youth culture – are learned, reinforced, or undermined in the course of leaving school and embarking on adult life. Since many of the 'traditional' ideas of gender identity – such as that of man as bread-winner with dependent spouse – are constructed around the idea of full employment, it is possible that 'traditional' gender identities are being challenged. The third hypothesis is therefore that there is likely to be a 'fracture' in the reproduction of gender roles.

Fourth, the restructuring of the labour market has implications for the reproduction of the family. Many studies have indicated the importance of the family for the activities and ideologies of workers (e.g. Goldthorpe *et al.* 1969) mostly taken from the viewpoint of the male bread-winner. More recently there have been a number of studies of women and the way in which the private and public spheres are connected in their experience (Hunt 1980; Porter 1983). The interrelationships of home and work-place are particularly important during the course of life-cycle transitions, for it has been traditionally assumed in our society that starting a family means that the male head of the household should have a job. Do young people start families on the 'dole'? In the case of young people two families are of relevance – that of origin and that of destination. Hence relationships with both sets of relatives are explored here. The fourth hypothesis is therefore that there is likely to be a 'fracture' in the reproduction of the family.

As with approaches to employment, studies of youth have

traditionally been studies of male youth only or have portrayed all young people in terms of masculine models. More recently studies have been undertaken of young women in an effort to compensate for this (Griffin 1985). This has led to some fresh insights into youth. The main one in this respect is that the issue of gender has been raised more generally as being a crucial, but neglected part of the process of social and cultural reproduction (MacDonald 1980). Indeed, feminists and others have laid emphasis upon a different aspect of social reproduction – they have focused upon the role of the family rather than the work-place in reproducing a class- and gender-divided society (Barratt 1980; Barratt *et al.* 1979).[2] By incorporating this expanded model of social and cultural reproduction into the study of young people, it is possible to provide a more comprehensive account of life-course transitions. Furthermore, in this research I have tried to apply some of the insights derived from feminist discourse to the study of young men as well as young women. Hence gender is taken to be a problematic category, a social construction, and issues of both male and female sexuality are explored along with the importance of domesticity for each gender.

The current restructuring of the labour market has implications for the way in which youth are studied sociologically. However, the growing youth 'industry' means that many of the issues raised here may also be of more general interest. The way in which youth have become of increasing interest to the outside world, and the attempts to structure their transitions through state intervention makes an appreciation of young people's own experiences all the more important. Moreover, the various 'moral panics' about youth that provide the backdrop to such interventions – panics about unemployment, drugs, riots, and potential teenage promiscuity – make a dispassionate appraisal of the *real* changes in the conditions of young people's lives essential.

How the research was done

Many studies of young people have tended to favour qualitative approaches, seeking to understand the subjective experiences of people being interviewed. This has become associated with a more 'feminist' or 'radical' approach to social science.[3] However, this assumes that samples are fairly small and makes it difficult to generalize trends. In this research I attempted to combine this kind of approach, which involves participant observation and lengthy in-depth interviews, with more quantitative survey data. Thus, qualitatively derived insights could be tested against the larger sample, whilst excerpts from interviews and research situations could be fitted into a framework of general trends.

A quantitative presentation of findings can also be valuable when collecting longitudinal data over a spread of people and social groups. This is not necessarily a less empathetic method. Indeed, it is arguable that people's experience can be de-contextualized, fragmented, and reified as much by isolated quotations as by numbers. In writing this book I was presented with a problem: how was it possible to portray both the subjective experiences of young people and the more general variations in responses across the sample at the same time? How could I be sure that I had understood these subjective experiences when the data was filtered through my own subjective experience of interviewing? I have attempted to overcome this difficulty as much as possible by presenting a variety of different data sources. Case studies, participant observation, and tabular information are presented at different points in the book, and in different ways. By allowing the reader to become familiar with the situation of young adults as described by them in their own words through the case studies, it should enable more theoretical issues and more quantitative data to be situated in context, making the intuitive, empathetic understanding a part of the reader's analysis as well as the researcher's. For this reason, I have included myself as a participant in the dialogue, since the researcher is also a part of the research process rather than a transparent, supposedly 'objective' analyst. This should allow the reader to form an impression of what it is like to be in a given situation. The names and personal details of all respondents have, of course, been altered to preserve confidentiality.

The presentation of the case studies in Chapters 5 and 8 also reflects my own methods of recording data at different points in time. The first round of interviews in 1979 and 1980 and the participant observation at the time was recorded in a detailed field diary or in notebooks. In the final round of interviewing in 1984 each interview was tape-recorded and I was able to transcribe many of them. Hence I am able to present edited transcripts.

The research was carried out on the Isle of Sheppey in Kent. The island was originally chosen as a research base because it had suffered high unemployment – roughly twice the national average – since the naval dockyard had closed some twenty years previously. From a practical point of view, this provided a readily identifiable community and local labour market to study. Moreover, there was one large comprehensive school containing 565 fifth-formers at the time and the staff there kindly gave me access to it.

There were three waves of surveys. In the first survey, begun as part of my Ph.D thesis in 1979, I contacted 153 sixteen-year-old school pupils, drawn from a mixed ability division at the local comprehensive school. This constituted approximately a quarter of that age group on the island. Roughly half of these were girls and roughly half were boys; some stayed on at school and later went to university, others went to college, but the majority left at the minimum age. The sample was skewed somewhat towards minimum age school leavers, as these were the ones that I was primarily interested in at the time.

For this reason I endeavoured to include the Easter leavers in the sample.[4] This research was combined with participant observation at the school, in youth clubs, and in the non-institutional spaces colonized by young people, including the beach, the coffee bars, and the high street. However, these 'spaces' were mainly populated by disaffected school students and truants; the more sheltered, 'respectable', and scholastically inclined youth were more likely to remain at home. Consequently, the survey was necessary in order to obtain a greater spread of responses and to compare different life-styles. The research was facilitated by the fact that I actually lived in the community for nearly a year and one of my addresses was an established meeting point for the young unemployed. The people of the household helped me to see a whole side of society of which I had hitherto been only dimly aware and I find it difficult to think of this phase of the field-work without visualizing some of our many conversations in the pub or the living room. This provided a wealth of material and an opportunity to check accounts given to me in interviews, but also inevitably led to some compromising situations. For example, I had to ignore some of the less officially sanctioned practices that were going on both in the so-called 'black' economy and elsewhere.

In 1980, I re-interviewed 103 of these young people after they had been in the labour market for one year.

In 1984 I obtained a grant from the Joseph Rowntree Memorial Trust that enabled me to carry out a third survey of the same young people. This time they were twenty-one and just entering adulthood. In this last survey I was more concerned with other aspects of social and cultural reproduction: how had patterns of work and unemployment affected the transition to marriage and parenthood? Only eighty-four of the original respondents could be traced in this last survey, but this is nevertheless a representative cross-section of the young people in the area, being a 15 per cent sample of all young people of that age on the Isle of Sheppey. These three rounds of interviews form the basis of the material to be presented in the book.

The sample drawn in this research is not large enough to make statistical predications about Great Britain as a whole, but it is large enough to indicate trends that might be occurring and to construct some tentative models of social reproduction. Furthermore, the combination of methods enables us to consider the lives of young people holistically rather than in the limited way afforded by surveys, and thus lends itself to other kinds of insights. Other more quantitative studies currently being carried out may well provide more generalizable evidence of these trends.[5]

This study was further supplemented by material collected through a large ESRC-sponsored project on the Isle of Sheppey. During this time, a team comprising Ray Pahl, Nick Buck, Jane Dennett, Frances Evans, Bill Gourley, and myself documented household work strategies through a sample survey and also assembled information about the local labour market, the history of the island, patterns of housing and residence, and so on, all of which provided invaluable background material for my study of young people.

The background to each of these questions and hypotheses will be explored more fully in the relevant chapters. First, however, this particular study needs to be set within its geographical context and so Chapter 2 provides a general description of the Isle of Sheppey – its geography, the labour market, and the education system. The remainder of the book is divided into two parts. Part One covers the period after leaving school using data from the

1979 and 1980 surveys. These are covered in Chapters 3 and 4 respectively. Part Two of the book covers the period when these young people were twenty-one, derived from the 1984 survey. Chapter 6 describes their experiences in and out of work and Chapter 7 concentrates upon their family and personal relationships. These are illustrated through case studies in Chapters 5 and 8.

2
Introducing the Isle of Sheppey

The Isle of Sheppey is set in the Thames estuary, separated from the rest of Kent by a muddy tidal stretch of water. On either side of the channel is an expanse of marshland, grazed by sheep. A road–rail bridge joins the island to the mainland, and driving across it means leaving behind the cosy patchwork of neat Kentish orchards, for Sheppey presents a very contrasting impression: that of a declining industrial area. At first sight the landscape, otherwise bare and treeless, appears to be littered with the debris of de-industrialization in the form of empty factories, abandoned machinery, and residential areas that have declined as industry and people moved elsewhere. However, the island has a colourful history, for, situated at the confluence of the Thames and Medway rivers, it has been of strategic military importance ever since it was first occupied by the Danes as a base for raiding England. [1]

The main road leading towards Sheerness docks, the major commercial port, is a busy thoroughfare with articulated lorries bringing goods in and out. Lines of Japanese-imported cars waiting to be taken away cover the land in every direction around the road. Approaching Sheerness, the steel mill looms ahead. Usually shrouded in a pall of orange-coloured smoke, it is a major source of employment for adult men and is surrounded by black piles of twisted metal and slag.

The population of 33,053 [2] is scattered around the four main residential areas with one or two farms and small villages between them. At the northernmost tip of the island lies the town of Sheerness. The older part, known as 'Marine Town' was built to house dockyard employees during the nineteenth century: the architecture of the houses reflects the periods of dockyard expansion. The streets are laid out in a grid-iron pattern with a network of narrow alleyways connecting them at the back. Some houses, freshly painted in bright colours, with picture windows and pebble dashing, reflect the attempts of their owners to refurbish them with the help of home improvement grants. Other houses are damp and decaying, as this part of the town has been subject to flooding from the sea. The more modern area of Sheerness, comprised mainly of council estates built since the war, is known as 'Mile Town'. Here houses are widely spaced along lengthy, wind-driven avenues, and residents have to endure long, uncomfortable walks to the nearest shop or pub in return for their larger gardens and increased privacy.

The town of Sheerness is the focus for teenage life on the island. A short walk up the high street enables people to encounter most of their acquaintances locally. Indeed, for teenagers, parading up and down the high street is a pastime in itself. At the centre stands the town clock, the site of drunken New Year revelries that occasioned the only arrest for rioting in Kent in 1981.[3] On each side of the high street are well-known pubs with particular reputations. At one end, is an old-fashioned mirrored bar where the local prostitutes consult the shipping almanacs to prepare themselves for the arrival of their customers from off the boats. Further along the high street is another pub that has become the local drugs mart. Still further along are the large, ostentatiously decorated pubs and discotheques where teenagers go on a Saturday night out. Dressed in smart and fashionably skimpy clothes that defy the weather, they move from one location to the next in a restless search for 'talent' and excitement. Meanwhile, many of their parents are in the smaller, shabbier 'locals' or working men's clubs where sing-songs are held at weekends.

At the end of town is the market-place and amusement park and from there one can walk onto the beach. In summer, the centre of adolescent life shifts to the sea front where young men and women walk up and down displaying their torsos and tattoos, or sunning themselves.

The old town of Queenborough is only two miles away, and yet it is claimed locally that the inhabitants speak with a different dialect. This is where all the older factories are found. The ancient high street was familiar to Lady Hamilton and Hogarth, but most of the population nowadays live in older terraced housing or council estates.

Moving towards the centre of the island on elevated land, lies Minster. Here, many of the houses are individually built and designed by the owners themselves or by small local builders, and give names such as 'Shangri-La' or 'Buona Vista' (Wallace with Pahl and Dennett 1981). Many of the more prosperous local people are able to move there: the image of the self-made, self-employed, and self-building man is a popular local archetype.

Between Minster, Queenborough, and Sheerness lies the aptly named 'Halfway', site of the Sheppey Comprehensive School and Careers Centre. Some new, tidy housing estates have sprouted around the fringes of Halfway and their relative cheapness attracts commuters.

Moving eastwards, we come to Leysdown, a traditional Londoner's holiday resort before cheap packaged tours tempted them abroad. The holiday camps take the form of lines of peeling chalets and caravans enclosed by grim, barbed-wire fences: some Londoners nevertheless return to enjoy the long, sandy beach and knees-ups in the local pubs. In winter Leysdown is boarded-up, but in summer there is a colourful parade of amusement arcades, fun-fairs, and bingo halls. Small stalls containing a cornucopia of balls, jaunty hats, and sticks of rock spill into the road. Most of these stands are staffed by young people, either still at school or after they have left, who find jobs through friends of friends. Leysdown's prosperity depends to a great extent upon this reservoir of juvenile labour.

For the teenager, one of the most important features of Leysdown is the discotheques, which attract bus-loads of visitors from as far away as London. Each disco is extravagantly constructed around an imaginary theme: a tropical island or a futuristic, science fiction fantasy. For the local residents and police these are better known for the fights that break out outside them.

From Sheerness there is a view across the Thames estuary towards the lights of Southend. When the tide is out, the beach is furrowed with lines of lumpy mud where lug-worm diggers and cocklers have been searching for a harvest. This can provide a convenient extra income for the young, who can earn £3.50 for

100 worms (in 1984). They now complain that as unemployment has risen, so the beach is becoming exhausted. The surrounding creeks and rivers also provide a living for fishermen and casual work for the young people and others who help them, whilst the marshes are full of rabbits that can be trapped and sold: many young boys own a couple of ferrets.

There are many myths about the Isle of Sheppey. Some refer to it as the 'Septic Isle' because of its reputation for social problems, and others claim that it is renowned for violence and juvenile delinquency. However, the 1981 census data, and those derived from a sample survey carried out by Social and Community Planning Research in the same year,[4] would suggest that Sheppey is fairly similar to the rest of England. The age structure is much like the national pattern, but the social structure is skewed slightly towards more working-class occupations and 88 per cent of the population had left school by the time they were sixteen (Pahl and Wilson 1984). Despite this predominance of working-class households, there is a slightly higher percentage of owner-occupiers on the island – 69 per cent – as against the national figure of 56 per cent. This is partly a consequence of the island tradition in home construction and partly a reflection of the low cost of housing locally. This is important because it offers the opportunity to pursue 'housing careers' or the gradual improvement of the living conditions of the household through moving home every few years. This also provides a basis for cultural divisions between 'rough' and 'respectable' households based upon the ownership and physical maintenance of property (Wallace 1984).

The island has two main youth clubs and one police station. Its reputation for juvenile crime led to its being chosen as the site of a 'community policing' style experiment involving co-ordination between the different agencies responsible for young people. However, many of the crimes prevalent on the island are those associated with poverty, such as breaking into gas meters, or 'stealing electricity' by tampering with the meter.[5]

The education system on Sheppey

Some of the most pernicious myths about Sheppey are those concerned with the education system. When I first arrived I was informed that the Sheppey school was a place from which children emerged as wild and undisciplined unemployables. This was contrasted to the 'good old days' when lads learned a skill and son followed father in a respectable tradition of dockyard employment. The 'good old days', however, were based upon the idea of full employment for men – for girls there appeared to be fewer opportunities than there are at present. Although the Sheppey school had adopted a progressive 'community school' approach to education it was held responsible by some for the educational and employment problems of its pupils. This can be explained to some extent by the cultural traditions in the community, and by the relationship between schooling and the local economy.

For nearly 200 years, until it closed in 1959, the naval dockyard had been the dominant employer on the island. The education system on the island had evolved to suit the needs of the dockyard so that the technical boys' school served to select apprentices for the dockyard through the examination system that continued for the purposes of promotion and selection within the dockyard itself.[6] Those who gained the highest grades could enter the prestige trades by becoming a shipwright, or an electrical or engine fitter, whilst those who failed became labourers or entered the local factories. It would be difficult to find an example of an education system so neatly reproducing the work-force as that in Sheerness.

Fathers encouraged their sons to do well and to enter prestige trades, for this secured the reputation of the family. An indication of the importance of this is given by the fact that ex-dockyard workers in their seventies and eighties remembered their precise grade and place in the examination system even to this day:

> 'Oh, if you passed the dockyard exam, then your name was on the front page of the *Guardian* when it was published. My father never forgave me. . . . I got 999 marks, and he never forgave me 'cause I didn't get the thousand, out of 1500. . . . I couldn't make the thousand mark and he never forgave me for it.'

> (Buck 1981: 76)

The dockyard shaped the character of the community in other ways too. Graduates of the dockyard apprenticeship system became teachers and local government officers, ensuring the continuity of traditions. The hierarchy of trades and skills was also reflected in the residential organization of the town. Dockyard workers dominated most of the social activities including the numerous chapels, the Co-operative Society and the working men's clubs. The structure and layout of different forms of housing in Sheerness mirrored the different grades of workers, so that positions within a competitive education system ultimately determined future life chances in a very direct and obvious way. This was a very male-dominated tradition of male-dominated employment and fitted with the 'traditional' conceptions of the male bread-winner determining the status of the family within the local community.

After the dockyard closed, the educational system was reorganized, and a new comprehensive system introduced in 1970. The first headmaster to be appointed was Cyril Poster, a respected advocate of community schooling. His book, *The School and the Community* was published in 1971, shortly after he took up his new post. In the book he argued that the community school should provide a broad-ranging inter-disciplinary curriculum and should aim to educate young and old on the same premises – the assumption being that education was good for both the individual and the community. He encouraged the development of links with the local community:

> 'The importance to the community school of these curricular developments cannot be underestimated because they identify needs and problems of society, they lead students to become concerned about the quality of that society. Education becomes relevant. . . . It is difficult to see how any school that aspires to the title of community school can fail to bring social service within the curriculum. Only thus can investigation of the needs of the community be linked with planning to meet those needs.'
>
> (Poster 1971: 81, 84)

This optimistic conception of education was based upon what Poster regarded as the problems of modern society. These he attributed to the decline of the traditional 'community', which resulted in social disintegration and anomie. The school, he argued, should compensate for this decline by providing an alternative community that could overcome many of the social problems associated with young people. The school was housed in a purpose-built 'campus' in the centre of the island. Although Cyril Poster is no longer the headmaster, many of the community school ideals live on, albeit in a manner modified to fit Sheppey.

By 1979, when I started conducting my field-work there, it was the largest school in Kent, with 1,846 pupils. The school was concerned to foster links with the local community and to provide an education sensitive to the needs of the locality.[7] This was put into practice in a number of ways. First, the school attempted to provide a wide-ranging, technologically and vocationally orientated curriculum: students were as likely to be taking 'Design Technology' as 'Maths'. They were also encouraged to undertake practical work in the community as part of their studies. Second, there was a policy of flexible sixth-form entry in order to be responsive to the needs of young people in a declining labour market, and a range of one- or two-year vocational courses were available at a post-compulsory level.[8] Those leavers who had not found jobs were allowed to drift back at the end of the summer, or even later than that, and sometimes drifted out again when they found that it did not suit them. Third, there was concern to develop a relationship with local industrialists so that the school could provide an education responsive to their needs. This was done through participation in committees and staging conferences that brought together educators and local businessmen.

Rising youth unemployment has made an impact upon the school. As Watts (1983) has indicated, it leads to an incipient crisis in educational goals: on the one hand there is a greater emphasis upon success in examinations in order to find a job, but on the other hand there are fewer jobs, and so this striving is likely to lead to more disappointed young people. The stress on qualifications at an individual level merely increases the competition for jobs at a collective level. This paradox was recognized by teachers at the school. As one told me in 1984: 'We have to balance educational needs with responsibility for the individual and these are in some ways incompatible. We've been successful so far in using the examination carrot, despite unemployment, but it's beginning to look increasingly dishonest'.

Thus, whereas the dockyard-based education system had evolved tight organic links with the local economy based upon access to jobs for boys, the comprehensive system tried to self-consciously recreate this sense of community and forge links with the local economy – only now there were fewer jobs for boys and the nature of jobs for everyone had changed.

From my interviews it appeared that whilst the more middle-class and educationally motivated students appreciated the open and liberal structure of the school and the wide range of subject options available, the more working-class students were often alienated eductionally and hence critical of the school. As Bazalgette (1975) has observed, those from less privileged backgrounds lacked the confidence to utilize the 'market' system of education effectively.

Some saw the solution in more coercive forms of schooling. They regretted the absence of corporal punishment and school uniforms, and they blamed the educational failure of their children on what they perceived to be the casual organization of the school. Thus, the open school did not overturn traditional attitudes and 'restricted' codes of behaviour. Paradoxically, they were reinforced.

Perhaps ultimately, the community school failed to achieve some of its more Utopian objectives because, whatever its organization, the school inevitably fulfils goals set outside its perimeter fence and many of these are antithetical to the 'community' ideal: it encourages competition rather than co-operation and individualism rather than communalism. To a great extent the social structure of the school inevitably reflects the divisions in society. Even an 'open' style school embodies a hierarchy of power and serves to grade and select students in such a way that some will be labelled as educational 'failures'. These tendencies have been accentuated in the context of economic decline as educational goals become more narrowly focused and pressure to pass examinations increases.

I have indicated that educational goals and experiences need to be situated in the context of the local economy and social structure. The reorganization of the education system on the island coincided with important changes in the local labour market and the social composition of the island. It is to this that I now turn.

The local labour market

The concept of a 'local labour market' generally presents a number of analytical problems, since it is difficult to define its boundaries. The local labour market on Sheppey, however, was relatively easy to define, since it covers all those industries on the island and a few on the nearby mainland which recruited people from the island. Being a relatively isolated location, a large number of local people work in a small number of local industries. Whilst a proportion of adult workers may commute elsewhere, young people's opportunities were concentrated more locally as they lack the transport and resources to move further field (Youthaid 1981).

There have been a number of models of labour market segmentation dividing jobs between the 'primary' and 'secondary' sectors. The primary sector contains internal labour markets with high pay leading to promotion and stable employment: dead-end, insecure, low-paid jobs are therefore found in the secondary sector (Barron and Norris 1976; Doeringer and Piore 1971). More recently, it has been argued that labour markets are segmented in more complex ways by sex, skill, age, and ethnicity rather than being divided into just two sections (Ashton, McGuire, and Garland 1982; Jenkins 1983). However, most of these studies are cross-sectional in nature – they look at labour market divisions at a single point in time. It is also helpful to consider how patterns of segmentation have changed over time. Despite the criticisms of the dual labour market concept, it is nevertheless useful for considering historical changes in the context of this study.

On Sheppey, the transition from a stable and prosperous, relatively 'full employment' economy to an unstable one with high unemployment occurred in 1959 when the dockyard closed (Pahl with Dennett 1981; Wallace 1985). The dockyard displaced 2,500 workers, and although many of the skilled craftsmen moved to other dockyards (especially Chatham, which later closed too), the island never recovered from the rise in unemployment this precipitated. Another important consequence was that the tradition of skilled craft training for boys, which had shaped the prevailing attitudes to education and the cultural ethos of the island, was broken. Careers Office records indicate that in 1979 nearly all the industrial training places were provided by firms elsewhere in Kent, whereas in the 1950s, these had been provided by the local dockyard as part of a father-to-son tradition.[9] Whilst in retrospect this was perceived by many locally as the 'golden age' of full employment, it should be remembered that the dockyard never did provide employment for all young people on the island, and what it did provide was mainly craft training for boys. [10]

After 1960, the firms that came to the island offered very different kinds of employment. For men, there was heavy, unskilled labouring with secure, high-paying jobs in some industries and insecure, low-paying jobs in others. School leavers were excluded from the high-paying sectors, being for the most part too young or not physically strong enough. Thus, whereas the primary labour market had previously been distinguished by internal promotion and training, it was now distinguished by high wage levels and job security. Young people were displaced into the secondary sector. For women, there was unskilled factory work, mainly in electrical assembly, and the garment manufacturing firms that arrived during the 1960s. Despite being described as 'semi-skilled' these jobs required considerable manual dexterity, but the wage levels were roughly half those of the average man (Pahl with Dennett 1981). Young girls competed for these jobs alongside older women. Unlike the naval dockyard, with its well-established ladders of internal promotion for young men, the new jobs offered little opportunity for individual advancement locally.

One important feature of this new labour market was that some firms subcontracted 'out work' to be undertaken for piece rates at home. It was more common to find women at home in the evening doing electrical assembly in front of the television than it was to find them knitting. Children and the young unemployed could help with this too.

One important contrast between the adult and youth labour market was in the size of the employers. Whereas most adults were employed in large industries (Pahl with Dennett 1981) Careers Office statistics covering all school leavers indicate that 43 per cent of young people were employed by small employers, some of whom were family members and some were seasonal. Small employers often provide insecure jobs and are less likely to provide formal training programmes or apprenticeships. Most of their training is of an informal nature. They are also likely to pay lower wages, are less likely to be unionized, and are perhaps more prone to exploitative practices. Moreover, these small businesses cannot offer 'internal' labour markets in the same way as large firms and are therefore 'secondary' in several senses.

Figure 1   Unemployment Rates 1961–1981

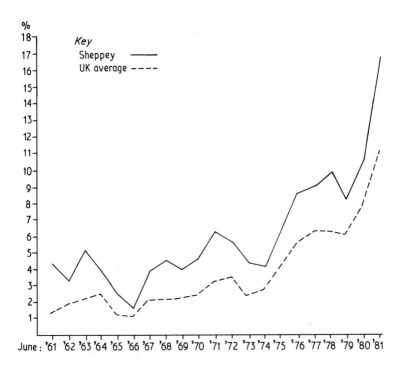

Sources: Manpower Services Commission; Sittingbourne Job Centre; Department of Employment Gazette

Unemployment on Sheppey

Some have argued that youth unemployment is an amplified version of adult unemployment (Makeham 1980; Raffe 1984), whilst others have argued that it is 'structural' in character, reflecting long-term changes in the labour market as a whole. On Sheppey, the rate of unemployment rose steadily in advance of national trends (see *Figure 1*) However, this should be seen in the context of the structural changes in the labour market already described.

The labour market on Sheppey can be compared to those described in a study by Youthaid (1981), which surveyed 250 young people in three different regional labour markets: Newcastle-upon-Tyne, London, and rural Northumberland. This survey, consisting half of girls and half of boys was carried out in the same year as my own first survey. The results are set out in *Figure 2*.

Figure 2   Comparison of skill levels between Youthaid survey and Sheppey

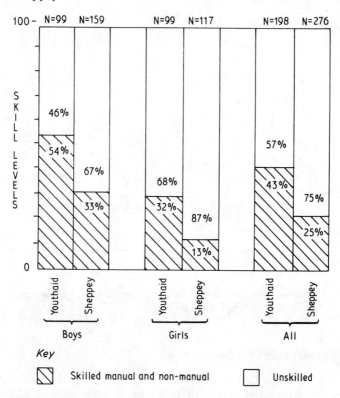

Sources: Youthaid (1981), vol. 1, tables 8.7, and 8.8, Sheppey Careers Office

Youthaid noted that there were regional variations in the search for apprenticeship training and that this reflected 'cultural labour market traditions' (1981: vol. 1, p.62) but in general, the demand for apprenticeship places outstripped the supply, especially in the declining areas. In Sheppey, only 25 per cent of all young people obtained apprenticeship and clerical places, as against 43 per cent elsewhere, which reflected the structure of the local labour market.

Special measures on Sheppey

Before concluding this description of the labour market, it is necessary to consider the role of government special measures, since many of the 1979 school leavers either went straight onto these schemes or were recruited later in their post-school careers. At this time, of course, such schemes mainly took the form of the Youth Opportunities Programme (YOP) lasting six months and intended only to 'mop up' the most disadvantaged unemployed teenagers. My respondents were able to enter the scheme direct from school because the Isle of Sheppey was granted a special status under Manpower Services Commission (MSC) regulations. This has since been replaced by the Youth Training Scheme (YTS) and a new package of measures designed to provide a comprehensive training programme for the first year after leaving school. [11] Despite this change in philosophy and in duration of the scheme, many have argued that it functions in a similar way to YOP in offering an alternative to the dole for school leavers and a source of cheap labour for employers. Here I shall discuss special measures in relation to the YOP scheme since this covers the period we are concerned with. However, many of the observations could also be extended to the YTS.

The YOP and related schemes aimed ostensibly to provide 'training' and work experience for otherwise unemployed school leavers, on the assumption that this will improve their job prospects. In the words of the Holland Report:

'Each individual opportunity within the programme should be designed so as to increase the options for the individual. . . . Each component of the new programme must therefore be designed to enable the individual to do more things, achieve higher level of skills, knowledge and performance and adapt more readily to changing circumstances or job requirements. The question should be "What is he capable of?" rather than "What is he qualified to do?" '

(Holland Report 1977: 34)

However, in the context of a declining labour market where there is little need for higher levels of skill, knowledge, and performance, it is difficult to see how they could fulfil the goals set out above. Indeed, since only a shrinking minority actually find work after leaving schemes, their function has been more one of 'containing' young workers.

The schemes are nationally co-ordinated but their implementation is regionally disparate. Therefore, whilst some schemes operating on Sheppey were the same as those elsewhere, others were distinctive.

The YOP schemes were divided into several distinct branches: short industrial courses, youth and community projects, and work experience programmes (WEP) many of which were carried out on employer's premises. The youth and community projects comprised some workshops for groups of young trainees and teams of young people under the supervision of an older trainer who travelled around the district undertaking non-profit-making ventures of benefit to the community in a broad sense. For example, they renovated a churchyard, rescued a scouts' hut from vandalism, and prepared a bird sanctuary. The girls were more likely to be sent to work for the social services, helping in nurseries , or old people's homes, and other kinds of feminized caring work. These youth and community projects were more person-orientated and they attempted to adapt the scheme to the needs of the individuals on them. However, because of the greater flexibility of these schemes, they often tended to receive those school leavers who were hard to place, or who were deemed to have behavioural or learning difficulties.

By far the most important YOP scheme was the Work Experience on Employer's Premises (WEEP). The WEEP schemes were the most numerous because they were popular with employers – being a means for screening potential recruits – and with the MSC because they were much cheaper than other schemes and more convenient to administer.[12] These schemes, however, were less popular with trainees who often thought of them as exploitative, since the trainee was paid an 'allowance' for doing a full-time job alongside workers who were often paid twice as much. Those who were taken onto these schemes needed to fit employers' needs, and the Careers Service and MSC were concerned to send them suitable trainees in order to retain their support, so the young people on these schemes tended to be the most competent and conventionally 'employable'.

It is difficult to estimate to what extent 'substitution' was taking place, since those employers who took young people under the YOP schemes tended to be the very ones that recruited large numbers of young people in any case. [13]

These schemes were similar to the national ones. The Youth Opportunities Programme has since been superseded by the YTS, which has been in turn restructured and extended to two years. The Short Industrial Courses (SIC) have been replaced by day-release components for all trainees. The tendency to expand Mode A at the expense of Mode B places however, reflects the same kinds of pressures as were described for the YOP. [14]

In addition to these nationally operated schemes there was also an initiative that was unique to Sheppey, a project called 'Swale Work Initiation Measures' (SWIM), which was launched by employers and the local authority together in July 1981. This initiative sought to create an infrastructure for new industries on the island. It was hoped that the schemes set up under the auspices of SWIM would become self-funding in time. It was applauded by Roger Moate, the local MP, and by the *Financial Times* as Kent's 'self-help' answer to youth unemployment, and it was opened by the then Employment Secretary, Jim Prior. In many ways this was perhaps an early prototype for other more profit-orientated schemes that became national policy later. At the time of my field-work in the area, SWIM was not able to provide all the employment originally hoped for, although it has since assumed far greater importance.

Indeed, it could be argued that to some extent the fortunes of government special measures depend upon the conditions in the local economy: in times of expansion they can provide a route to employment, but in times of contraction they are often merely a poor substitute for real jobs. Nevertheless, such measures have now become an important intermediary stage in the transition from school to work and there are important differences in the quality of the different schemes currently operating.

The emphasis on schemes of a 'work experience' rather than 'job creation' variety may in fact have served to diminish the real employment opportunities for young people through substitution, rather than increasing them. One effect they will certainly have had is to redistribute employment and unemployment across a broader range of young people by providing temporary rather than permanent employment. Moreover, two-thirds of the YOP places went to boys, reflecting the gender imbalance observed nationally (Deem 1978).

Conclusions

I have tried to show the interrelationships of education, the labour market, and the MSC at a local level in order to provide a context for the experiences of school leavers to be discussed in subsequent chapters.

In the local labour market there has been an historical tendency towards re-segmentation and de-skilling. Whilst the naval dockyard was in existence, the labour market was segmented according to one model: the primary sector may have been low-paying but it led to a 'career' for some men. Young people had access to this primary labour market as well as the secondary one, depending upon their school performance. Since 1960, however, the pattern of segmentation has changed. The primary sector now consists of high-paying, secure but not necessarily skilled jobs for adult men. Young people and women are relegated to the secondary sector. Their school performance is less relevant to these labour market sectors.

The nature of changes in employment had important implications for the education system. The tri-partite system had served to reinforce the division between primary and secondary labour markets, whereas the segmentation in the labour market at present is based more upon gender, age, and the nature of the industry than upon qualifications (except for that small minority who went on to further training). Consequently, despite the efforts of the Sheppey school to integrate education with the needs of industry, these were constrained by the nature of the local and national economy.

This serves to create one form of disjunction in the course of the transitions that are the subject of this book. Whilst the dockyard exerted its hegemony, family ideals and traditions, educational careers, employment careers, and positions in the community, all served to reinforce one another for men. This in turn reinforced the position of the male head of household, transmitter of craft traditions, and the importance of craft skills generally in determining masculine status. Education served as a form of 'legitimation' for other roles and positions. However, under present conditions, the sort of cultural reproduction necessary to produce heavy unskilled labour for men and a docile but dexterous work-force amongst women is irrelevant or even antithetical to meritocratic and individualistic educational goals. School becomes less relevant to the needs of the community not because it fails to impart sufficiently high educational standards, but because the values it attempts to transmit are not required for most jobs. This serves to de-legitimize education: it can no longer provide the ticket to a good job, or indeed – in some cases – to any job.

PART ONE

After school 1979–1980

Who when looking over
Faces in the subway
Each with its uniqueness
Would not, did he dare,
Ask what forms exactly
Suited to their weakness
Love and Desperation
Take to govern there

Would not like to know what
Influence occupation
Has on human vision
Of the human fate:
Do clerks for instance
Pigeon-hole creation,
Brokers see the Ding-an-Sich
As Real Estate?

(*From* 'Heavy Date', *W.H. Auden 1939, reprinted by permission of Faber & Faber from* Collected Poems *by W.H. Auden.*)

3
Into work

The transition from school to work has been the subject of numerous studies in the post-war period (Clarke 1978). These studies are inevitably based upon an assumption of full employment: that there should be a job for every school leaver was axiomatic. The question was: what kind of job?

Some answered this question by showing how the values school leavers derived from their homes would determine their future careers (Ashton and Field 1976; Carter 1962, 1966). Later studies showed how capitalism was reproduced through the education system, which divided young people into working and middle class (Corrigan 1979; Willis 1977). Most agreed, however, that labour market destinations were based not upon 'occupational choice' so much as upon socialization processes taking place *prior* to leaving school (Roberts 1968). Thus home backgrounds imparted sets of values that were either affirmed (in the case of middle-class youth) or disaffirmed (in the case of working-class youth) once they arrived at school. On leaving school young people replicated the values embodied in their home and school experience, and so working-class youth accepted that they were going to do working-class jobs and middle-class youth, middle-class jobs. Subjective perceptions of status fitted with objective labour market conditions. The subdivisions within these two classes operated in the same way, with upwardly aspiring youth heading for short-term manual careers via apprenticeships or clerical training and 'rough' youth heading towards unskilled labouring jobs (Ashton and Field 1976). This can be termed the 'equilibrium model' and represented diagrammatically in *Figure 3* on p. 32.

Figure 3 The Equilibrium Model

The home	Education	Employment
Middle class: professional and managerial workers	Higher education Grammar school Top streams of comprehensive school	→ Professional and managerial training 'Extended career orientation'
Lower middle/upper working class: skilled manual and clerical workers	Specialist vocational courses Lower streams grammar school Middle streams comprehensive schools Top streams secondary modern school	→ Apprenticeships and clerical training 'Short-term career orientation'
Working class: manual workers	Bottom streams comprehensive and secondary modern schools Leave at minimum age General vocational courses	→ Manual work 'Careerless orientation'

Source: Adapted from Ashton and Field (1976: 21)

In the 1960s, this process was thought by some to lead to a 'wastage of talent' amongst working-class young people and this was a source of some concern. For example, the Newsom Report (1963) argued that the economy would expand and society would benefit generally if school leavers at the bottom end of the spectrum could be persuaded not to pursue 'dead-end' jobs but to raise their aspirations and continue at school or pursue further training. However, this was in the context of an expanding economy. No one doubted that there would be jobs for all those with raised aspirations to fill.

Others argued, however, that at a global level the education system merely served to reproduce the needs of the capitalist economy, the main one being for a docile and divided labour force (Apple 1982; Althusser 1971; Bourdieu and Passeron 1977; Bowles and Gintis 1976). This was the context in which the concept of social and cultural reproduction was developed, for it provided a wider theoretical framework within which to situate the transition from school to work, and thus constituted an advance in the conceptualization of this field (Cohen 1985). However, even this model of social reproduction assumed that there are jobs there to fill. Furthermore, it presented social reproduction as a smooth, circular, and timeless process – in other words, it emphasized the *continuities* between school and work rather than the *discontinuities*, leading to criticisms that it was functionalist (Jenkins 1983).

Rising unemployment served to challenge these assumptions. Employers complained that young people were not being socialized to their satisfaction whilst the educational currency was devalued through certificate inflation: 'Employers are reluctant to recruit young people into permanent jobs. They complain that young people are not sufficiently motivated before the age of 25 to justify expenditure on training programmes and give them job security' (OECD 1977: 42).

Employers also claimed that school leavers lacked the kinds of work skills that would make them employable (Colledge 1977; Holland 1977). Rather than the work-force being functionally reproduced, there is a *mismatch* between school and work for which both young people and the education system are blamed (Finn 1982). This can be termed the 'mismatch model' and is represented diagrammatically in *Figure 4* on p. 34.

Figure 4 The mismatch model

The home	Education	Employment
Middle class	→ Higher education Leave school with A-levels	→ Professional and managerial training
Lower middle and upper working class	→ Vocational courses Leave school with CSEs and O-levels	Apprenticeships and clerical training Skilled 'better' training schemes
Working class	→ Leave school minimum age with few or no qualifications	Manual work and unskilled training schemes Unemployed

What emerges from these accounts is the idea that young people are in some way deficient. It is argued that young people are unemployed because they are undisciplined, lack the right skills, and are expensive to train. Paradoxically, although sociologists had shown how young people had been socialized to accept their positions in the occupational hierarchy, employers argued otherwise.

All the studies of the transition from school to work have been criticized for failing to consider adequately young women's experiences. They have either explicitly excluded girls or simply assumed that young men and young women were the same.[1] Feminist critics, by contrast, have argued that the transition from school to work, is structured by patriarchal relations – the domination of men over women – so that young women's experiences and work trajectories are very different from those of young men and require a separate set of explanations (Griffin 1985; Griffiths 1986).

To begin with, processes of socialization are different between boys and girls, with girls being encouraged both directly and indirectly to take more 'feminine' subjects at school, such as arts and domestic subjects, and to subordinate their long-term careers to the interests of marriage and a family (Deem 1978; Griffin 1985; Sharpe 1976; Spender and Sarah 1980). The general conclusion from those who have addressed this issue is that girls are therefore doubly oppressed: by class and by sex.

Once they leave school, girls' opportunities are circumscribed by patriarchal assumptions in the labour market including indirect as well as overt sexism. Because employers believe that their lives will be dominated by domesticity, girls are not considered worth training. They get the lower status, lower paid jobs with little in the way of 'internal career ladders' and generally poorer prospects. These assumptions are reflected in girls' own preoccupations with romance and motherhood (Deem 1978; McRobbie 1978; McRobbie and Garber 1976; Sharpe 1976).

With these general models in mind, how was the transition from school to work experienced by young men and young women on Sheppey?

Empirical work on the Isle of Sheppey

The original 1979 sample comprised 75 boys and 78 girls. *Figure 4* indicates that some three-quarters of them left school at sixteen

Figure 5   Qualification levels of Sheppey School leavers on leaving school 1979

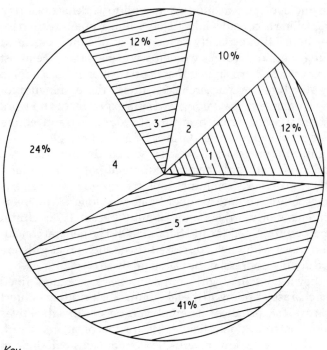

Key
1. A-levels
2. Entering further education
3. Leave school with O-levels
4. Leave school with CSEs
5. Leave school unqualified or do not know exam grades

Source: Sample survey of Sheppey School Leavers 1979, Total = 153

with O-levels, CSEs, or no qualifications. Some minimum age school leavers had enjoyed their school days but were looking forward to starting work and beginning the next phase of their lives. However, many others were seeking to escape from school, especially those fifty-three who left at Easter without any qualifications. They had little prospect of doing well at school and felt disassociated from educational values. They often resented the arbitrary restrictions imposed by the school and expressed their discontent by playing truant or doing spare-time 'odd jobs' instead. Many claimed to be looking for work rather than going to school. Ten per cent of all school leavers stayed on at school or went into colleges of further education in order to pursue vocational education such as secretarial or pre-nursing courses. More girls than boys pursued this route, although boys were more likely to obtain training at work. The remaining 12 per cent stayed on at school in order to take A-levels and go on to higher education.

All school leavers were asked what sort of work they were seeking. The results are set out in *Figure 6* along with the way in which they hoped to pursue that kind of work. It would be wrong perhaps to describe their replies as ambitions, for it has been convincingly argued that minimum age school leavers do not have 'ambitions' or 'choices' in the same way as middle-class ones do (Corrigan 1979; Roberts 1968; Youthaid 1981). Nevertheless, many of them did have specific employment goals, which might be described as 'aspirations', and even those without specific aspirations often had clear ideas about which kind of work they preferred to do.[2] These preferences could be negative as well as positive in nature, and young men and women often began by stating emphatically what kinds of work they were *not* going to do.[3]

It can be seen from *Figure 6* that a small minority of the sample (14 per cent) sought professional training of some variety, such as managerial and technical jobs, or teaching, mostly by remaining at school to take A-levels. In addition, 7 per cent sought clerical work either through staying on at school for a one-year training course, or by leaving to seek work. A further 9 per cent wanted to join the armed forces and 26 per cent expected to find unskilled work. However, the most popular jobs were in skilled work, sought by 43 per cent of the sample. In this category I included girls who were intending to become nurses, most of whom went to further education colleges first. Others tried to find jobs as apprentice hairdressers or working with animals in some specialized capacity. For boys 'skilled work' mainly took

Figure 6 Employment aspirations and the pathways into work

Aspirations 1979	Methods of achieving aspirations		Total school leavers		
Professional and managerial work	Via higher education	18	Boys	13	⎫
	Via employment post	4	Girls	9	⎬ 14%
Clerical work	Via further education	5	Boys	1	⎫
	Via employment	6	Girls	10	⎬ 7%
Skilled work and caring work with training	Via further education	12	Boys	41	⎫
	Via formal training	35	Girls	25	⎬ 43%
	Via informal training	19			
Unskilled work	Shop	10	Boys	11	⎫
	Outdoor labouring	14	Girls	29	⎬ 26%
	Factory	10			
	Other	6			
Armed forces			Boys	9	⎫
			Girls	5	⎬ 9%

Source: Sheppey School Leavers Survey 1979. Total = 153

the form of craft skills such as carpentry, welding, plumbing, mechanics, and so on.

Occupational aspirations broadly fitted educational credentials and parental background, although parents and children from all sorts of manual backgrounds tended to see skilled work as a good trade for a young man. This perhaps reflected the more long-term historical patterns of employment for men in this particular labour market. Longer-term social mobility will be explored later, but at this stage young people appeared to fit the 'equilibrium' model.

Aspirations and destinations

Those adopting the 'equilibrium' model argue that the aspirations are attuned to labour market conditions: most school leavers more or less get the jobs they expect. What jobs did they get on Sheppey?

Table 1 cross-tabulates first jobs found with occupational aspirations for all those for whom I had information. The numbers along the diagonal axis represent those who found the jobs they sought. Those to the left of the line are the ones who found better or equivalent jobs, and those to the right of the line are the ones whose first jobs were at lower level than that to which they had aspired. It can be seen that only a minority of school leavers found the jobs they wanted. The majority had to settle for less – many of them entering unskilled work. Altogether, over one-half of those who had sought craft or office training were disappointed. This led them to modify their aspirations. Those who had sought to secure places on formal company training programmes faced fierce competition, with up to seventy applicants for each place. By September, many of them had applied to a dozen or so companies and, when they failed to secure a place, sought inferior apprenticeships with small local employers. A further strategy to emerge after young people had left school was to enter the YOP in the hope of securing suitable training and work experience. Consequently, there were two kinds of YOP trainees: those who were 'instrumentally' orientated and therefore enthusiastic and those who joined to avoid becoming unemployed and were therefore more likely to become disaffected.[4]

By the time they left school, young people no longer fitted the 'equilibrium' model, for labour market conditions had changed. There would thus appear to be evidence of a 'mismatch' between levels of aspiration and labour market conditions in this locality in 1979. This is because there were very few training or clerical places available in the labour market and even those which had existed had been cut back severely during the 1970s, as was demonstrated in the previous chapter. There was thus a *disjunction* between socialization processes in education (which in turn reinforced home background) and opportunities in the labour market. In other words, subjective perceptions of status did not fit objective labour market conditions. Given the nature of these preferences and the mismatch between aspirations and destinations identified in the survey, it seems appropriate now to consider some of these job aspirations in more detail.

However, it should first be noted that a number of these disappointed school leavers explained that they were doing seasonal or 'filling in' jobs that they regarded as temporary whilst they continued to search for other employment. For this reason job

Table 1 Aspirations by first jobs found: 1979 school leavers

Aspirations	First job found							
	Professional/ managerial	Clerical	Formal skilled and caring	Informal skilled and caring	Armed forces	Unskilled	YOP scheme	%
Professional managerial	(4)							4
Clerical		(4)				3		6
Formal skilled and caring		2	(9)	10		11	2	49
Informal skilled and caring			1	(5)		10	3	
Armed forces		1			(7)	3	1	11
Unskilled						(28)	5	30
%	4	6	9	14	6	50	10	109

Notes: Ten of the 119 minimum age school leavers are not included here, having emigrated, fallen pregnant, or their destinations were not known. Total = 109

Figure 7   Job destinations of 1979 and 1980 school leavers

Kinds of work sought		First job 1979[a]		Numbers having done that work by 1980[b] †	
			%		%
Professional and managerial work		4	4	3	3
Clerical work		7	6	10	10
Skilled work and caring work with training	Via formal training	10 }	23 }	12	12
	Via informal training	15 }			
Unskilled work	Shop	55 }	50 }	22	21
	Outdoor labouring			21	20
	Factory			33	32
Armed forces		7	6	13	13
YOP schemes		11	10		
		N = 109*			

Sources: a Sheppey School Leavers Survey 1979. N = 153
          b Sheppey School Leavers Survey 1980. N = 103

Notes: * Only 109 people actually *entered* the labour market in 1979 from total of 153
          † These do not add up to 100 per cent because people may have done more than one kind of job, in which case they are counted more than once in this column only

preferences will be discussed with reference to the 1980 survey when young people had been one year in the labour market. These are set out in *Figure 7*.

The kinds of job preferences held by school leavers reflected the kinds of identities they saw themselves as having. These were determined by the occupational culture of the job and by the kinds of definitions of masculinity and femininity these served to construct. They also depended upon 'rough' and 'respectable' orientations, as Jenkins (1983) has shown. Here I shall describe the main categories of employment mentioned by school leavers, excluding those who continued in education and had not yet entered the labour market. The classification is therefore defined by them.

Why did school leavers choose different jobs?

Clerical work

It is evident from *Figure 6* that 7 per cent preferred clerical work and these were generally girls who saw themselves as having a neat, respectable image. Whilst not being particularly scholastically oriented they accepted the importance of qualifications on the whole and were well liked by teachers. One group preferred to stay on at school in order to improve their record of qualifications and undertake the short two-year business training course available in the sixth form.

Sharpe (1976) has indicated that girls often preferred clerical work because they had unrealistically glamorized impressions of what it entailed. They thought that it was an opportunity to dress up and meet people when in fact it often involved very menial, monotonous, and increasingly deskilled work. This may be the case, but it was certainly cleaner work than that in most factories, and at least offered some prospects for training and promotion. However, despite being higher in status, office work was lower paid – a sacrifice which many girls were prepared to make, since the majority of these preferred to be unemployed or even to take part-time work or YOP schemes than to resort to factory work. These were often the alternatives that faced them, for due to the short supply of office work locally, nearly all of these girls had had to endure periods of unemployment by the following year (*Figure 7*). The six who had resorted to factory work to avoid unemployment had soon left these jobs, which they lacked the cultural resources to endure. This will be considered later.

For the two boys who undertook clerical work, it was an alternative to skilled manual apprenticeship training, when they failed to find places.

Skilled manual and caring work

The majority of boys and girls, however, preferred skilled work of some variety. For boys, this included the traditional craft trades, such as carpentry and mechanics, whilst for girls this included clerical work and one of the several caring 'semi-professions', such as nursing or nursery work. There were three different strategies for pursuing skilled, caring, and clerical work. The first was to remain in the education system and improve qualifications either at school or at college. Half of those seeking clerical work followed this route, and most of them were girls. Girls pursuing the caring semi-professions usually began with a pre-nursing course at college to fill time until they were old enough to commence formal on-the-job training. The second way was to secure a place on a formal training programme as the majority of this group of school leavers tried to do. A third strategy was to seek some kind of informal training whilst learning on the job, without necessarily signing indentures or acquiring a certificate. This was the preferred strategy for those school leavers who had been strongly discontented with school and looked forward to starting work as a means of escaping from the classroom. They could obtain the skill without the burden of more studying. One-third of boys seeking craft skills pursued this avenue. It is not surprising perhaps that those pursuing the first two strategies emphasized the importance of educational qualifications, whilst those following the third saw them as irrelevant. Some school leavers resorted to the armed forces as the most reliable way of acquiring useful and thorough training of some kind.

Those pursuing the third strategy had problems explaining their aspirations to a careers officer, who invariably encouraged them to go on to further education or otherwise improve their record of qualifications. This was greeted with little enthusiasm by such school leavers, for whilst they had broadly realistic aspirations – in the sense that they recognized that becoming a carpenter, for example, was a realizable prospect whilst becoming an astronaut was not – they did not necessarily recognize formal qualifications as the way to achieving these goals. They regarded the possession of a practical concrete knowledge as being of a different order to the abstract intellectual capacities necessary in order to pass examinations. They thus maintained the division between mental and manual labour by arguing that they were 'good with their hands' whilst qualifications were for 'brainy' people. Some jobs, they argued, only needed people 'good with their hands' whilst others needed 'brains'. This argument is perhaps based on a fallacy, for even digging a hole in the road requires considerable mental as well as manual dexterity, but it did provide a way of inverting the emphasis placed on manual and mental skills by the education system and thereby rejecting the negative status this had imposed upon them. Whilst teachers saw them as 'fit only for manual work', in the words of one respondent, young men regarded some manual work as embodying an enviable status. However, at the same time it implicitly accepted the educational classification imposed upon them and reinforced the mental/manual division of labour (Browne 1981). It should be noted that this fitted masculine conceptions of power and status within the community. For girls, the sources of status to be derived from clerical work or the caring professions were rather different.

Why was skilled and caring work so popular? One answer would be related to the point just made: it demonstrated a capacity to create and to transform the world, and ultimately to earn a living. It thus preserved a sense of self-esteem through building an alternative identity based upon occupational cultures.

Responses were gender specific. For girls, their skill preferences were extentions of feminine roles more generally. Hence, hairdressing was related to a concern with appearance and nursing or caring for animals, the sick, or the handicapped was an extension of maternal roles within the home. However, at the same time girls had very positive commitments to these jobs in occupational terms. They offered a secure professional identity and a career structure:

> Jane: 'The job satisfaction is the most important and you do get that in nursing. It's not like factory work where you're trapped in. And you can always aim higher in nursing, there's a career structure.'

Young women were likely to mention that they saw such jobs as being more intrinsically worthwhile in the social division of labour generally and that it gave them a chance to be involved with people:

Mandy: 'It's the job satisfaction, not the pay that's important. I like meeting people, and you meet more in nursing. Just working at Canning Town Factory (her present employment) would drive me batty, it's not going anywhere. I have to go and do something, not sitting there all the time, doing the same thing. There's more variety in nursing. You're always learning something, not like in a factory.'

Thus, aiming for a traditionally feminine occupation was not incompatible with a career orientation. However, girls appeared to have a more humanistic orientation to their work in the sense that caring for, or meeting people, was more important than financial rewards. In this way they perhaps implicitly accepted the dominance of the male 'bread-winner' ideology in which they would not have to support others on their income. This is despite the fact that women very often do play an important economic role in the household, so that Land (1978) has estimated that one in six households are wholly or partially dependent upon a female wage-earner. This humanistic devotion to a job almost as a 'vocation' also stems perhaps from the nineteenth-century view of women's professions such as nursing as embodying a sense of self-sacrifice and feminine duty. This too contributes towards an anti-instrumental approach to feminine careers.

Hairdressing was the most popular craft aspiration for girls as it offered both a skill and, in the long term, considerable flexibility in exercising it. Eight girls sought apprenticeships in this trade and recruitment was mostly informal in character, vacancies being notified through personal contacts. Most girls who found hairdressing vacancies had been working in these shops on Saturdays already in the hope of being taken on permanently.

Some girls however did not seek traditional feminine employment. Three girls wishing to become mechanics had applied to garages but they were unsuccessful as no garages were recruiting apprentices at the time. Two of these girls then applied for YOP schemes in the hope of finding the right kind of training, but were sent to work in shops instead – to which they strongly protested. The third girl joined the army as a trainee driver. A fourth girl applied to a merchant navy training course, and was told to apply again when she had improved her maths sufficiently to pass the entrance test, but she abandoned the idea at that stage.

Instead she went to work temporarily as a deck hand aboard a sailing yacht in the Mediterranean.

Clearly, these girls were exceptional but they did represent just over 6 per cent of all female school leavers and illustrate the point that whilst for some girls occupational preference reinforced traditional feminine roles, other girls resisted them. This is an issue that also emerged in relation to domestic roles, as I shall demonstrate later.

It is significant, perhaps, that although girls were keen to undertake traditionally masculine crafts, boys showed no inclination to pursue traditionally feminine ones at this stage. On the one hand this reflects the higher status and rewards associated with masculine crafts, and on the other it is consistent with the tendency – described elsewhere in this study – for boys to maintain more rigid gender stereotypes than girls.

Boys, like girls, regarded skilled work as more varied, creative, and interesting than other employment. Like girls, too, they saw craftsmen as being people with status in the community and performing jobs that were more useful and important in their perception of the social division of labour as a whole:

'I just want an apprenticeship. It doesn't matter what, but not in stupid things. You see, you need metal work for instance. Some things there's no need for, like painting, but you need metal work to make tools. It's useful, and there are career prospects as well. And job satisfaction.'

But skilled work had another crucial advantage. Acquiring a skill allowed a man to become self-employed later and thus have greater independence and control over his work. As one lad put it: 'Well, you're your own boss, aren't you; You do what *you* want.'

Furthermore, in a declining labour market craftsmen would be the last out of work: even if they found themselves unemployed, they could always resort to doing jobs 'on the side' if necessary:

'I would like to get a career. The pay's not very high (in an apprenticeship). It could be better, but you earn quite a bit when you come out. And you can do little bits on the side too, when you come out . . . You see, labouring's all right, but it's not secure.'

As one boy said: 'There'll always be a need for plumbers, won't there? Even if all the firms close down.'

Paradoxically, the importance of acquiring craft skills – both in terms of social status and job security – increased in conditions of declining employment, the same conditions that led to craft training being cut back. However, for those who found the training they sought there were considerable personal rewards, as this lad describes it after having worked for his brother's building firm for a year:

'I thought I wanted to *be* something. There's carpentry and there's bricklaying in building. I thought you didn't need much intelligence to be a bricklayer, but it's quite hard really. But it's outside, and I like that. I did a bit before I left school. You've got to stick at something and do it well, that's my motto. It's always at the back of my mind that. My brother's a bricklayer, and the other one is a carpenter, so I did bricklaying too . . . there's more enjoyment in bricklaying, I enjoy doing it. It's more outdoors really, more achievement. You see what you've done and you think to yourself, "I built that, I have!" I do lots of jobs – painting and that to help out, glazing and artexing. I'd crack up in a factory. We had a job down the steel mill one time. . . . they were like morons walking around in there, as if there was no time of day. I would never work in a place like that, it would crucify me. I like my freedom.'

How did those seeking craft skills fare after a year in the labour market?

There were forty-seven school leavers originally seeking craft skills who were followed up in 1980. The first group – roughly one-third – did find some form of training, although not many of them had stayed for long. Only two boys had managed to secure a place with one of the large regional employers. Others applied to some of the small local employers, including some of those who had been unable to find a place with one of the larger employers. Small employers more often recruited by personal contact, and two boys were employed directly by their own families. Small employers therefore used particularistic recruitment strategies and they were responsible for employing a high proportion of male school leavers. Large employers, on the other hand, were more reliant on formal credentials or entrance tests:

they used universalistic selection criteria. This helps to explain why boys with no qualifications were just as likely to secure a training place as those with qualifications at this level of the labour market.

However, these small local employers proved to be an unreliable source of training – several of them defaulted on their promises of training and two went bankrupt. This left only seven young people altogether who had managed to find training places that were still secure one year later. Three young workers left their apprenticeship complaining that they did not like the employers or the conditions of work: it appears that an 'apprentice' was often a euphemism for a cheap young assistant.

Forty per cent had abandoned their aspirations and most of these were girls. This was partly because there were fewer opportunities for girls to pursue alternative strategies and, as is evident from the case study of Michelle in Chapter 8, they were more likely to face opposition and discouragement. The girls who had wanted to train in traditionally male crafts were amongst this group.

Altogether, roughly half had pursued their training in other ways. These included joining the army, joining a YOP course that appeared to offer the skills they were seeking, and working in establishments in an unskilled capacity but with the hope of learning skills informally or eventually becoming an apprentice. Examples of this latter strategy were two boys who sought to become carpenters by working in furniture assembly factories. Yet others undertook a range of informal work by helping family, friends, or small craftsmen in their work and this could be either paid or unpaid. Some sought casual or labouring jobs that provided similar training: for example, working on a building site was a means for learning bricklaying or painting and decorating. In this way they acquired informal rather than formal training, but they felt on the whole that this was acceptable, since it did not involve the attendance at college and low wages endured by apprentices. Many of those adopting alternative strategies still hoped vaguely that an opportunity for a formal apprenticeship might arise, but had lowered their sights and accepted semi-skilled work instead. Labouring jobs on boats, building sites, or with local 'cowboys' were the best alternatives, because, like skilled work, they allowed some autonomy and variety.

The job careers of this third group of young people are difficult to classify because they involved formal and informal employment (some of it being undeclared), 'self-employed' work (meaning in this case being hired on a sub-contractual basis rather than a regular employee), part-time work, voluntary work, seasonal employment, periods unemployed or on YOP schemes, periods of undertaking unskilled work just to 'fill in' until something better came up, and so on. These patterns are best illustrated through the case studies in Chapters 5 and 8.

Unskilled work

Unskilled work is often thought to be undifferentiated: one manual job is much the same as another. In Marxist analysis it appears as general 'labour power', a view which, according to Willis (1977), his lads also shared. For the Registrar General and others who classify occupations, the large majority of manual jobs appear under social classes 4 and 5, although more skilled and clerical work – which many have argued is also 'proletarianized' – is entered under social class 3. For teachers and other professionals by whom young people are advised, much manual work – from cleaning to car mechanics, from factory work to fish fryer – appears to be much of a muchness. However, from the vantage point of the school leaver, there were important distinctions to be made between different kinds of manual work, both in terms of the social status they implied and in terms of the kinds of masculine and feminine identities they conferred.

One of the main distinctions, as I have already indicated, was between the 'better' jobs, such as skilled or clerical work and other kinds of employment. Other important distinctions occurred within the general category of unskilled work, and here I shall consider the main three – shop work, outdoor labouring, and factory work.

Shop work

Shops were among the main employers of young people. Ten young people, all of them girls, mentioned shop work as a preference, for it was thought to offer 'clean', 'nice', and 'respectable' employment. Hence, it provided an acceptable alternative for those girls who had been unable to find clerical posts. Shop work was also considered more interesting than factory work because it did not involve being dominated by a machine:

'I would do shop work if I could – any kind really, especially a clothes shop. Just sitting on a till all day would be boring, but in a clothes shop you're helping customers – giving opinions and that, and staying up to date with all the fashions.'

Girls who preferred shop work saw factory work as vulgar and unfeminine, preferring the person-oriented atmosphere of the shop to the raunchy collectivism of the factory. They also distinguished between different kinds of shops. Supermarkets were thought to encourage the same collective vulgarity as factories, and tasks were equally as fragmented and meaningless, whereas small shops were thought to be 'friendlier'. However, many of these girls were disappointed with their experiences of shop work, which was less interesting than they had first imagined. Moreover, because of the 'respectable' image, shops and restaurants imposed strict codes of feminine dress and conduct, which some girls welcomed but others found irksome, for they preferred to dress in a way that suited them:

'I left because they complained about my clothes. I had a T-shirt on – a nice one, with frills round the top – it looked smart. And they said: "Oh, going up the beach are you?" They said I looked scruffy, but I looked okay. The only thing I could wear was a blouse which had to be buttoned up to the neck.'

Although ten girls had wanted to do retail work, many others were forced to do it for lack of an alternative, so that 21 per cent of the sample altogether had done some kind of retail work by 1980 (*Figure 7*). The wages were generally much lower than jobs in factories, for example. However, shop work offered a respectable 'feminine' employment that was in many ways preferable to factory work.

Outdoor labouring

Twenty per cent of the 1980 sample had undertaken labouring work by 1980. All of them were boys. This was an emergent category, for boys who had been seeking informal skills or who were dissatisfied with their experiences of factory work found outdoor labouring to be a desirable alternative. It was therefore mentioned specifically as a preference by fourteen boys in 1980. Much of this outdoor labouring was casually hired and some of the boys described themselves as 'self-employed', a reflection of the movement towards casualized labour in a number of industries, especially construction (Gill 1985). However, this was regarded as an advantage rather than disadvantage, for it provided the individual with maximum flexibility to come and go. Examples of this kind of work included painting and decorating, working on boats, on farms, or in scrap yards. However, work on building sites was prized most highly. Whilst some labourers were regular employees, others were paid in cash or worked for a share of the profits.

There were a number of reasons for preferring this kind of work. First, it was associated with a tough, masculine, individualistic status. Second, it was thought to be more interesting and varied than other forms of employment: a young person might be moved around a building site and have the opportunity to see the fruits of their labour before them. Third, it was a means of acquiring a range of useful skills that could be used 'on the side' later as a source of extra income. Finally, it appeared to provide more freedom from supervision: on a building site boys could move around and avoid the watchful eye of the foreman whereas on a production line they were trapped. As one explained:

'I wouldn't work in a factory. I don't like being shut in – like my mate – working on a machine all day. That's all he does. I couldn't stand that. I would rather be unemployed. No, there again, I would rather be at work.'

And another said:

'I wouldn't like to work inside. I just like it out in the open and I don't mind the weather. I couldn't stand being locked in all day, doing the same old job all the time, so it's more interesting, you can talk to people at the same time. You have a good laugh when you're working.'

There was no feminine equivalent of outdoor labouring, although some girls preferred outdoor work such as fruit picking. In general, outdoor work represented the quintessence of a certain kind of masculine image in the same way as clerical work did a feminine one. Thus, outdoor labouring was associated with a culture of heavy masculine labour and offered a kind of individualistic autonomy along with the fellowship of other workers. It was the ideal compromise between the struggle to assert independence from the arbitrary regimes and authority of the workplace on the one hand and the need to earn some money on the other.

Factory work

Eighty per cent of school leavers saw factory work as the kind of job they would least like to do: other jobs were judged according to their degree of contrast to factory work. Nevertheless, factories were some of the major employers in the area, and 32 per cent of the 1980 survey had worked in a factory by the time they had completed their first year in the labour market.

Why was factory work rejected? Thirteen school leavers had reacted negatively to their experiences of factory work by leaving the job, and they gave the same reasons for this as those who had refused to do it in the first place. They felt that the work involved spending too much time indoors, having to perform meaningless and repetitive tasks, too much supervision and being tied to a machine. In the words of one girl:

> 'Well I stayed six months, but I was so pissed off with it I left. I'm just not cut out for factory work. It was terrible doing the same thing all the time and all those fiddling little bits you had to do (making fuses). You couldn't stop for breath and I started getting headaches. It was just so boring – and the dirt and noise and that. It is like a rabbit hutch in there – no windows and it's so hot. I never thought it would be so awful.'

Male school leavers came to similar conclusions:

> 'I went to work in the rubber factory in March for six weeks, but I didn't like it. It was too hot in there and I don't like being told what to do. That's why I left. You're doing one job and they tell you to do another. It was the same at school and that's why I left that.'

Factory work was associated with a raunchy collective culture that could be either masculine or feminine in character depending upon the labour force employed in different factories. This involved a form of aggressive sexual humour and remorseless teasing and horseplay that some of the young people with quieter temperaments found difficult to tolerate. Many girls reported having to suffer sexual harassment in a variety of work-places and this emerges in the case studies in Chapter 8. Boys too became victims of the sexually harassing banter developed by factory women, which they found intimidating:

'Oh, that. . . . It was terrible working with the women all day. I had to go round emptying the trucks and I had to pass all the women. It's hard on you, they get mouthy with you and you can't mouth 'em back because there's too many of them. Mind you, I didn't get bullied as much as some of the others. I wouldn't put up with that. I used to hate it, having to walk along the rows past thirty women, all giggling at me. I just ignore 'em.'

And another boy received similar treatment from male workers for it appeared that bullying and gruesome initiation rituals for young men were a standard part of male occupational cultures:

'They were horrible to me, so I left. They put petrol in my tea one time . . . this bloke called Nigel, a rough lout of about twenty, tried to strangle me. I think he must have been a bit demented.'

Others resented what they saw as the vulgar and crude culture of the factory. In women this was thought to be 'unfeminine' as this girl explains:

'People in there were what I call stupid. It's like that in a factory, they were all shouting and loudmouthed. Shouting all around the place.'

Given this general antipathy towards factory culture amongst the majority of the sample, how did those who remained in such jobs accommodate them?

Willis (1977) argues that the collective solidaristic culture of the factory was precisely what made this work attractive to his 'lads'. The factory culture was fused with a sense of masculinity through the espousal of an inverted ideology: other kinds of work were regarded as effeminate. Some in my sample also voiced this orientation:

> 'The management, they dress smart because they think they run the place. Of course they don't. They don't make the paper do they? The workers do that. . . . I'd like to do packing jobs again, it's a cushy job. In a factory, I like working in a factory, I wouldn't work anywhere else. I would have liked to have been a mechanic, but not out on the streets. I'm supposed to be a working-class person, it's something I believe in, like some people believe in God.'
>
> CW: 'Can you explain that?'
>
> 'Well, you've got your working class and you've got your upper class. You don't do nothing you should do and stuff you shouldn't do, you do it. If there's any trouble going, I'm in it. If there's anything you're supposed to do, I don't do it. Do what you feel and not what anyone else wants you to.'

Similarly, boys identified some factory jobs as being better than others because they implied the same sort of strong masculine power associated with outdoor labouring. Hence, work at the steel mill was attractive to some, not only because the wages were high, but also because of the association with a form of strong elemental masculine toughness. Wrestling with fire and steel was more 'macho' than minding machines: it possessed an almost heroic quality of control and mastery over the environment.

However, others were more ambivalent. They resigned themselves to factory work by arguing that the wages were some consolation and any job was better than nothing. They cited the same disadvantages as those who rejected such work, but regarded it as something that simply had to be endured as these statements from young factory workers illustrate:

> CW: 'What sort of work would you prefer?'
>
> Shawn: 'Factory work. Or otherwise labouring on building sites, in the summer, out in the fresh air. All the money seems to be there these days and you get a sun-tan. It's the money and the general picture of it I suppose, in summer anyway. Not stuck in a factory like I am now. That's one thing about factory work, you never see the daylight. You're in there from 7 a.m. until 6 in the evening and it's hot and sweaty in

summer and freezing in winter.

Danny: 'I didn't have no ambitions, I just wanted to get out of school and get a job. I don't have no ambitions now, I just live from day to day at the moment.'

Dave: 'I always wanted to work outdoors or else factory work. I went for this job because I thought it was outdoors, but I suppose I would have taken it anyway. Now I have been doing this work, I think it is probably better than outdoor work anyway. All the lads want to do outdoor work because they get well built and a suntan.'

Willis (1977) posed the question, 'Why do working class kids do working class jobs?' His answer was that his 'lads' were able to embrace the culture of masculinity and celebrate unskilled labour by working in a factory. However, it is evident from my interviews that only a small minority perceived such qualities in factory work and that there was a hierarchy of 'desirable' manual jobs. The positive orientation towards manual – and particularly factory – jobs voiced by Willis's 'lads' did not fit the majority of young working-class school leavers on Sheppey. Other explanations have to be found as to why they accepted this kind of work.

Given these possible compensations for boys, how did girls adjust? Pollert (1981) has argued that becoming a factory worker was both low status and unfeminine and consequently girls could not resort to the gender-linked inverted ideology espoused by the boys. Rather, they sought to escape from the realities of factory life through domestic roles – that is marriage and motherhood – and the ideology of romance. Some girls on Sheppey were certainly dissatisfied with factory work and they also sought to escape by leaving jobs altogether. However, other girls valued the sense of collective feminine comradeship provided by the factory – the very feature some other girls had rejected. There were opportunities for companionship, merriment, and works outings:

CW: 'Why do you like factory work?'

Sandra: 'Because in a factory you can have a laugh, you can please yourself. You can sit down with all your mates in the canteen together. You meet friends and you can go drinking with them in the evening.'

However, the most common way of 'adjusting' to factory work,

for both boys and girls, was to leave it. Factory work was accommodated only with reluctance despite the fact that factories were
among the main employers on the island.

Thus, factory work was associated with a collective solidaristic
culture that could be either masculine or feminine in character
and involved a measure of aggressive banter and teasing by both
genders, which some young people found difficulty in accommo-
dating, but which others saw as the main advantage of this kind
of work. Whilst Willis and others at the Centre for Contemporary
Cultural Studies have emphasized the sense of collective solidarity sought by working-class male teenagers and reproduced
through subcultural activities, in Sheppey there was also a
strong streak of individualism. Many school leavers felt appalled
at the prospect of being reduced to a small unit of labour in a vast
process and swamped by the collective culture of the factory that
had evolved to accommodate this. They sought instead jobs
through which they could exert a direct sense of individual control. For girls, this took the form of a preference for individual-
ized, person-oriented contact with people in shops or feminized
professions. For boys, this was associated with the independent
masculine identity which craft work and outdoor labouring provided. The value placed upon being 'self-employed' was one
expression of this and fitted with the 'self-made' traditions of the
building industry locally, whereby ordinary men who were able
to make their own fortunes through their own initiatives were
regarded with a mixture of envy and admiration. The tradition of
working-class male individualism therefore valued individual
entrepreneurial talents more than submission to the demands of
employment. Although there undoubtedly existed the kind of
collective masculine and feminine solidarity described elsewhere, this was not incompatible with a kind of working-class
individualism that existed along side it.

The armed forces

A significant minority of school leavers – seven boys and six girls
– had joined the armed forces by 1980 (*Figure 6*). The girls generally waited until they were seventeen, whilst the boys mainly
joined straight from school. Two boys had left the forces by 1980
– one because he disliked the atmosphere in the navy and the

other was discharged for an injury. The majority chose to join the army.

There were a number of reasons for joining. Some followed family traditions, for the island had a long military heritage. A number of boys had been members of the army or sea cadets for a number of years and so joining the forces represented a continuation of their interests. Paradoxically, these were often boys who most resented what they regarded as the petty tyranny of authority at school!

There was both a 'pull' and a 'push' effect associated with wanting to join the armed forces and the nature of these factors differed between genders. For boys, the armed forces were popular because they provided opportunities for travel, excitement and a career:

> CW: 'Why do you want to join the army?'
> Steve: 'To get off the island and make new friends. I've always wanted to do that – it's the best job going.'

As well as these positive attractions, there were also negative factors that propelled young people into the armed forces, for in a labour market with rising unemployment and unrewarding jobs, the army offers a secure alternative. As one lad put it, 'There's nothing going on round here anyway, is there?'

One 'push' reason for joining the armed forces was that by 1980 a number of young people were disappointed in the experiences of employment and were seeking a more interesting alternative. Others regarded it as the only means for finding the skilled training that was not being provided locally. For girls, the armed forces held different attractions.

They were more often propelled out of the island by a desire to escape the constraints of domestic life and unhappy family circumstances. For example, one girl, after a year of working in a factory, said that she was joining the army,

> 'To get away from home and be independent. You learn to live on your own and to cope, but your expenses are all taken care of, so you're better off really, in the long run. And you meet lots of people – it's easy to meet people in the army. Also you've got chances of promotion – you can get on if you want. Then there's the chance to travel. You go all over Britain and

you get cheap holidays abroad . . . it's a good life if you work hard at it.'

Thus, for male and female school leavers, the army had many positive attractions: it offered job security, training and the possibility of adventure.

I have shown how different kinds of work were associated with different kinds of occupational cultures, which in turn determined social identities. These work cultures were differentiated along the following dimensions: degrees of 'roughness' or 'respectability', models of masculinity and femininity, and different forms of collectivism or individualism. They did not therefore constitute an homogeneous class culture. Rather, different dimensions could be conflicting and incompatible.

Strategies of job search

There were three main strategies of job search: through formal agencies, through informal agencies, and by contacting employers directly.

Formal mediating agencies included the Job Centre, the Careers Service, and the local newspapers. Those seeking formal craft apprenticeships, office jobs, or careers in the armed forces had to use these formal agencies. The careers officers themselves tended to emphasize the importance of formal training and further education in the search for employment, and hence their values clashed with those of young people who were antipathetic to school goals or preferred informal training or casual work. These young people complained that the career officer 'put you off things' or 'persuaded you out of things'.

Informal job search strategies involved the mediation of informal networks of friends and relatives. These were used for seeking jobs in factories, as labourers, in shops, and with small local employers: I was frequently informed that in a tight labour market 'who you know is better than what you know'. Local networks were alerted before a young person left school and even if this was not successful in securing a first job it might lead to the second or third. Parents often 'spoke for' their children at their places of employment, but they complained that as jobs became scarcer, so even this 'traditional' pattern of recruitment became more difficult.

The third strategy of job search was to contact the employer directly and this was more often used for recruitment to factories and building sites. This involved going round to local employers and 'putting your name down', usually a number of times. When young people described themselves as 'out looking for work' they were often doing a circuit of the factories or shops depending upon which type of employment they sought. The circuit had to be continued indefinitely since employers tended to recruit individuals on the spot.

It is impossible to count the numbers using each kind of strategy since most individuals tended to use a combination of these strategies simultaneously. Friends or relatives would hear of a potential vacancy because someone was leaving or because the firm was expanding and ensure that social networks were alerted even before the vacancy officially arose. For this reason, may complained of the futility of applying for jobs through the Job Centre when most of the vacancies had been informally filled before they even reached the display board. New firms, such as Tesco, which opened during my period of field-work, used the Job Centre for recruitment, but more established industries with extensive pre-existing communications networks seldom needed to do so.

An aspect of the transition from school to work that has caused concern in recent years is the lack of qualifications held by today's school leavers. Many teachers and others subscribe to what Ashton and McGuire (1981) have termed the 'tightening bond thesis': that as opportunities decline, so the importance of educational qualifications increases. One reason for reaching this conclusion is that surveys of the young unemployed have shown that they are in general less qualified than employed school leavers and it is therefore these unqualified school leavers that have been the object of most social inquiry and comment (Colledge 1977; National Youth Employment Council 1974). From these results it is assumed that lack of qualifications causes unemployment, and for the unemployed to become employable once more they just need a few more certificates. This is based upon a false premise. Whilst at an individual level it might be advisable for the school leaver to equip herself or himself with qualifications before seeking work, at a general level this simply increases the competition for the jobs available, for the reduction of unemployment depends ultimately on the supply of jobs, rather than upon the characteristics of young people.

Furthermore, as this study has shown, only some firms require qualifications for minimum age entry. Large regional employers offering formal apprenticeship or other training and those recruiting clerical workers are likely to inspect qualifications. However, those firms that recruit school leavers 'on spec' or through particularistic informal networks rather than universalistic procedures, did not require qualifications. This has been noted in other studies of the labour market too (Ashton and McGuire 1980; Jenkins 1982).

These results would therefore support those of Ashton and McGuire, that there is indeed a 'tightening bond' at some levels: for formal apprenticeships, academic posts, and so on, more qualifications are needed. However, in other sectors of the labour market this is not the case, and indeed it would appear that the importance of informal criteria as a method of screening applicants has if anything grown stronger (Jenkins 1982). This would imply that those entering the latter sectors of the labour market would be better off spending their last year at school looking for work or doing part-time jobs than sitting examinations. Indeed, some of my respondents had come to the same conclusion.[5] For example, one particularly determined young man explained that he would not go back to school after being suspended 'unless they give me something useful to do'. According to his version of events, he was finally tempted back by being offered some concreting!

Young people perceived this lack of consonance between educational goals and labour market opportunities themselves, for it confirmed their distinction between concrete and abstract intellectual skills:

> Mick: 'I applied to garages and that, but they'd already been filled in. Or I didn't have the right qualifications to suit them. You know, like they say you need O-level English and things like that, but I don't see what it's got to do with mechanics.'
>
> RP: 'Is that what they say?'
>
> Mick: 'Yer. You know, you see them up on a noticeboard, "Apprentice mechanic required, O-level Maths, English

and Science", things like that. But I find you don't need them. I mean you ain't going to go out to a motor car, are you, and start writing on the top of it, and hope that it's going to work! or say, "Two plus two is four – you're fixed!", are you? You know, you've got to get down in it.'

RP: 'Well what kind of skill do you think you need to fix cars?'

Mick: 'Yes, it's a matter of having the right sort of mind about you. Think about things before you get into it. You know, think what you can do about it, and where – how to take it apart, and what bits to get and that. You know you've got to keep it in your head you know.'

This was evidently one way in which Mick rejected educational labelling, seeing it as irrelevant to the world of work. However, it was also to some extent an accurate perception of the structure of opportunities. For the kinds of jobs Mick was likely to get, having a good all round practical knowledge was perhaps more useful. In this way, rising unemployment can lead to a de-legitimation of educational values. Some minimum age school leavers become increasingly sceptical about the value of qualifications as they come closer to leaving. Hence, I heard endless stories about those who had O-levels but were nevertheless unemployed. There were in fact less of these in my survey than the stories implied, but these were cited as evidence of the futility of formal schooling, a rumour that was only partially correct.

Patterns of job departure

Job changing has been regarded as evidence of a deficiency amongst young people or amongst the agencies that serve them. Some conclude that it could be overcome by providing a better Careers Service (Carter 1966; Maizels 1970). Others argued that it was a problem with some young people themselves, being associated with social problems such as deprived homes or poor education (Baxter 1975), or individual problems such as minor psychiatric or nervous disorders (Cherry 1976; Gray, Smith, and Rutter 1980). In the context of rising unemployment, leaving jobs has been identified as one of the factors leading to a decline in young people's employment opportunities as bad job records lead to lengthening periods out of work (Markall 1980; OECD 1977)

In the Sheppey survey, less than one-third had been in the same job continuously for the entire year after leaving school, and many of these were in jobs it was difficult to leave, such as the army. Others who had been regularly employed had found apprenticeships and office training: those who remained employed were often in the most secure and rewarding jobs. A further 17 per cent had held only one job, although they might also have been unemployed or participated in a government scheme, but the majority had held two jobs or more.

What were the reasons for job departure? After counting up all the ninety-seven job departures in the sample, I found that 44 per cent were voluntary in nature – mostly a consequence of disliking the work or the supervisors – and more than half were involuntary. This latter group of job departures were caused by redundancy or by young people being recruited to specifically temporary employment. Dismissals accounted for 6 per cent of all job departures, and these could be regarded as partly voluntary, partly involuntary.[7] There was therefore some considerable turbulence in the early careers of beginning workers, much of which was not their fault. Government schemes contributed towards these rather fragmented and unstable patterns of employment: only five out of the sixteen school leavers who had been on YOP schemes found regular employment after leaving them. However, using a 'deficiency' model did not seem to be the best way of accounting for job departure.

Some forms of job departure were economically rational. They were means by which an individual could maximize their labour market position by finding better jobs or seeking special training. The social psychologists West and Newton (1973) have argued that job departure could be a rational strategy in other ways too. Their model assumes that what individuals lose in income or employment, they compensate for in other, less easily calculable ways. Job departure is therefore a trade-off between loss of income from employment and improved status in other respects. However, more often than not, young people left jobs as a reaction against what they perceived to be unacceptable employment and bad conditions. The culturally valued trait of 'standing up for yourself' on Sheppey led to friction in young people as well as at school. It demanded redress for what were seen as infringements of personal dignity and could lead to arguments resulting in either dismissal or the young person leaving. The West and Newton thesis is perhaps borne out by the way in which many of these walk-outs and conflicts were embellished on being retold. For example, a girl who had been a hairdresser's apprentice reported:

'I was going to the apprenticeship, but I got sacked and then I got angry about that. She was going to give me my job back, but I gave her a load of mouth and left. They're a bit high and mighty in those hairdressers' places.'

Another girl who had left a shop job explained:

'You see, I don't like being told what to do. That's why I'm going into the army, to get away.'

And one boy who had left his job in a butcher's shop described it like this:

'I didn't like it there. I didn't like the manager who kept bossing me about. I got locked in the fridge one day for a joke and I dropped the lamb once. He told me off, right in front of all the customers for that, so I left.'

In the case of young men, some of the job changes were due to the fact that they preferred casual labouring, which was inherently unstable in nature. Indeed, its lack of permanence was regarded as an advantage rather than a disadvantage. In jobs where young people were regarded as easily dispensable labour, personal dignity and a sense of self-worth could often be better preserved by leaving jobs (Roberts, Duggan, and Noble 1981, 1982b, 1982c).

The higher level of job departures by girls was also related to the fact that girls' jobs were lower paid and were less likely to provide training than were boys' jobs. Moreover, it was more difficult for them to resort to casual labouring, and introduce a degree of flexibility into their employment careers, than it was for boys. Altogether then, job changing could be seen in the context of unstable and unrewarding employment. Rather than looking at why young people leave jobs – as many of these studies have done – and thus seeing 'job-hopping' as a problem with young people, we should perhaps consider it the other way round: why do young people accept the employment available and how do they come to 'settle down' to it? This raises the issue of social and cultural reproduction once more, for it enables us to see job departure as part of the process of becoming an adult worker. I address this question more fully in Chapter 6.

Job changing *could* therefore be subjected to a social psychological 'cost-benefit' analysis as Newton and West (1983) have suggested, but this was more often a rationalization that took place after the event rather than a rational calculation beforehand. Furthermore, job departure was a way of experimenting with employment and the culturally conferred status that went with different kinds of employment. Some girls, for example, felt that they could not conform to the kind of culture required of factory women – they were not *that* kind of girl. It was also one strategy for preserving a sense of self-worth in a situation where the individual was technically reduced to an expendable unit of labour: it demonstrated that they could still act upon their environment and be self-determining. It gave them a way of fighting back.

Odd jobs

The transition from school to work is normally conceptualized as a transition from full-time education to full-time employment. Indeed, some of the recent government intervention in the process is intended to bridge this alleged gulf by introducing work experience into schools. However, school leavers in Sheppey already had extensive working experience before they left school: every young person I interviewed had undertaken some kind of part-time or casual job. Such jobs included: assisting with clay pigeon shooting, game beating, farm labouring, working on fishing boats, lug-worm digging, seasonal agricultural work, car cleaning, window cleaning, working on ice-cream vans, fish and chip shops and vans, cellar boy in bars, golf caddying, paper rounds, working on market stalls, café attendants, shop assistants, leaflet delivery, and gardening. In addition, a number did factory out-work for their families. This list does not cover all the jobs undertaken by young people, but it is broadly representative. I have termed such informal and casual activities 'odd jobs'. [8] Those who persistently truanted from school were often the ones who were most heavily engaged in this kind of work. They felt that this was better preparation for employment than they could have found at school, as the following extract from the local paper makes clear:

'*Father Pays Son a Regular Wage*
'Rather than allow his 16-year-old son to play truant or roam the streets, Henry Payne ''apprenticed'' him to a trade and paid him a regular wage, magistrates heard on Friday. But by the law, the boy is not entitled to leave school until Easter, and Payne of Cliff Gardens, Minster, was fined £50 for failing to ensure his regular attendance. Payne, who pleaded guilty to not insisting that the boy was at school, told the court that he was happier to have him working with him learning some basic skills rather than be idle, possibly get into trouble, or play truant from school.'
(*Sheerness Times-Guardian*, 21 March 1980)'

Casual and informal work could be one means of securing a permanent job after leaving school, for nineteen individuals, or 17 per cent of the 1979 sample, found jobs that were in some way related to their previous casual experience. Some, like the hair-dressing apprentices, were taken on full-time as a result of this experience and for this reason it became part of a deliberate job search strategy. This then explains why many of the unqualified school leavers were just as successful in securing training places as those who were qualified.

Moreover, many young people continued this pattern of doing casual, informal work and part-time employment after they had left school. Some were able to pursue alternative careers through working 'on the side' or through petty crime. For boys, jobs 'on the side' included casual labouring, digging for lug-worms, mending cars and motorbikes, or helping on boats. For girls, there was fruit-picking or caring for children as an informal 'nanny'. These jobs were often pursued during periods in which they were not registered as unemployed, and altogether eleven boys and three girls out of the 1980 sample (14 per cent) had undertaken informal work that may or may not have been remu-nerated since leaving school. It appeared that the majority of young people were better able to find these kinds of jobs whilst they were still at school and could work occasional hours and school holidays for a little cash. This pattern of activity was also discovered in a study of four inner-city neighbourhoods by

Roberts, Duggan, and Noble (1981, 1982c). They found that the propensity to engage in informal and occasional work varied from area to area, ranging from 25 per cent in Moss-side, Manchester, to 11 per cent in Wolverhampton. However, they emphasize that 'hustling', as it was known in these areas, was a strictly minority career: most young people had neither the inclination nor the resources to engage in it. One of this minority described the kinds of skills he acquired in this way:

> Mick: 'I have worked up at Ruislip. I got a girlfriend up there, and I've worked for her Dad, doing building, you know, like plastering and concreting.'
> RP: 'What sort of things can you do?'
> Mick: 'Well, I can do mechanics, woodwork, you know, bookshelves and things like that. Bit o' concreting, plastering, painting, you know. The only thing I can't really do and that's hang wallpaper.... What I really like to do is plastering.'
> RP: 'That's quite tricky!'
> Mick: 'As I say, me girlfriend's Dad learned us. You know, he does things up on ceilings. Like you get faces, up on ceilings, and things like that, he re-moulds them and builds them up and that. You know, he's *really* good. That's the sort of thing I'd like to do.'

It has been argued that informal work is less available to young people than to adults because they lack the contacts and the expertise (Roberts 1984). However, certain marginal occasional jobs were *more* likely to be done by young people than by adults because it was worth their while to work for a few extra pounds whilst they were living at home subsidized by parents. This implied that a whole sector of the local economy was probably staffed by young people in low-paid 'runabout' informal positions, particularly small shops, instant food vans, and the holiday trade. There appear to be forms of segmentation in the informal labour market as well as the formal one, although since this sector is by definition 'hidden' it is impossible to know the total size and shape of it (Wallace and Pahl 1986). Nevertheless, it appears that school leavers find the lower-paid and more marginal jobs in the informal sector.

Informal work thus had a number of functions for young people after they had left school. First, it provided some extra income and a source of activity whilst they were unemployed, as illustrated below:

CW: 'Did you keep busy though?'

Martin: 'I did, I used to go out, like when I was at school. I used to go round doing cars and that. I helped out with that at weekends, so I went there (to the yard) and helped at weekends or in the evening and that. I started on one car, the car was all smashed up, it had gone straight through a wall . . . and I started rebuilding it.'

'CW: 'Are you doing that at the moment?'

Martin: 'Yes, I'm doing up this Cortina at the moment. (He goes into a lengthy description of the car.) It keeps me busy, I can't have nothing to do.'

Second, as I have already indicated, it could be a strategy for learning skills informally. Third, some young people undertook this casual work – either paid or unpaid – in the hope that it might lead to permanent employment. The boundary between some forms of casual and 'self-employed' labouring and informal jobs was a blurred one. Teenagers would spend periods drifting from formal to casual employment and back again even with the same employer. Some employers preferred to hire a young person but not to declare this. Hence, employees were often unclear about their own status.

A further important advantage of doing informal jobs was the opportunity for control and autonomy over their employment, which some young people valued in a similar way to those who prized skilled and outdoor work.

Conclusions

To summarize, then, the study has identified a 'mismatch' between school and work. This mismatch was due not to the fact that young people were underqualified and underexperienced – they had considerable work experience and did not appear to require qualifications for many of the jobs locally. Nor was it due to the fact that the school had filled their heads with esoteric academic information: school had endeavoured to equip them with useful knowledge. The reason for the mismatch was that despite young people's own enthusiasm for skilled jobs, there were few such jobs for them to fill. In this respect, then, the 'mismatch' identified here has to be seen as something distinct from the 'mismatch' between young people's and employers' needs identified by the Holland Report (1977) and elsewhere – the alleged mismatch for which MSC schemes are designed to compensate. Indeed the 'officially' identified mismatch based upon employers' needs may have served to obscure an appreciation of the lack of fulfilment of young people's needs and is used as a way of blaming them, rather than the labour market, for youth unemployment (Finn 1982).

Whereas the 'transition from school to work' is usually portrayed as being a smooth process, with a clean break between full-time education and full-time employment, it can be seen that in circumstances such as those on Sheppey it is a 'ragged' transition stretching both sides of the official divide. A substantial proportion of young people had often effectively left school before they reached sixteen and often did not begin work until some time later. In between there might be a whole variety of part-time and casual jobs, interspersed with periods of 'doing nothing'. This has been identified as a pattern in a recent study in the north-east of England too (Coffield, Borrill, and Marshall 1986).

Moreover, young people were selective about the kind of employment they were prepared to take. The job needed to fit the self-image they had constructed, and these self-images were gendered ones. At this stage, most young people still held some hope of finding rewarding employment that would lead them towards excitement, adventure, and would introduce them to a world of new and interesting people. For this reason they were critical of many local jobs. They rejected much of the 'slave labour' locally because they hoped for something better.

Third, there were important differences between male and female school leavers in their search for work. Girls had a different, more humanistic commitment to jobs than boys. However, this did not mean that they were any less committed to their employment. Girls were subject to socialization into 'feminine' roles. Whilst some girls accepted this, others kicked against it, so that acceptance of these roles was by no means unproblematical.

It will be evident that the transition from school was a period of evolving gender identities in relation to prevailing labour market conditions. This involved a struggle to assert a sense of pride, individuality, and dignity in situations where this was continually threatened. This theme will be explored further in the course of their response to unemployment.

Finally, the experiences of Sheppey school leavers may lead us to modify the idea of 'social reproduction'. Workers are no longer simply 'reproduced' when they leave school because the job market has changed. This then relates to my first hypothesis, outlined in Chapter 1, that there is likely to be a fracture in the patterns of reproduction of work roles. This hypothesis would appear to be confirmed in this study. Furthermore, gender is a crucial variable in conceptualizing reproduction, since it was gendered labour that was being reproduced.

However, we can go further than simply identifying a disjunction in the transition from school to work. It would appear that this calls into question the whole notion that 'reproduction' is an on-going smooth, circular process as was originally argued. Nor are young people entirely socialized to accept their places in the work-force *before* they leave school. Rather, it is evident that the way in which young workers receive and incorporate work-place values and ideologies is problematical and subject to some resistance. Social and cultural reproduction – contrary to what those such as Willis, or Bowles and Gintis, or Bourdieu and Passeron have argued – is a longer-term process, one that continues *after* young people have left school. Young people do not readily accept their positions as alienated labour in the workforce, as is reflected in their search for something more satisfying. Nor – as we shall see later – do they unproblematically accept their roles as men and women.

4
From school to no work

The Hero rides to heaven the public merely rot
for a fraction of forever in a designated spot
eternally paralysed the morbid orbit shifts
halfway to paradise stuck in the lift
some smart cracking bimbo says you can't be employed
sends you off to limbo in a stairway to a void.
        (From 'Limbo', John Cooper Clarke, 1983 reprinted by
permission of Century Hutchinson from *Ten Years in an Open-
Necked Shirt* by John Cooper Clarke)

George Orwell, one of the original ethnographers of the unemployment in the 1930s described the effects thus:

'When I first saw unemployed men at close quarters, the thing
that horrified and amazed me was to find that many of them
were ashamed of being unemployed. . . . I remember the
shock of astonishment it gave me when I first mingled with
tramps and beggars to find that a fair proportion of them, perhaps even a quarter, of these beings whom I had been taught
to regard as cynical parasites, were decent young miners and
cotton workers gazing at their destiny with the same sort of
dumb amazement as an animal in a trap. They simply could
not understand what was happening to them. They had been
brought up to work, and behold! it seemed as if they were
never going to have the chance of work again.'
        (Orwell 1937: 76, 1977 edition)

A similar picture of despair and calamity is presented in Walter
Greenwood's 'Love on the dole' in the 1930s. Large-scale and

systematic surveys by the Social and Applied Psychology Unit at Sheffield University and by Breakwell (1985) have indicated that the young unemployed suffer from a loss of psychological well-being when compared to equivalent young workers.[1] This includes depression, anxiety, loss of self-esteem, and other psycho-social disturbance. But why do they suffer from being unemployed? After all, a life of full-time employment has only been considered 'normal' for the last hundred years or so (Pahl 1984) and many people also suffer from the kinds of employment which they undertake (Jahoda 1982).

Marie Jahoda has provided a systematic framework for answering this question from her studies of unemployed adults in the 1930s and 1980s. She argues that employment has both a manifest function – providing us with money to live on – and latent functions that are social and psychological. She lists five main functions work provides:

> 'it imposes a time structure on the waking day; it enlarges the scope of social relations beyond the often highly emotionally charged family relations and those of the immediate neighbourhood; by virtue of the division of labour it demonstrates that the purposes and achievements of collectivity transcend those for which an individual can aim; it assigns social status and clarifies personal identity; it requires regular activity.'
>
> (Jahoda 1982: 83)

Hence, she argues that unemployment means that individuals suffer from the loss of these things, which in turn leads to loss of psychological well-being. But does unemployment affect young people in the same way as adults and can these models derived from male experience of unemployment be equally applied to women? Women have a status – a domestic one – that is not provided by employment and could potentially fulfil at least some of these functions. Some have argued that this is one reason why unemployment does not affect young women as badly as it does young men.[2] This highlights the fact that 'work' is not necessarily the same as 'employment' (Pahl 1984). Could all these functions be derived from work outside of employment too?

These latent functions of employment were explored in relation to the experience of young people on the Isle of Sheppey after they had been one year in the labour market.

A year after leaving school, roughly half of the sample had

been unemployed. Given the patterns of job instability and turn-over already described, it can be seen that school leavers were neither wholly employed, nor wholly unemployed. Rather, they were in and out of work. This has been described as 'sub-employment' (Roberts, Duggan, and Noble 1982b) and has implications for their responses to unemployment.

The loss of the five latent functions of work

The loss of a time structure

School leavers are familiar with two kinds of externally imposed time structure: those of school and those of employment. That imposed by schooling, however, was often resented and one way to resist this was by truanting:

> Gary: 'I truanted all the time at school. I got bored with it. I get bored very easily. You get into a routine, and then it's boring. At school it was always the same pattern, every week. I was bored at school, but I was also bored, after a while, truanting as well.'

The time structure imposed by employment could be equally oppressive and one of the main areas of conflict between young people and their employers was precisely over time: young people were concerned to balance their personal time with the structure imposed by employment and one of the advantages of casual labouring or being 'self-employed' was that it allowed the freedom to do this:

> 'The plumber and the carpenter are going self-employed and they want to take me with them. I'd like to be my own boss, be self-employed, because you can knock off when you want and not lose a day's pay.'

For working-class school leavers employment involved exchanging units of their time for a wage. In this way, 'their' time became the property of others and, unless the rewards were sufficient, it was time 'wasted':

> Jenny: 'There's Tesco's, the shirt factory, and shit like that. Boring, repetitive jobs, sewing jeans and stacking shelves.

I wouldn't do a lot of factory work unless I was really desperate, because I think it would be a waste of my life. In a factory . . . doing the same thing all day. You need an awful lot of money to be able to stand that.'

For these reasons, then, time structures could be a source of domination as well as social-psychological fulfilment, and they were consequently resisted.

Being unemployed, however, did not necessarily provide a satisfactory alternative. Time was still 'structured' by the need to eat, sleep, and 'sign on'. The unemployed described regular patterns of activity, which in turn became 'routines':

Mike: 'I used to get up in the morning, go down the pub, or walk down the town first, see if we could con anybody for ten pounds, then stay there till the pub closes. Walk up the town, walk back down it, walk up it again, walk down it. At one stage we got to, we just used to turn round at a certain point, walk up and down, go round someone else's house, have something to eat or a cup of tea there, go out, go to another house. Used to be all right.'

Getting up was invariably mentioned as the first significant event of the day, for the unemployed slept longer hours than those who went to work:

Gary: 'When unemployed – I don't want to sound like I was giving up, I didn't want to stay on the dole – but I just lost interest. I don't know how to describe it really. I just got up at ten-thirty to eleven o'clock, then I'd work on the bikes in the mornings, walk round the town in the afternoon and then go round the pub in the evening. I was sort of getting into a rut, I think. It was just the same every day. I was bored on and off. It was okay when I was doing something but I go out more now I am at work, you feel like a nice pint afterwards.'

Thus, whilst externally imposed time structures were resented, the time spent unemployed seemed purposeless. This daily pattern was punctuated by the arrival of the Giro every other week or by other unexpected windfalls of money or goods that provided the opportunity for frenzied bursts of spending:

CW: 'How much do you drink each day?'

Mike: 'All me money's worth. I got twenty-five quid the other week and I went out, no one was out, so I decided to get drunk on me own. I just – as soon as I've got money – I just blow it all. Oh yeah, and on the machines. Half of that money went on the machines and the other half went on drink.'

Since income was irregular, this encouraged patterns of hedonistic overconsumption followed by periods of compulsory underconsumption, for it was not possible to plan anything very far in advance. This pattern, forced upon them by necessity, was also justified as a way of life.

Those who were regularly employed for the entire period, by contrast, invariably told me of their long-term goals and plans, which included buying houses and cars. Long-term life structures in terms of personal life projects were therefore available to those in regular employment, but not available to the sub-employed.

Jenny, who is quoted more fully as a case study in Chapter 5, illustrates the fact that at this stage many of the effects of unemployment were the same for girls as they were for boys. However, for other girls, domestic duties did serve to impose their own rhythm, giving the loss of a time structure a different significance. This is discussed later.

Thompson (1967) has argued that industrial capitalism imposes a time discipline upon the otherwise 'natural' rhythm of pre-industrial life. Whilst the young unemployed were certainly aware of time discipline, and resisted it, the alternative was not a 'natural' rhythm, but a sense of emptiness and a pattern of activity dictated by the irregular availability of money.

The reduction of social contacts

Unemployment, it is argued, leads to social isolation. However, the young unemployed I interviewed on Sheppey at the ages of sixteen and seventeen did not depend solely upon the workplace for their sources of social contact. In a small community, with large numbers of young people being unemployed for at least some period in their teenage years, there was no shortage of social contacts. Indeed, some complained that going to work

interfered with their social lives, and at times the latter took precedence over the former:

> Danny: 'Yer, I got sacked 'cause I kept going in late. I'd go to
> work in the morning and then I'd see some of me mates and
> start talking. And then I'd think, "I'll just stay half an
> hour," and then it was an hour, and time creeps away. After
> a while you don't want to go in all day.'

Those who did complain of isolation were young people who
had lost contact with their friends from school, who were kept at
home deliberately by parents for fear of them drifting into bad
ways, who lived in isolated locations, or whose friends were all
working full-time. This affected girls in a different way to boys,
for girls were more likely to spend more time at home and to pursue home-bound pastimes such as reading novels or magazines,
and collecting things such as key rings. Boys, by contrast, were
likely to have hobbies, such as fishing or ferreting, which took
them out of the home. On the one hand this could be seen as a
source of strength for girls, who had a more secure sense of
belonging somewhere, but on the other hand it also led to isolation from peers who were not already close friends and increasing dependence upon the home – particularly upon mothers –
for emotional and social support. However, in general, most
respondents agreed that the presence of unemployed contemporaries served to mitigate some of the worst features of
unemployment:

> Gary: 'No, I wasn't on me own when I was unemployed, because
> three of my mates had broken legs and were off sick for ages.
> I was bothered to get a job, and yet I couldn't be bothered. I
> was having fun, but I also wanted a job, if you see what I
> mean. My friend was disabled for a year, and he was in the
> merchant navy, and he got really fed up.'

> Mike: 'No, it used to be all right when everybody used to be
> unemployed 'cos we all used to go down the pub and that,
> but now everyone's employed, no one's a dosser. And every-
> body used to go out every day of the week, but now they
> don't, they all stay indoors. Till Friday or Saturday.'

Loss of participation in collective purposes

Employment is not the only source of collective purpose. Some of the young unemployed had collective projects of their own and this provided them with what they regarded as meaningful activity. For example, involvement in music bands, bike gangs, and the CND[3] provided more satisfactory and genuinely collective participation than employment did, for as I have indicated, employment was regarded as time sold to someone else at a personal cost rather than as a source of fulfilment. Those with such recreational pursuits were sometimes able to pursue them whilst they were unemployed as well. However, most young people did not have such absorbing pastimes and their lack of financial resources meant that they were unable to develop any. Such collective projects as did exist were ones that could be pursued whilst they were either employed or unemployed. Moreover, collective pursuits were more often a characteristic of male leisure patterns than of female ones. Questions about the way in which young people spent their leisure time revealed that young men were more likely to be involved in 'project'-type activities with specific goals to them – such as doing up an old motorbike, or joining a football team – than girls were. This perhaps reflects the fact that leisure itself is often seen as something geared around masculine pursuits (Deem 1982).

The loss of status

The loss of an acceptable status has implications for the unemployed person's personal identity too. Here I interpret 'status' to mean the judgement of others, whilst 'personal identity' refers to the individual's own perception of their status. It has been argued that unemployment leads to a loss of a sense of well-being because individuals attribute unemployment to their own failure (Bloxham 1983; Stokes 1981). To what extent did young people on Sheppey blame themselves for unemployment?

In conditions of high unemployment, such as existed on the Isle of Sheppey, roughly half of all school leavers were likely to find themselves unemployed within a year. Most of these reacted with incomprehension when I asked them if they ever felt ashamed or embarrassed about being unemployed. It was a fact of life. However, there was some tension between their own perception of their status and negative labelling by others. Whilst parents and elders often berated them for their inability to find a job, young people themselves did not always readily accept such definitions:

> Jenny: 'Old people are prejudiced against you. You've only got to be standing in the pub and the old gits come in and say, "Oh, so that's who I'm supporting, is it? That's where all my taxes are going?" But a lot of people try to understand. I don't care what they think. I just try to get on with what I'm doing.'

They were more inclined to blame external circumstances familiar to everyone, such as the state of the economy:

> Mike: 'No, I don't think there's no hope now. Unless you get a shop job or something. See, there's everyone being laid off, and made redundant. In the main factories on the island – 'cept for Abbotts, and then you have to join a big waiting list. Twinlocks, Arthur Millers, that typewriting place, all just laying people off. . . . I s'pose it's got to get worse before it gets better.'

Furthermore, employment was not the only source of status for teenagers immediately after they had left school. Status amongst peers was judged by positions in the local subcultures. These alternative sources of status resulted in some teenagers adopting self images which were deliberately antithetical to those required by employers, such as the 'punk' image:

> Mike: 'Then there was this bloke above. He was a good bloke. He always tried to talk me out of being silly and that. Being a punk. But that was what I wanted. That was part of the trouble. I wouldn't give in to him, by changing and coming in all nicely dressed and that.'

> Jenny: 'And what else came up? Oh, I went for the job at the White House. I had to go down that Farm Shop, the one in the Broadway, and the bloke who interviewed me said, "Well, of course, you know, if you get this job you've got to have a very smart appearance – you've got to wear a skirt

every day and be really smart and no cheekiness,'' and this and that. ''And if you don't hear from us by Saturday you'll know you haven't got the job.'' And I didn't hear from them and that was that. (She laughs.) I look smart when I want now.'

At times this determination to assert individual identity at the risk of losing jobs could enhance status in the peer group: both male and female teenages would recount with pride how they confronted employers, even when it involved losing their jobs. However, this was in a context where employment did not offer a secure status and failed to fulfil the aspirations young people had held. An alternative status provided a means of appearing to reject employment before they were rejected by it. This was therefore a short-term defensive strategy.

The part played by ideologies of femininity and masculinity in constructing these alternative statuses is explored later.

The loss of regular activity

Unemployed teenagers on Sheppey complained that one of the worst features of being unemployed was the boredom that resulted from having no worthwhile activity. Leisure is a commodity bought and sold on the market-place, a luxury they could not afford. Hence the absence of an income was exacerbated by the need to fill large tracts of time. I have already indicated that some young people were able to pursue alternative occasional and informal activities but these seldom consumed all of their time. Most of the time was spent 'doing nothing'. Doing nothing involved a regular pattern of activity, but it was not defined as worthwhile activity. For unemployed teenagers 'doing nothing' was contrasted to 'doing something'. 'Something' involved some departure from routine activity.

Jenny: 'When I've got no money, I stay in and wait and see if anyone comes round. No, I just stay in, play records, go round Kevin and Janet's, go up me mum's, go round and see someone, or just wait here; do some washing. Don't know, it depends, you can never tell, 'cause things always sort of crop up, and you think, ''God, I've got to see her again.'' Doing nothing, then something sort of happens.'

CW: 'So you're never really sitting around doing nothing for
    long?'

Jenny: 'No more than a day.'

CW: 'Then you go somewhere else and do nothing?'

Jenny: 'Yes. There's always something really, it never gets that
    bad.'

CW: 'You feel most bored when you haven't been doing a lot?'

Jenny: 'Yer. Well. I just sort of . . . before, when I used to get
    bored I just used to jump the trains and go up to London or
    something. Or do something. But now I've got a bit lazy and
    I've not been doing much. Been more sort of boring. If I get
    bored I just go and have an argument with someone.'

CW: 'You'd do something to sort of liven things up a bit?'

Jenny: 'Yes. Well, I wouldn't do anything drastic, nothing – '

CW: 'Like smash a window?'

Jenny: 'No. Just sort of, just something. There's always some-
    thing you can do.'

Such 'somethings' could either occur spontaneously in the
course of the day or had to be created through wild adventures
that might otherwise appear irrational.

Boredom was the corollary of doing nothing. Indeed, boredom
was mentioned so frequently that I began to inquire as to its
meaning. Boredom was used to describe a range of undesirable
states of being, but there were two main kinds of boredom: boredom imposed by others and boredom that was self-generated.
Having to perform tasks under the authority of others – whether
at school or at work – was boring:

CW: 'Did you ever get bored?'

Mike: 'Yes. Sometimes. I used to fall asleep. At Abbotts they
    used to give you the women's job. Just sticking labels on
    bottles or just putting bottles on a conveyor belt. Just doing
    that all day. Just sitting there. Your mind wandered, you're
    thinking of something, you fall asleep.'

However, escape from the supervision of others could also be
boring if there was no meaningful activity to fill the space, as
Mike goes on to explain:

CW: 'Were you more bored working than on the dole, or the
    other way round?'

Mike: 'I was bored in a different way. Just sitting there doing bottles all day. Just get totally bored. It just drives you mad. You're not doing nothing. Just sitting there doing the same actions all the time.'

CW: 'Would you rather be at home doing nothing then?'

Mike: 'Yer, because you're not doing nothing. You're doing something. You can get bored at your own expense. Like you can do what you like there, but when you're at work, you have to do that. When you're at home you can do something and not bore yourself. Play records, or read a book, or something like that, or go out for a walk.'

Any kind of routine activity could become boring, whether it was imposed by employment or caused by having nothing else to do. The latter kind of boredom however was at least under the control of the individual and, as with the control of time, young people felt they needed to assert control over their activities. Whilst the absence of each of these latent functions of employment was experienced as a loss under some circumstances, there was considerable ambivalence in responses. Nor did young people necessarily regard employment as providing an acceptable alternative. They were thus trapped between unemployment and work, dissatisfied with both.

It was evident that they recognized certain life-styles as being associated with being unemployed, but they did not necessarily welcome these as being an alternative to employment. For example, when asked how they felt about others who were unemployed, nearly every school leaver replied like this one:

'Most of 'em, it's not their fault, so you can't blame them. But some of 'em, they just don't *wanna* work. They've been years like that and they won't ever change.'

They also condemned this life-style of permanent joblessness as purposeless:

Jenny: 'I wouldn't want to be like Andy. He's just vegetating, I think. He's been like that for years. Not going nowhere.'

Consequently, whilst young people adapted fairly readily to life without work through creating alternative life-styles and even valued these as a means of controlling personal time and activity, this was no long-term 'solution' to unemployment.

Thus the experience of the young unemployed would appear to be different to that of adults in some respects but similar in others. Much depended upon the position of the young person within the family – a theme I address later. Perhaps one of the main differences is that whilst for adults employment may be regrded as a *loss* – if they had built their lives around the expectation of a regular job they would need to reorientate their lives considerably after losing it – for young people who had never had full-time employment, the situation was rather different.

However, the main loss for young people was of the *manifest* function of work – money. Without money they were not able to participate in many of the collective activities young people were supposed to do – unable to buy the symbols of status, or to fund their social contacts with other people, or to purchase activities to fill their long empty days. Money could help to fill the social and psychological vacuum left by the lack of employment.

As Jenkins (1983) has argued, responses to unemployment also vary according to the contrasts between 'rough' living and 'respectable' living. Parents often attempted to control the social lives of unemployed offspring for fear of them falling into a 'rough' life-style of the kind described in Northern Ireland.

So far, the responses of male and female school leavers to unemployment would appear to be similar in so far as both groups were looking for full-time work and were just as disappointed when they could not find it. However, unemployment also had implications for masculinity, femininity, and the social construction of gender identities more generally.

Femininity

It has been argued that whereas male youth cultures took public forms – such as fighting on the beaches or parading on the streets – working-class girls adopted a more passive consumer subculture, although little is known about the subcultural activities of middle-class girls (McRobbie 1978; McRobbie and Garber 1976). This involved such things as becoming the fans of male pop idols and their activities were restricted to things that could be carried out in the home. Moreover, such activities often involved a preoccupation with clothes and make-up involved in an ideology of romance, which in turn was concerned with finding a boyfriend. This, it was argued, led to girls not forming recognizable 'youth subcultures' in the same way that boys did. This had led Jenkins (1983) to argue in his study of school leavers in Belfast that girls were almost entirely absent from the 'rough' street culture of the 'lads' and were more often found amongst the more conformist and 'respectable' 'citizens'.

Despite the force of these arguments and their evident basis in empirical research, they appear to represent girls as somewhat passive and retreatist, as less rebellious than male youth. Other studies that have concentrated upon girls in particular have provided a rather different picture. In Griffin's (1985) and Davies's (1983) studies, girls are portrayed as *resisting* pressures to conformity imposed by them by institutions such as school. However, they do this in different ways to male youth – for example by emphasizing their sexuality in clothes and cosmetics – in situations where it is restricted. Their social and occupational lives are circumscribed by domestic duties. Furthermore, the more informal collective solidarity they create is undermined by 'deffing out' – that is the withdrawal of those who become part of a couple and start to go around with the boyfriend's friends instead. This too, presents a rather dismal picture of defeated femininity. For these reasons, I was particularly interested in girls' responses and in ways in which 'femininity' was reproduced. My concern to understand how this happened led me to particularly focus upon young women who had distinctive or 'non-conformist' approaches to femininity – but these were not difficult to find.

I described some of the ways in which employment served to create models of feminine identity in Chapter 3. Other sociologists who have focused upon the reproduction of gender roles amongst girls have argued that it is important to take both their roles as workers and their domestic status into account. Young women are growing up into a society where women are increasingly taking on the burden of both roles for the major part of their lives. Although young women do not become 'housewives' until they are married, Griffin (1985) has shown that teenagers' lives too can be crucially affected by the need to do domestic labour. However, in general there were important distinctions between their role as domestic assistant in their mother's home, and their role as houseworker in their own home – with the possibilities of status, independence, and control that this implied.

Some girls on Sheppey embraced this domestic status whole-heartedly, regarding it as the evidence of a mature femininity. As we have seen, a home of one's own had a special status and this was traditionally achieved through marriage. Two girls got married immediately on leaving school, and others were saving up to do so. This indeed reflected national trends, since many of the daughters of manual workers get married in their teens (Dunnell 1976). For these girls employment came second to domestic careers and one girl did not want to go out into employment at all.

However, the majority of girls wanted to find a job and have a period of independence and freedom before 'settling down':

'Of course you want to travel a bit first, see the world, do something exciting. . . . I don't want to end up like my mum – she never gets to do anything.'

Whilst sixteen-year-old girls recognized that ultimately they would have family responsibilities, they insisted that they wanted to 'live a bit' first. Thus, in a number of discussions between girls at school, they claimed that they would not have children until their mid-twenties in order to enable them to do this. This desire for independence was based upon the assumption that employment would provide a regular income enabling them to pursue other life goals:

'Oh, I want to get a flat up in London. As soon as I've got some money together. Not just staying here all the time, that's too boring.'

Thus, whilst in the *long term* girls recognized that they would have to fulfil traditional domestic roles, in the *short term* they resisted them. Indeed, many were very critical of domestic roles and only a tiny minority saw this as a woman's only career.[4] Despite the pervasiveness of the ideology of romance, girls had very prosaic expectations of married life. For example, when I asked a group of girls at school what qualities they looked for in a husband, they chorused, '*No* drinking, *no* gambling, *no* violence!' This unromantic fatalism has been observed by others too (Griffin 1985). Many have documented the importance of romantic escapism for young women (McRobbie and Garber 1976; Pollert 1981; Sharpe 1976). However, the way in which romance oper- ated in the lives of young women was complex. They did not simply swallow it whole – indeed, many were very sceptical. Romance did however play a part in structuring feminine roles for it helped to construct the 'imaginary' reality through which young people constructed their roles in real life (Cohen 1985): it provided the fantasy escape and yet it had 'real' consequences for their behaviour. It could be said that 'romance' was both accepted and rejected simultaneously. This is evident in the case studies in Chapters 5 and 8.

Just as ideas of work were structured by roles in the family, so roles in the family were structured by the expectation of work. Hence, they argued that women who were working should expect men to perform some of the domestic labour:

> 'Well, it's not fair. If the man's at home and the woman's working then he should help with the housework . . . 'cos you can't do it all otherwise.'

There was evidence that this may lead to some conflict how- ever, for boys were uniformly more conservative in their opin- ions: they insisted that a woman's place was at home whilst a man's was out at work:

> 'Well, it stands to reason, don't it? If the bloke's out working he should have his dinner ready for him when he gets back. A wife should be at home. That's what they're for. A man's a bread-winner.'

At the time, this was greeted by vociferous protest by the girls in the class, but one year after leaving school, half the girls in the 1980 sample were engaged in 'courting' and one-fifth had got married, had babies, or were cohabiting with their boyfriends. Despite initial resistance these girls had entered domestic roles at an earlier age than they had anticipated.

Jenkins (1983) has indicated that in his study there were two roads to the altar from the point of view of young men: the planned and the precipitous. There were examples of both strategies in this sample of young women, for a year later some girls were confi- dently planning their marriages, their houses, their cars, their children, and their holidays in comprehensive life strategies:

'I'm getting engaged in October – that's my eighteenth birthday – and then we're getting married in the following year. We've been saving up since before Chistmas and we've put in for our own house so we should get that before we're married and have the reception round there. We want to get a car first really though.'

Such girls tended to see rushing into parenthood as foolish:

CW: 'Who would you not like to be like?'

Tracy: 'Carol. I wouldn't like to be like her. She's ruined her life completely. I wouldn't want a kid at her age and living in that house she's in now. And he's never going to work. And she was quite clever at school, but she never got no qualifications after she went with him. He won't get a good job. She's had no enjoyment at all.'

However, others sought to demonstrate their maturity and independence through having a recognized domestic role. This could even be seen as a form of rebellion *against* 'respectable' femininity:

'You know, I was rebelling really. I had to prove something. I had to show them all, show them that I could do it, could do it all on me own. They just think, "Oh, that Alison', she's a wild one, she'll never do anything," but you see I got a family now and I can do it on me own.'

Others however, continued to be critical of domestic roles:

CW: 'What would you want to do?'

Marie: 'Not just stay on this island and get married and have a husband and a baby and get out to work; dinner on the table and, "What did you do today?" That's terribly boring. I want to do something different. Do something with my life. Families are boring altogether. You know it's "My family's better than yours, my baby's better than yours." I live next door to a young family and it's all hassle all the time. The young girl up the road, she's got two children and she's worrying all the time about how she can pay the bills, because her husband's not living with her.'

As I have argued elsewhere (Wallace 1986), we can examine the reproduction of gender roles as taking place on three dimensions.

Gender roles were reinforced *materially* by the fact that girls received lower wages than boys and were therefore obliged to be supported either by family or by a male partner, *socially* through the expectations of appropriate adult behaviour, and *symbolically* through codes of conduct that prescribed social behaviour for both genders. These symbolic codes of behaviour have been documented for deviant girls (Shacklady Smith 1978; Wilson 1978) but can also be applied to other girls as the way in which sexuality is symbolically represented in subcultures and in cultural reproduction more generally. Hence, the powerful symbols of 'nice girl' and 'whore' are pervasive in school leavers's cosmology, and the codes of behaviour – such as shouting and swearing or styles of dress – that define girls as being in one category rather than another are clearly understood and prescribe their behaviour. However, the fact that these repressive symbolic codes of conduct existed did not mean that girls accepted them uncritically, as we can see in the examples of girls from Sheppey.

The transition to family life took place at a much earlier stage for girls than for boys, for in their first year after leaving school about half were in stable relationships, often with boys they hd known whilst still at school (Griffiths 1986). Their boyfriends and fiancés were normally some years older. Consequently, girls were expected to behave as adult women and become initiated into adult social activities. This often led them to see boys as immature or foolish and to resent the junior sexual status imposed upon them by school.

Girls' behaviour was also circumscribed by the risk of sexual labelling, in particular the universal distinction between 'nice girls' and 'slags' (Cowie and Lees 1981). One means of avoiding negative sexual labelling was through ideologies of romantic love, for to be too sexually available was to risk a loss of status, but being 'in love' – a recognized status – allowed for more intimate relations between young men and women which were socially sanctioned. Indeed, being 'in love' could boost a girl's social status, and so relationships were translated into appropriately romantic terms involving the appropriate kind of 'in love' behaviour. The ideology of romantic love thus held various instrumental functions as well as serving to construct fantasized identities, as I have argued previously. This ideology of romantic love had other functions too. Girls sought to exert proprietorial rights over male partners, for if their men were seen to be a 'bit of a lad' this could undermine their own status. Girls were not unaware of the hypocrisy this involved. As one girl said, 'If I was a bloke, I would screw everything in sight, but as a girl you've got to be more careful.' Romantic love could therefore at times be a strategy in the same way as Shacklady Smith (1978) and Wilson (1978) found in their studies of deviant girls in gangs. For this reason, it sometimes took exaggerated public forms, such as histrionic displays of grief or jealousy. At other times, romantic love could be a way of describing sexual desire (Lees 1986) or more complex feelings of belonging or possessiveness.

Studies of girls' subcultures have been criticized for portraying girls as passively dominated by patriarchal culture (Griffiths 1986; Wallace 1986). Girls on Sheppey however often actively asserted their position, as the following extract from the local paper makes clear:

> '*Girl Hurt in Fight over Boy*
> 'A fifteen-year-old girl, who took exception to remarks made about her boyfriend, pulled another girl to the ground and kicked her. At Sheerness juvenile court last Thursday the girl admitted the assault, causing actual bodily harm. . . . When questioned by police, the girl said, ''I know I shouldn't fight over a boy. I should have just walked away. I would like to apologise for the harm I caused her.'' '
> (*Sheerness Times-Guardian*, Friday, 19 October 1979)

This forceful femininity and the manipulation of codes of romantic love is very different from the more passive 'retreat' into romance described elsewhere, for they did not simply moon around in a helpless fashion, but nevertheless the powerlessness of young women's position was reinforced.

Collective codes of behaviour defined within subcultures could also be cruel and intolerant towards those who did not conform. Girls who did not subscribe to the subculturally acceptable definitions of femininity by not adopting fashion styles, rejecting codes of romance altogether, and appearing to be too dominated by parents – especially girls who seemed to the rest to be aloof – were isolated, persecuted, and at times physically threatened. Hence, one girl who sought to forge an alternative identity that was not sanctioned by the subcultural majority, expressed her pain and isolation thus:

Sarah: 'You see, they don't like me because I don't have stories of boyfriends to exchange. They just ask each other, ''Who are you going out with?'' all the time . . . and because I don't go out, ''Look at you, you don't ever go out.'' '

Whilst girls' subcultures and ideologies did express resistance, this had to be channelled into acceptable forms. It can be seen that when looking at young women, 'femininity' and 'romance' are important cultural strands, but the way in which they are adopted by young women can take complex and contradictory forms.

Masculinity

Work by Willis (1977) and Brake (1980) has indicated that masculinity needs to be seen as a social and cultural construct. They illustrated how this was often done – like femininity – in a dialectical relationship of opposition to dominant and conformist models of masculine behaviour. Hence, young men used masculinity as a form of resistance at school and elsewhere by adopting adult cultural symbols and codes of behaviour, such as smoking and aggressive sexual banter.

In Sheppey, sexual identities amongst boys had to be aggressively asserted. This was acheived through codes of prowess that were highly ritualized and were communicated publicly by the retailing of stories. Honour could be won through grand Quixotic gestures of defiance against those in authority – such as employers, the school, or the police – and many of their supposedly deviant activities could be explained in these terms. Although the young man might risk suffering punishment it nevertheless enhanced his status in the community. Honour could also be won through predatory sexuality – by aggressive sexism and by 'pulling the birds' – and hence was inversely related to girls' sexual honour. This too had to be publicly displayed, leading boys to invent or exaggerate their conquests when they retold them afterwards.

For boys, masculinity was lost, won, or redeemed through their status in the peer group. Consequently, the male peer group was bonded through the celebration of wild behaviour. This included embellished stories of fighting, or more commonly, excessive bouts of drinking or drug-taking that could perhaps be described as self-immolating heroism.

Thus, it would appear that the male teenager's sense of masculinity was insecure – it needed to be continually reaffirmed or 'proved'. This imposed rigid rules upon masculine behaviour with those who refused to conform being labelled as 'poofs', not because any of them were homosexual, but because homosexuality implied an ambiguous masculinity. Hence, 'masculinity' was often defined against an imaginary idea of homosexuality, not a consideration that ever arose for girls.

Male sexuality was also defined through women. Whilst women exerted proprietorial rights through romantic love, men often asserted control through threats of violence. If their wife or girlfriend betrayed them, they were expected to exact revenge through an 'irrational' frenzied burst of rage, mostly against the other man. The papers, cafes and pubs were full of stories of these *crimes passionnels*. Violent threats and actual violence might also be used against a girlfriend, for this was a recognized feature of some courting as well as some marital relationships.

These characteristics of masculinity have been interpreted as ritualized resistance or the 'magical' reconstruction of forms of working-class solidarity (Hall and Jefferson 1976; Mungham and Pearson 1976). However, they could also be interpreted as attempts to assert and reinforce an otherwise fragile masculinity (Brake 1980).

The combination of ostentatiously predatory male sexuality and defensive female sexuality produced an in-built tension into courting relationships. Girls attempted to control male behaviour by curbing their more excessive escapades and the public presentation of their relationship in the male peer group. They presented themselves as 'in love' with the partner although this could cover a whole variety of feelings. Boys resisted being seen to be 'under the thumb' of a girlfriend. Thus boys would describe themselves as being 'tied down' to girlfriends if they were courting and look back wistfully to their wilder days or insist that they preferred their freedom if they were not courting. Nevertheless, as we shall see, a domestic status was just as important to young men as it was to young women. Boys believed in a different kind of masculine romanticism, which, like female romanticism, embodied sets of fantasized relationships and a fantasized status.

Whilst in the short run masculinity could be asserted through symbolic codes of behaviour, in the long run it was validated through the adoption of more 'traditional' domestic roles, which led to wilder activities being dropped or lessened. This was partly on account of changes in expenditure (money was put into the building society rather than consumed in drinking bouts) and also because masculinity did not need to be 'proved' quite so emphatically.

Boys who did not conform to such expectations of masculinity could be brutally persecuted – as the case study of Martin in Chapter 8 makes clear. As in the case of girls, sexuality had to be presented in forms acceptable within the subculture.

Masculinity, feminity, and employment status

How were these sexual identities related to employment status?

The reproduction of gender roles amongst girls has been the subject of much debate, but for boys it has been regarded as unproblematical as long as employment was available. Some have discussed the importance of the wage packet and employment for maintaining a sense of masculine power and the impotence associated with the loss of these things (Walsgrove 1984; Willis 1984a, b). I have indicated that the reproduction of family roles for girls also has implications for male roles and that both boys and girls held very traditional conceptions of what the male role should be: that of 'bread-winner'. Boys therefore expected to take girls out, pay for them, and to be economically dominant within the relationship. Boys who were unable to find employment were both excluded from the masculine sources of power associated with the work-place and the wage packet, but were also disadvantaged in relationships with girls. It was likely that the girls would have a more regular income than they did.

Hence for boys, the *material* and *social* bases of masculinity were undermined – they had no money and no status as wage-earners – and consequently perhaps the *symbolic* expressions of their status were exaggerated. The stories through which masculine status were communicated were much dramatized amongst young men who were sub-employed. This was partly a result of the need to create incidents in order to avoid 'doing nothing' and partly a consequence of the fact that story-telling was one way of filling time. Stories about otherwise unremarkable incidents were therefore elaborated into ever more fantastical forms. Such stories fitted identifiable ritualized patterns, the form of which remained similar even when the content varied between accounts. These tales were almost entirely about male adventures, and whilst girls enjoyed them too, they were more inclined to dismiss them as fatuous or further evidence of the boys' immaturity.

A number of these tales covered confrontations with those in authority, such as the police, employers, staff at the DHSS. They transformed potentially humiliating encounters with those in power into personal triumphs through their reconstruction in narrative form. The narrator, who would normally be the victim in such encounters, was thereby elevated into a hero and could exact symbolic revenge. Consequently, a number of stories about frenzied bursts of rage at the DHSS offices circulated in the community even though in practice such incidents were rare. Outwitting the authorities was likewise a popular theme, although in practice the unemployed lived in conspicuous poverty, and many of them did not even get the minimal benefits to which they were entitled.

Being marginal to mainstream adult society themselves, unemployed teenagers identified vicariously with the romantic rebels whose spirit remained uncrushed:

CW: 'What sort of songs are they?' (That Mike sings in his punk band.)

Mike: 'Adverts, you know, adverts on the telly. Like just about that. And crime, you know, just about people going out, and famous criminals and that, doing things on the run.'

CW: 'What famous criminals?'

Mike: 'The Ripper, a few other ones. There's "On the Run". That's about being tied down, the bloke gets out, kills a few people. And just about life in general, that's all. It's not just fantasizing.'

CW: 'But it's not about your lives, is it?'

Mike: 'No, er, just about life in general. You get something about speed and the way it affects you. And there are songs about nuclear war, and about politicians, "Politicians make you sick, they think they know it all, but they don't know nothing at all" sort of thing. "Always telling lies, they say we're going to do such and such, but it never happens. It's just a waste of time." '

Fights were a popular source of such mythology, but the young unemployed also had dramatized accounts of *self*-destruction and 'excess' hedonism:

CW: 'Where do you get the money from then, apart from the dole and odd jobs?'

Mike: 'Er, sold all, virtually all, me belongings to a second-hand shop and that. Push bike, er, things, I sell me records, stuff like that. I don't buy no records now, I used to be always buying records. I just go out and blow all me money . . . er, didn't know the value of money, all me belongings.'

CW: 'Do you regret that?'

Mike: 'No, I haven't got no value for it, 'cos I just go out and sell them. . . . I think, if I want some money, I'll just sell it.'

CW: 'Has that been since you were unemployed then?'

Mike: 'Yep'.

CW: 'So when you were working you were collecting things and since you've been unemployed you've been selling them?'

Mike: 'No, I didn't collect nothing – I was working. Used to buy the odd record, used to just sort of, say, go out and blow all me money as usual – pay-day. Get paid Thursday night, Friday morning I'd be borrowing and the next week.'

For some groups there were pill-popping as well as drinking binges. Slimming and sleeping tablets or tranquillizers stolen from mum's and aunty's medicine cabinet, or obtained on prescription, could occasionally be supplemented with dope, 'blues' (amphetamines), glue, and inhaled commercial cleaners. Hence, doctor's surgeries and chemists shops were favourite targets for break-ins. When available these were swallowed by the handful and washed down with cheap plonk. Combined with alcohol, these substances could induce a state of frenetic activity or vacant unconsciousness and thus accelerate the effects of ordinary drinking. They often appeared to be taken not so much in order to heighten sensibility, but rather in order to deaden awareness. In this semi-conscious state young men were capable of the wild and reckless deeds they were able to relate with such gusto later.

However, psychotropic drugs did not seem to have the same deli-quescent effect on young women. The occasional suicide attempts that took place were mainly due to deliberate overdoses by girls, implying that they took these drugs more in order to dull perso-nal miseries than in order to become wild and ostentatiously reckless. Masochism too appears to take gendered forms.

It could be argued that tattooing provided the opportunity for a similar kind of masochistic heroism, since tender parts of the body – nipples and penises – were reputedly tattooed as well as arms and hands. As well as the traditional scrolls, daggers, and tigers there were home-made tattoos, supposedly the mark of having been in a penal institution of some kind. (One respondent tattooed himself in eager anticipation of being sent to a detention centre but in the end was never sent!)

By using this interpretation of story-telling as a means for asserting an increasingly insecure sense of masculine identity, the accounts of informal and occasional work can be likewise re-evaluated. Survival skills were highly prized, expressing the same ideal of independent individualism as was embodied in the self-made, self-employed orientation to outdoor labouring and craft work. Far from concealing this, many young men boasted or hinted of their abilities to 'get by'. Consequently, there were stories of how they had refurbished old cars and sold them for a profit or managed clever and perhaps slightly shady deals:

'So I went down there to sign on, with me painting and artexing gear, didn't I? Parked the van outside. Covered in paint I was. I says, ''Hurry up, mate, I'm busy. Got things to do, money to spend. I can't afford to hang about in here all day.'' That makes them mad, see? 'Cause they can't pin nothing on me. I just like to see their faces.''

The rewards from this were more social than financial for these individuals appeared to be no more affluent than the rest and many did not even get the paltry benefits to which they were entitled.

Young people from the more 'respectable' end of the continuum were more likely to spend more time at home. Some parents kept them in to prevent them from joining these 'rough' subcultures, and others preferred to stay at home themselves. Going out to visit friends, the pub or the disco, or pursuing their hobbies – such as fishing, horse riding, sailing could be carried on in the normal way. Spending time at the beach was a popular pastime, especially in the summer months, and for this reason it was sometimes difficult to track down unemployed respondents. Many regarded their period of unemployment immediately after leaving school as one of relaxation, a break between leaving school and starting work (Hendry and Raymond 1983). For the first two months they hardly really considered themselves as unemployed and were often looked upon with envy by their contemporaries who had started work. At this stage, they wanted jobs, but they wanted jobs of the right kind, and hence were prepared to wait until the right job came up. Hence, this initial period of unemployment would not appear to fit the 'calamitous' model presented by George Orwell in the 1930s.

It might be argued that I – like many professional employed people – have biased the results by describing periods of unemployment as vacuous and negative, and that this represents my own value system more than the subject's. Indeed this is a criticism that has been levelled at Jahoda's conceptualization of the five categories of experience that are somehow 'lacking' for the unemployed. It is evident, however, that whilst some of the young unemployed did feel negatively about their status, feelings were ambivalent and complicated. Moreover, unemployment affected them in a different way to that described for adults. This is illustrated more clearly in the case studies in the next chapter.

However, the experience of unemployment depended upon the young person's relationship with their family, especially in the case of 'ordinary kids' (Brown 1987; Jenkins 1983) who spent more time at home. It is to this that I now turn.

Unemployment and the family

Some parents supported their children quite generously, so that their life-style was little different to those in employment. These tended to be amongst the more contented young unemployed, for they had financial and moral support from within the home (Pahl and Wallace 1980). This financial support enabled them to continue with their hobbies and pursue social lives so that they did not suffer the social-psychological consequences described by Jahoda. These were often from the more affluent families. Poorer families were not able to be as financially supportive and were more likely to need the young person's contribution, and hence, for these young people, unemployment was more stressful.

The young person's unemployment could lead to potential sources of misunderstanding between parents and children, as this young woman explains:

'You see, they (her parents) don't understand. They don't understand what it's like to be unemployed. They think I'm not looking for work. It wasn't like this when they left school. It's not their fault really though, I suppose – it's just the way they were brought up.'

Thus, it was not coincidence, perhaps, that by 1980, 29 per cent, or nearly one-third of the sample had left home at least once – although they mostly returned again – and roughly half of these departures could be attributed to family tensions of one kind or another. When this happened, the young man or woman mostly went to live with friends or relatives until they were able to move back again.

From the moment the young person started to receive an income – either from employment or from supplementary benefits – they were expected to pay 'keep' to their parents. This was usually set at a nominal level and not according to the earnings of the young person. Hence, in 1980 it was normally between £5 and £10 per week, when in fact it cost more than this to keep a young person. Some of the more affluent parents reduced the level of 'keep' when the young person was unemployed, and others gave it all back to them in other forms – such as driving lessons – or put it into a building society or into insurance schemes on their behalf. However, they seldom dropped it by more than a couple of pounds. Any money earned over the 'keep' was disposable income for the young person. Those earning a reasonable wage could spend it whilst those without an income had little surplus if they came from poorer families. 'Keep' was paid to the mother as part of the housekeeping budget and regulated by her. Some parents subsidized children (either employed or unemployed) in other ways, too, such as by buying them cigarettes or clothes.

CW: 'Do you ever get help from anyone in your family?'

Jenny: 'What close family? Well, I can just go up me mum's any time, and just sort of open the fridge and eat anything I want to and, I mean, I do that, I don't feel guilty about doing that, 'cause I know me mum won't mind at all. If I go into her and say, "Is it all right if I have such and such?" she says, "Yer silly cow, you can have what you bloody well like. Just take it" sort of thing. And if I haven't got any money, she'll always lend me some. I never sort of borrow a lot of money off her, but, like, if she gives me fifty pence here and there, or a quid here and there, and she'll say, "No, forget it, I don't want it back" sort of thing.'

This indirect subsidization served to shelter young people from some of the more brutal consequences of unemployment: they did not have to face accumulating bills and court orders, or to dread the knock on the door from the debt collector in the way that adult unemployed householders did. It was this security provided by the natal home that perhaps allowed young people the confidence to be critical of employment conditions, to adopt alternative identities, and to leave jobs they did not like.

However, parents did exert moral pressure upon young people to find jobs and remain in them, for they often found it difficult to understand why their children rejected jobs. The following comment from a boy who had been unemployed during most of his first year since leaving school illustrates this:

Mark: 'I told me mum about the apprenticeship and she got me to go for it. Dad said the same thing. They all say it. That's the main reason I actually got the job. You keep having people nagging at you and in the end I got fed up with it. Me mum and me dad wanted me to prove that I could do it to the other relatives, like me gran and grandad (he lives with them). They're old fashioned, me gran and grandad and they believe in doing a steady job and all that sort of thing. It's their generation, I suppose.'

Other parents found jobs for their children and were angry when their children failed to keep them, as the following incident from the interview with a boy who had left a number of jobs indicates:

CW (to the boy): 'What would you like to do?'

Boy's mother (interrupting): 'Precisely what he's doing now – nothing! Because he's got no interest in sticking a job for longer than two weeks. It makes me mad! He's just left all of them. I would never help him to get another job.'

Parents resented their children adapting to a life without work and this frequently caused arguments in the home. They also tried to encourage young people to do work around the home, partly as a contribution toward the household, and partly as a moral discipline. Boys were expected to mow the lawn and girls were expected to do housework or babysitting, and indirect subsidization of incomes was justified in this way:

Sally's mother: 'She's all right, she helps me with the washing and cleaning and ironing. I don't let her sit around all day doing nothing.'

However, girls were expected to do a great deal more housework than boys were and unemployed girls did a lot more than employed ones. Hence one of the incentives for girls to find a job was to escape from domestic labour. Thus, whilst girls had alternative roles to turn to, these were not necessarily welcome ones.

Indirect subsidization by parents was an ambiguous advantage. Earning a wage had traditionally been a means by which the young person's status within the home was transformed. They could go out where and when they liked because they did so with their own money. Therefore unemployment led to greater dependence on, and domination by, parents.

This phenomenon of 'spoiling', as Leonard (1980) has called it, is a feature of changes in the reproduction of family life more generally. Whereas before the second world war young people's wages were an essential part of the houshold budget – they were only given 'pocket money' out of this – in the 1980s it was more common for parents to be subsidizing them. The flow of resources between parents and children was reversed, and material gifts and subsidies came to be regarded as evidence of parental affection. Although these changes may not have been universal (and nor are they even throughout the country), it could be said that in general post-war affluence has led to expectations of much higher standards of living on the part of teenagers, and that parents play an important part in ensuring that their children do not fall behind in the race for consumer goods. This is perhaps a product of our more 'child-centred' family and the way in which this has developed within consumer capitalism (Harris 1977).

Conclusions

Experiences of unemployment therefore differed between young workers and their parents, between male and females, between those adopting 'rough' life-styles and those adopting 'respectable' ones, and between those from affluent families and those from less affluent families. This raises the question: to what extent were young people suffering from the loss of various *latent* functions of employment, and to what extent did they miss the very obviously *manifest* one – money. Clive Jenkins is reputed to have said, 'If work were so wonderful, the rich would have found a way of keeping it for themselves.' Indeed, the leisured classes have historically despised work, but then the idle wealthy do not face as many problems as the idle poor. Given the lack of a suitable group for comparison, it is difficult to answer this question, but it illustrates the limitations of looking for 'universal' responses to joblessness. Perhaps, ironically, studies of unemployment serve merely to reinforce the work ethic?

At this stage, there did indeed appear to be a 'fracture' in the reproduction of gender roles, particularly for young men. The conventional symbols of masculinity, obtained through access to a wage, were no longer available and girls were increasingly trapped within roles they had hoped to transcend. However, we need to distinguish a number of levels in this process of the reproduction of gender roles. As well as the material, social, and symbolic levels, there were the levels of fantasy roles and real roles. What was missing on one plane could sometime be compensated for on others. Moreover, there was certainly a fracture in the sense that youth cultures of affluence were available only to those in work. Others (in this context) appeared to adopt anti-affluent subcultures or to long forlornly for the kind of leisure pursuits made possible with a wage. In this respect, they resembled Presdee's teenagers in Australia who spent their time drifting around the supermarkets and centres of commerce from which they were excluded through lack of income (Presdee 1986).

Many aspects of these responses to both employment and unemployment could be explained by young people's struggle to maintain a sense of status and dignity in situations that threatened to crush them. As Jenny said, 'You've got to be you, got to be you.' Unemployment was one such situation since it implied negative labelling by parents, peers, and others, and a lack of status in the community. Some young people therefore responded by rejecting conventional status and criticizing the work ethic. However, these alternative identities appeared to be fragile and experimental. Most of them, it later turned out, were short lived.

This was illustrated by their answers to the question: what do you think you will be doing in five years' time? Whilst their present life-styles appeared to accept and adapt to unemployment, their views of the future did not. When pressed, they rejected the scenario of growing up and starting families 'on the dole':

Gary: 'Yes, because I want, like everyone else, I want everything in life. I don't want to get married to a girl and have nothing behind me. You know, I want something behind me before I get married and you're on the dole. 'Cause it's no use getting married and you're on the dole, you ain't working or anything like that, I mean you've got nothing to look forward to. I'd sooner have a job behind me, the money behind me, before I get married anyway.'

Mark: 'I wouldn't get married if I didn't have a job. I'd feel cheap living off me wife's work. I'd want to get a job behind me.'

Mike: 'I wouldn't get married on the dole. Where would you live? How would you get food in? You couldn't build nothing up on the dole. You're stuck with what you've got.'

Most of the girls similarly expected to be married to conventionally employed young men:

'I suppose I shall be married by that time. All me sisters were married by then. . . . I suppose he would have to be working, wouldn't he?'

'I'll have three children and a house by then, I suppose. I hope it will all be finished by then. . . . I would like to have a house like my mum's, she's got a lovely house. . . . It wouldn't be much fun on the dole, 'cause you don't get much money, do you?

'Being a housewife, married with me own home. I'm saving up for it now in fact. I don't know if I'll be working, because it all depends on if I have children or not. Hopefully, I'll have children as well. I want about two children. . . . I would like to be like my sister, she's got two kids and she's still full of life. . . . She's got a council house up the road, twenty-one and happily married.'

and others were wary of having a family on the dole:

'I always said that I would never never have a family on the dole. Get a good house and a good job behind you first. 'Cause I could see what my mum went through. She got in trouble with the Social Security and it caused her no end of trouble. Somebody grassed her up because she had a boyfriend. I never, ever, want to get in that situation.'

At the time that I asked this question I never imagined that I would be able to find out what happened to them five years later. Neither did they. However, in 1984 I was able to return to do another survey. This is the subject of Part Two of this book.

5
Some case studies

Sally

I remembered Sally from the previous year (1979) as a warm-hearted, vivacious, and irrepressibly mischievous girl. I call round for her at her parent's council house. The garden contains an overgrown vegetable patch, an old pram, and a child's tricycle. Its circumference is marked by a chicken-wire fence that serves to keep the dog in and stray children out. I walk round to the side of the house, and the dog barks noisily, hurling itself against the half-panelled door. A shadow moves behind the frosted glass, hushes the dog, and opens the door a crack – simultaneously inspecting the caller and restraining the dog. I explain my purpose and they let me in.

Inside, the house is dingy, with little on the walls to conceal the stained and yellowing wallpaper. We sit round a dining table in a cramped living room, trapped between the hallway and the kitchen. A scratched, varnished sideboard on one side displays a collection of small ornaments among which are a Spanish dancer and some souvenir mugs. Lying on the floor between two armchairs are some piles of 'Klippons' homework: little brown plastic units that are assembled into larger brown plastic units like three-dimensional jigsaws, the ultimate purpose of which is obscure.

Sally, by contrast, is immaculately made-up and coiffured. She seems fresh and wholesome amidst the generally worn, drab furnishing. She wears a tight, clinging skirt, a light blouse and strappy, high-heeled sandals. She models herself on her sisters –

factory girls – who spend their money on clothes, discos, drinking, and 'having a good time'. However, Sally cannot join in with most of these activities, much as she would like to, because she is unemployed.

Her mother is present throughout the interview and hovers around interrupting or even taking over the conversation altogether. She is a slight, gnarled, and worried-looking woman, who appears much older than her fifty-odd years due to a hard life and ill-health. Her wrinkled white hair is stained yellow at the front by tobacco. She draws frequently on a No. 10 miniature cigarette, sucking in her cheeks as if to drain the last drop of solace from each drag. Sally takes one occasionally too, flicking it nervously, compulsively, into the pub ashtray in the centre of the table.

The interview is awkward and embarrassing, for it is evident that Sally's mother is using it as an opportunity to upbraid Sally. She holds her as an example of failure before her brothers and sisters because she has not managed to find a job. Sally worked at a local factory for some six months after leaving school, but she was made redundant at Christmas. It is now June, and she has been unable to find work since that time, despite prodigious efforts. During the course of the interview, Sally's response changes. Under continual haranguing from her mother, she sinks from being lively and voluble at the beginning to becoming faltering and resigned by the end. Sally gives the impression that everyone is pressurizing her. Being eager to please, she is confused as to how to satisfy these demands, for as well as enduring scolding from her mother, she is frequently summoned for interviews by the Job Centre:

'I've been around all the factories all the time, and I've got my name down at all of them, but there is never anything going. I haven't been to see the careers officer yet, because the phone is out of order. I've been going up the Job Centre and I've got to see Mr Chandler again tomorrow 'cause he wrote me another letter. I go up there every week and I sign on, but I can't phone up because we haven't got a phone and the kids have got to the one on the corner. I'm embarrassed to go to the careers officer now, I wouldn't know what to say to him. That's the third time I've gone to see Mr Chandler. He always asks me, ''Have you been anywhere?'' I have been *everywhere*. I tried the bottle-works' canteen today but there were no jobs there. I went down Wasso's and down the shirt factory. I don't know where else to go. They are standing people off everywhere now, there is no work. All the factories are on half time. And it's getting worse as well. R's made the whole night-shift redundant. Me dad was on that. . . . He won't get another job now because he's nearly sixty.'

Sally frequently played truant from school. She belonged to a group of girls for whom 'bunking off' provided far better enter-tainment than sitting in a classroom and there is a slight gleam in Sally's eye as she tells me:

'Yer, I truanted a lot. I used to go down the cafes, in the churchyard, anywhere. In the caravan classrooms. Used to have a laugh. But I used to dread coming home in case me dad found out. My dad wouldn't let me stay at home. They used to put me on the bus. Mr A. (the educational welfare officer) said they should take me to school, but I'd just get off the bus again and sneak out.'

As a result of this, Sally's parents were prosecuted and Sally's mother is still angry at what she perceives to be Sally's flippant attitude towards school. She feels that Sally is now suffering unemployment as her rightful punishment:

Mother: 'Yer, she cost me a lot of money that one – in fines!'
Sally: 'I just didn't like school. It's a big school, and it's a job finding your way round. There's all different lessons and by the time you'd found the lesson, it was finished.'
Mother (interrupting): 'She cost her father a lot of money with not going to school, and you see what happens.'
Sally: 'I was all right at the Lady Anne school!'
Mother: 'Yeah, and I say to the others, ''If you don't go to school and learn properly, you'll end up like Sally, and look at her!'' '

The mother's somewhat censorious attitude is due to her own worries about the financial situation of the family. Her husband and son have just been made redundant from a local factory where they both worked, and her other son is on short time. 'I just don't know how to make the money go round any more. I've got three of them out of work, and the little one still at school.' Not surprisingly, her resentment tended to focus at times on Sally.

Since being unemployed, Sally has stayed at home most of the time, and is put to work by the rest of the family.

> 'I've not been doing nothing really. Just sitting indoors or going down the club occasionally and having a game of pool with me mum and dad. It's a very boring life. Just going shopping with me mum. And I do for me mum. I do people's hair 'n' all sometimes. Set and wash it, roll it and that, I like doing that. I do it just to help them out, just for something to do. I always tong me sister's hair at the back for her.'

Sally's parents don't like the idea of her seeing her previous group of friends from school and consequently she has become very isolated. As her mother explained firmly,

> 'It's just as well she's not seeing them any more. She was led astray by them. They weren't going to school, so she didn't go either. They were a bad influence on her.'

Sally's social life has been severely curtailed by her lack of an income. She is forced to take her recreation with the family – which she accepts unenthusiastically – or rely upon the charity of her friend's boyfriend:

> Sally: 'I stay at home mostly. Sometimes I go out with Debby and her John, and she gets him to get me drinks. I've got no money. I get £25.90 for two weeks from the dole. I give five pound to me mum and what I've got left after I've paid me mum goes on fags and clothes.'
>
> Mother: 'And it's not enough either. She smokes all mine an' all.'
>
> Sally: 'Oh, I buy fags and that. Sometimes I buy a top if I see one I like. I'm mad on clothes. My dad used to buy me things now and then and give them to me, but he can't afford to do it now.'

Sally desperately wants to find a job. She would prefer to do factory work, partly because her sisters all work in factories. The advantage of factory work is that it offers opportunities for companionship and 'having a laugh'. Sally's sisters found her a job at L's and provided support for her whilst she was there. Consequently, this is the factory where she would most like to work:

'I was all right at L's. I liked the work, but they kept moving me around all the time. As soon as I got used to a job, I was moved onto something else, so I never settled down really. I had to know how to do everything in case they got a rush job on. Three of me sisters work there. There is one in the office. I told Mr Chandler, "Where else have I got to go? That's where all me sisters work, so if I can't get a job there, what chance do I stand anywhere else?" '

Sally also enjoys hairdressing but could not imagine working as a hairdresser, as this would involve going to college, which she thinks would be too similar to school:

'I wouldn't have minded being a hairdresser, but I wouldn't have gone to college, so I didn't apply. I wouldn't have liked it in a shop either, not standing in front of everyone else, and I am no good at reckoning up and that. I don't like standing around all the time either.'

Sally is more circumspect about accepting work at other factories, especially those that are notorious for bad conditions and low pay, but at the moment she will accept any job just to get out of the house. For this reason she regrets not having worked at school:

'If I had learned to read more, it would have been useful. I would make my children go so they wouldn't turn out like me.'

However, it is difficult to see how qualifications would have improved her plight. But she feels that at least she has turned out better than some of her friends.

'Some of the girls I used to go to school with, they've got kids and they're not married. Norma Daley, she's on the boats already (i.e. she is a casual prostitute) and Joanne Smith, she's all tarty, and they are only my age as well.'

Evidently, sexual honour was worth more than easy money, and Sally prides herself on remaining 'respectable.'

Shortly before I interviewed her, Sally had started seeing a boyfriend called Rob, an unemployed lad of twenty. She explains that her life has become more interesting since then:

> 'Since I started seeing Rob, I go out a bit more. When his giro comes through, we go out down the pub or down the club. Otherwise we go up his mum's house and watch telly. He was a friend of me mate Paula. He did have a job up at Towmasters', but he got laid off. It ain't his fault that there aren't no jobs.'

Steve

I have arranged to see Steve in the evening after he has finished work and eaten his supper. His family have recently moved into a 1920s semi-detached house, which they are in the process of refurbishing. Steve belongs to a very close-knit family and they are all involved in the interview. They usher me inside, hand me a cup of tea, ask me whether I would prefer to sit at a table, and are generally very solicitous about my comfort. I am also introduced to Steve's younger sister, for they are very proud of the fact that she is a clever girl who is taking O-levels at school. She is plucked from her homework to 'say hello to the lady who is doing a survey'. The parents seem disappointed that I did not want to interview her as well.

I had to make an appointment to see Steve, for he is a busy lad and the family perhaps wanted to prepare themselves. They show me enthusiastically around the house, which is warm and comfortably decorated. We sit in a kitchen-diner with french windows opening out onto a small but orderly garden with a greenhouse. They indicated the improvements they have made and tell me how Steve helped his father to put up all the wooden panelling. On the wall are some framed examples of Steve's handiwork in the form of geometric designs made of strands of coloured cotton and mounted on wooden plaques. Although they are keen to show me more of Steve's artwork, we postpone this for another time.

The room smells of the dinner that had been prepared. Steve's mother bustles about at the far end of the room in the kitchen section, keeping half an ear on the conversation and occasionally interjecting comments. 'He's a good little worker,' she calls out.

Steve's father sits on the other side of Steve and does much of the talking. Steve himself sits in a chair sipping his cup of tea. He is a sharp-featured, slightly built lad, with short, neat hair, pressed jeans, a clean, checked shirt and a gentle smile. Every now and then he has to cut short his garrulous father in order to answer questions in his own way.

He tells me that he is not interested in punks 'or any of that stuff. Going around dressed up like nutters,' but he still sees his friends from school. His friends are similarly respectable, quiet and hardworking, although some of them have suffered unemployment in the last year. Everyone agrees that they did not deserve this because they always 'do their best'.

Steve very much wanted to find an apprenticeship on leaving school, because as his father explained:

'It's a trade, and with a trade you can't go wrong, can you? It's always something under your belt. And then, even if you're unemployed, you can always make a bit of extra. Nah, nah, they can't take that away from you. You see, look at me. I mean, I didn't get a trade but I did learn sign writing when I first started. I don't do that now, but it is always useful to have a trade behind you. You don't see many tradesmen out of work, do you?'

Steve and his father tell me that they get considerable satisfaction from working with their hands, and point to the evidence around the home. Steve worked hard at school and, although not a high achiever, was liked by his teachers. He attended regularly and worked conscientiously for his four CSEs in woodwork, metalwork, maths and technical drawing, all useful, practical subjects he hoped would lead to an apprenticeship. He had enjoyed school well enough, but his main complaint was:

'There was not enough discipline, I don't think. They should've made you work more. And the other kids, some of 'em, they were always mucking about in class and that. They (the teachers) didn't bother much with them, but they put you off what you were doing. I would've done better if someone had made me.'

Steve had originally wanted to become a carpenter, as he thought that this was a trade he could apply at home or informally for others, but he was happy to do any kind of apprenticeship if necessary. A tradesman was a man with status in the community, someone who possessed useful knowledge and could do a job well. Steve saw manual work in terms of a particular kind of career:

> 'I wouldn't like to be like Mick (a friend). He's not getting any-where at that job (working in a timber yard). I would get another job if I was him, but he thinks only of today and tomorrow. . . . He's not looking ahead.'

This led Steve to reject many jobs as 'dead-end' and insuffer-ably boring. He regarded those who did them as lacking in ambi-tion, foresight, and intelligence. However, he is prepared to endure unsatisfying work with little money, if he thought it might lead to an apprenticeship. He had considered applying for a place with one of the leading regional employers, such as Mar-coni Avionics or Chatham Dockyard (both now closed down), but he thought that the competition, with over seventy applica-tions for each place, might be too fierce.

So Steve's father 'put a word in' for him at a firm where he used to work and was on good terms with the foreman. This was a small furniture manufacturing business and they recruited Steve as soon as he left school, promising him an apprenticeship if he performed well. Had he not found this job, he might have considered stopping at school to improve his grades, but he felt confident that a sturdy, intelligent and capable boy would be able to find something. Besides, it was well known that in these mat-ters, 'who you know is better than what you know.'

Thus, Steve had joined his present firm a year ago on the under-standing that he would be signing indentures later. He began by working hard and enthusiastically, coming in early in the morn-ing, leaving late, and always being available for extra duties and errands. He made himself the personal assistant of the foreman. In this way, he demonstrated his enthusiasm, even though the work itself was not very interesting. At the moment he is just doing routine assembly work, but he feels he needs to under-stand that sort of work to go on and do a proper apprenticeship:

> 'I started at the bottom making drawers, and I've worked me way through chests and cabinets until I was on wardrobes. It's

like assembly work really, though, but the bloke who owns it (the firm) calls it 'cabinet making'. It's not really, though, because the blokes down on the mill just cut all the wood to the right size and all I do is slot it together.'

From this he has moved onto machining wood, but has found this equally undemanding.

After one whole year of this work he has still not been asked to sign indentures or sent away to college to learn the principles of woodworking. Steve feels rather anxious about this, since he is rapidly approaching the legal age limit. His employers have not even mentioned the apprenticeship since he started work there, nor is there any indication that they intend to send him away to college as they have made no provision for his absence:

'When I started, I believed that I would be doing an apprenticeship, but instead they put me on the machines. I got a bit fed up with that, so I went up to the office in January to have a word with them and they told me I had to wait until the work picks up before they could train me, 'cause they can't take anyone else on. See, it's a bit slack now.'

Steve feels satisfied that he is getting some kind of work with wood that provides informal training, and there is still a chance that some apprenticeships may become available. He explains that the foreman is teaching him everything he knows; 'He's been very good to me.'

In his spare time, Steve goes out with a regular group of friends he has known from school. They play tennis together, go to the 'pictures', and then on Friday or Saturday evenings they might go down to one of the local pubs for a drink. His mother wants Steve to find a nice girl to take out, and asks me jokingly if I could recommend one from the survey. Steve says he prefers to go fishing.

Steve's earnings, low though they are, are accounted for in various projects. He is learning to drive with the money from his Christmas bonus and, apart from this, he gives £10 to his mother, £2 goes on clubs and catalogues, and £2 per week his mother pays into life assurance and endowment policies on his behalf. I ask him about these but he says he doesn't know what they are really, as his mother takes care of that.

Steve says that he wants to 'build something up. I'm careful with me money. I don't waste it all on the machines and stupid things like that, and yet I still enjoy myself.' One reason why Steve feels that he will achieve his goal is that he would not leave a job – no matter how boring it was – unless he had another to go to.

Steve's ultimate ambition is to become a self-employed crafts-man, as this would give him greater independence and responsi-bility. If he does not achieve this goal, he thinks he might become a foreman instead:

CW: 'What do you think you will be doing in ten years' time?'

Steve: 'I'd like to be a craftsman, self-employed preferably. I'd just like to work for myself. Like Eddy Watts – someone I know – he's a self employed joiner. He seems happy enough, working for himself. He's got his own house and every-thing.'

Mother: 'And now, you see, he's been working this length of time, he knows what he wants to do.'

Steve: 'Yes, you see, it's the independence I want – '

Mother: 'He's a good little worker!'

One month later, at the beginning of September as I was finish-ing this survey, I heard that the firm where Steve was working had closed down.

Gary

Gary lives with his parents in a run-down terrace in Queen-borough. Once a salubrious row of nineteenth-century houses, they have since fallen into decay, many of them being sub-let several times over or multi-occupied. Gary's house has a number painted on the wall in lop-sided digits and it is shared by grand-mother, a grown-up sister, a younger brother, and both parents. Gary, however, is not at home. He is usually to be found together with a group of youths who are everlastingly overhauling their motorbikes. I walk round the block and find them working on the pavement outside his mate's house. Their tools and the dismantled parts of the motorbikes spill over the road in a tangle of twisted metal. There are about six lads of various ages gathered around the dismembered bikes. Those who do not own motorbikes lean against their push-bikes and pass comment, listen or lend a hand where they can.

Gary is a keen adherent of 'heavy metal' music and styles. Permed and bleached curls tumble over his shoulders in a manner modelled on popular heavy metal heroes. He wears a black torn T-shirt, with a faded skull and crossbones motif discernible on the front. His jeans are blackened and greasy from working on the bikes and his leather jacket is tossed carelessly into the side of the road.

I interview him sitting on the pavement, whilst the lads turn over pieces of equipment in a desultory manner, for the object of dismantling the bikes seems less to mend them than to provide a rallying point.

After leaving school, Gary was unemployed for the duration of the summer until joining a YOP for a few months. He left that to start a labouring job, rebuilding the sea wall, but left that after only a couple of weeks complaining of the bad weather conditions and low pay. After this, he was unemployed for another period before finding his present job in a building firm through his father, telling them that he was twenty-five. Gary sports a fresh tattoo on his forearm.

When Gary first left school, he wanted to become a builder's labourer. Fortunately, his experience and his contacts were an advantage, for he had already worked with his father, who was himself a self-employed builder.

Gary truanted for most of his final year at school, for he did not feel that he possessed much talent for studying and saw the curriculum as irrelevant to his life plans.

His parents have been consistently supportive towards him, helping to find jobs by activating their networks and preferring to use positive reinforcement as a tactic to keep him straight. His father helped him to find his present position and bought him a new motorbike and music centre, which he will withdraw if Gary does not keep his job.

On the Youth Opportunities Scheme on which he was involved Gary learned about building by travelling around with a team renovating buildings. Whilst he enjoyed being with the team, he felt the training was of limited use because he had already gained extensive experience of building through helping his father. This made him feel sceptical about the value of the Youth Opportunities Scheme in general:

'I reckon the Careers (Service) palmed me off with that scheme in the end. Someone told me that there were seven or eight courses you could take, specializing in one thing, which would have been much better, but I didn't know about that. I have got a feeling that they wanted to get rid of me. They probably through to themselves, ''Oh, that Gary Moore's a nuisance, let's get him out of the way.'' '

Gary's main problem whilst being unemployed was boredom, although his circle of 'heavy metal' and motorbike friends helped to ease this. He observed himself slipping into a frame of mind whereby employment seemed less and less important and the chances of finding a job more and more remote. His leisure activities stretched to fill the entire day.

However, Gary is keen to emphasize that he is not a scrounger, and thinks that scroungers deserve little sympathy. He intends, very firmly, to do manual work. He justifies this by his lack of achievement at school, but also regards manual work as both more generally useful to society and as requiring more skill than non-manual work. For this reason he rejects the authority of those who, although employed, do no useful work:

'I wouldn't like to be a foreman, because I don't want to end up like a cabbage. Not doing any work. Foremen generally don't do any. I've no ambition to make my way up to the top and be in charge of everything. That doesn't interest me. If people want to be at the top, then that's up to them.'

Indeed, this mental–manual division features strongly in Gary's cosmology, for he claims that whilst he was not good at school, he is 'good with his hands'.

CW: 'What would you really like to be then?'
Gary: (Long silence, then he sighs.): 'A painter. That's what I would like to be. If I was offered an apprenticeship in that, I would take it. I've always liked art, and I used to be good at art in school. I'm always drawing at home. I used to want to be a commercial artist, but then I found out you have to have lots of O-levels and things for that. I'm not brainy enough. Most people who are good with their hands haven't got it up top.'

He hesitates here and thinks before continuing, because the

contradictions in this inverted ideology begin to become apparent.

'There again, I suppose brains are nothing to do with drawing. (He pauses again to think.) For instance, being a drummer. . . . I suppose I got on all right at school.'

He pauses again and I question him more closely.

'It's difficult to know if it is just laziness really or whether I didn't really want to do it at school. I had a good education, but I don't want to do anything spectacular, just earn a living. They don't seem to teach you what you want to learn at school. I mean, we had music, but it was Beethoven and that, and rock music isn't really like that, so it was irrelevant.'

Gary had some difficulty in specifying the precise trade he would like to do, but he knew which *kinds* of trades he is interested in:

Gary: 'I have always wanted to be a builder's labourer. You can watch and learn what everyone is doing (on a building site) that way, and then you get an idea of what you want to do. I would only want to specialize afterwards.'

Hence, Gary was offered a college course in building through the Youth Opportunities Scheme, but turned it down. He prefers some form of informal training, as it does not involve going to college. In general, he feels that there are more advantages in being able to turn your hand to a number of tasks on the building site rather than specializing in just one. Gary contrasts the advantages of labouring with the disadvantages of factory work:

'I wouldn't like to work inside. I just like it out in the open and I don't mind the weather. I couldn't stand being locked up all day, doing the same job all the time. In building you can do different jobs all the time, so it's interesting, you can talk to people at the same time. You have a good laugh when you're working.'

Gary also feels that it is important to be treated with respect and courtesy at work

'I don't mind if someone asks me to do something. It's the way they treat you is important. Like this foreman at the moment, he doesn' ask, ''Can you do something,'' but, ''Do this!'' That brings out the negative in me. I'll do it, but they won't get the best out of me. I'll be too narked to concentrate.'

He also has a sense of being exploited:

'I'm a builder's labourer, but I do all the proper jobs. I'm cheap labour for them really, because they only pay me a labourer's rate and they don't have to pay a tradesman.'

Nevertheless, he works hard, leaving at six o'clock in the morning and returning at six o'clock in the evening. Even his social life has had to be sacrificed to these long and exhausting hours, for he is aware that under the present circumstances it would be difficult to find another job.

His real ambition, however, is to become self-employed. Rather than seeing this as insecure and as casual work 'on the lump', Gary sees it as providing a very positive status. Becoming self-employed would enable him to earn a living without being tied down to an employer, and therefore subject to petty restrictions and an externally imposed timetable. Moreover, he thinks he can also earn more money this way, or work 'on the side' if necessary to boost his earnings.

'I would like to be self-employed, working with this bloke, the chippy. You get jobs through other builders. You're hired out when you're self-employed. You do price work, or you get a basic day's pay. There's no messing about, putting it in the books and that, and you earn a lot more. You get more work, and more free time, and you're not sacked for taking a day off, like you are at L and B (his present firm). I run the risk of being sacked every time I go for a job. At this place you have to work at one job until it's finished, and they are all very big jobs, so I get bored. I would rather do something for two weeks and then do something else at another place. That way, there's more variety.'

Therefore, by being self-employed he can avoid monotonous routines, being able to come and go as he pleases. In this way, he could adapt his working hours to suit his social life.

Whilst he seems generally contented with life, at present,

Gary's main problem is how to cope with boredom. Whilst school was boring, so was playing truant. Unemployment was occasionally boring, but not as boring as working in a factory subject to machines. The difference was that in a factory you were paid for being bored. Some of his tasks at work at present are boring because they seem repetitive and purposeless.

The things in life that are not boring, however, are those that are actively chosen and engage his creative capacities. Playing in a heavy metal band is one such activity. Gary is a member of a band called 'Torment' and he talks enthusiastically about it. Since starting his present job, however, he has not been able to practise as much as whilst he was unemployed, and consequently he was ejected from this band and forced to join an inferior one.

> 'There are at least twenty young musicians on the island and there is nowhere for them to go. The hall (where they have been practising and have caused complaints) is so old that all the sound escapes. There are two punk bands and two heavy metal bands. All the other kids are getting drunk and having fights, smashing the place up, and we have an interest. We don't want to end up on the streets, and there's not much alternative.'

Gary's future plans encompass a range of goals, including leisure pursuits, housing, and employment. These objectives complement one another in so far as they lead towards a self-determining and independent life-style.

> CW: 'What do you think you will be doing in ten years' time?'
> Gary: 'Playing at Hammersmith Odeon, I hope! I won't be on the island. I want to buy some land and build my own house and have another house somewhere else which is nearer London. I'm determined to go on with one band or another. I'm a drummer. The group I'm in now is not so good, but I feel I ought to stay with them and anyway, I got chucked out of the other group for not practising enough. I will advertise all round the Medway area and get a really good band together. . . . I might be working in building, I suppose, but I don't know what at.'

Jenny [1]

In order to find Jenny, I first make a visit to her local pub, a place where the punks congregate. They give me an address in Sheerness. After walking along one of the nineteenth-century terraces in Marine Town, I finally stop before a narrow, shabby house that fits the description given to me in the pub (I have not been given a number). I rattle the rickety door, for there is no knocker. There is a long wait whilst I am inspected from behind a curtain in the room adjacent to the door. Will they answer? Eventually, the door is opened suspiciously by a girl in leopard-spotted slacks and hair. It is Jenny's unemployed house-mate and she leads me upstairs. The room is dingy with one dusty sash window overlooking walled back yards and a bleak parade of grey brick houses. It is a dull winter's day and Jenny's room is bitterly cold. We both sit huddled in overcoats – Jenny on an unmade bed and I on the kitchen chair – as she explains that she has no money today to buy paraffin for the heater.

Jenny contributes £5 per week towards the rent, and until recently the DHSS gave her only £7, although they have now raised this to £11 per week. This leaves her little surplus.

Lying around on the floor are a number of books on psychology borrowed from the school library, where she worked until recently on a WEP. They include titles such as *Adolescent Breakdown* and *Depression and Breakdown*; R.D. Laing rubs covers with *Brighton Rock* and the poems of Leonard Cohen. There are also a number of exercise books full of poems she has written.

A light bulb hangs from the centre of the ceiling illuminating the tangle of clothes and books on the floor. She explains that when she gets around to it she will paint the room black. On the wall is a newspaper cutting of her and a number of punk friends at the 'Hoppit' club in Holland.

Last time I met her, Jenny was a punk. She had cut a rather dramatic pose at the local pub with her hair dyed black at the front and sharpened into fine needles whilst the rest was back-combed and lacquered so that it stuck out from her head in a petrified helmet, like a parody of a 1960s beehive. On these occasions all the punks had white, mask-like faces and black circled eyes in carefully crafted expressions of frozen horror. For a while they also wore red kilts and black trousers. However, Jenny has now left the punks, finding that they had become too dandified.

Today her demeanour is muted by a head cold that adds to her natural pallor, blunts her voice, and causes her speech to be punctuated by frequent sniffs. But her eyes are bright and challenging beneath a shaggy fringe. She compensates for this relatively mild appearance by wearing a black sweatshirt inside out. It makes life 'less boring' she explains:

> Jenny: 'Yeah. You've got to wear your leather jacket and your such-and-such trousers and have your hair like this, then you're all right. If you're different to them, they don't like it. Can't just be you.'
>
> CW: 'D'you think you're more you now, then?'
>
> Jenny: 'No, because now I'm just sort of being like this because I don't want to be the same as they are. . . . I want to be something different, but you can't. If you wear this you're such and such and if you wear that you're something else, you can't just be you, you've got to have a label.'

This determined search for an authentic identity leads her to reject conventional images of femininity:

> CW: 'Do you prefer to be with blokes or girls?'
>
> Jenny: 'Depends what sort of girls they are. There's a lot of girls I wouldn't like to be with, the sort of typical (she mimics a childish voice), "Oh I want to go out, what can I do?", "My boyfriend said this to me," or "I want to get engaged." I can't stick girls like that. "What can I wear to the disco?" "Oh, I've got to get my hair cut and don't know what style" "Oh, what do you think of my new make-up?" "Look at my new nail-varnish" "Oh, I've got some new curtains for my bedroom". I can't stand people like that.'

Likewise, she rejects conventional views of marriage and the family.

> 'I don't believe in it. Marriage is – oh! – awful. I mean, I can't see how you can really think that much of one person anyway. It's just jealousy. It's sort of a little bit of paper saying, "You belong to me" sort of, it's just, it isn't fair – if you think about it. It's better to live with them and get on with it, whenever it comes up. It's just a bit of paper isn't it? Just like ownership. Yeah. Like having a dog licence.'

Jenny's rejection of conformity leads her to question patterns of regular work, respectable living and polite language. These views are particularly reinforced when Kevin, a friend with strong opinions drops by. Kevin is hostile towards me, making the interview situation uncomfortable. Kevin is a tall, stooping, prickly man in his early twenties, who is remorselessly and articulately caustic. He has been unemployed for a number of years, and his hunched figure in a battered duffle coat is a familiar one in the nearby pubs and streets. He sits on the floor for a while, mocks my questions, makes blistering attacks upon the 'disco crowd', the London tourists and the 'Social Security' before he abruptly strides out again.

Jenny has developed her own rhythms of life. Much of her day is spent in bed and she prefers to be up at night. She dreams of becoming a professional writer or poet, which would fit with the kind of times she chooses to keep and the kind of life-style she wants to develop.

'If I've got nothing at all planned and nothing to do I get up around twelve, one. It depends on if I've got any money.'

Her weeks lurch from peaks to troughs depending upon the availability of money and of 'events' that might happen. If someone has got some money then they can all go up the pub and have a good time, otherwise it means staying in and finding cheaper diversions such as reading and sleeping. In general, pleasure takes precedence over subsistence:

'See, it depends, it depends how much money we get and what we decide to spend it on, sort of thing. It's either buy food, stay in, and be bored, or go down the pub, get pissed, and starve.'

Like many of the young unemployed, she is concerned to get her kicks where she can and this involves spending money whilst you've got it, because it may be some time before you get any more. In this way, no one has any money for very long, but they can all share in the good fortune of others. Jenny can always scrounge money from the landlord of the local pub, or from her mum, if necessary.

Hence, most of her time is spent 'doing nothing' or waiting around for 'something' to happen. When 'something' fails to just happen, Jenny and her friends go down the pub to look for it.

CW: 'Do you go down the pub when you've got no money?'

Jenny: 'Say if I had fifty pence, I'd go down the pub and buy them some drinks. Well, I mean, it depends who it is. I mean, it's usually you go out with a lot of money and everyone buys you drinks, and you go out with nothing and nobody buys you drinks. I don't buy just anyone a drink. If someone buys me one, I buy them one.'

CW: 'So you get them all back, it evens out?'

Jenny: 'Well, it depends how many foreigners are about!' (She laughs.)

CW: 'They buy drinks for you?'

Jenny: 'Well, the past couple of nights they have had a few. It's all right if that's all they want.'

Jenny did not lack for company in her present life-style, for friends could be easily accommodated. Indeed, at one stage their house had become one of the local teenage 'drop-in houses': a place where anyone on the run from parents, school, or trouble of any kind could sleep for the night, the sort of house Jenny herself had taken advantage of at one time.

'Yes, various people come to crash out on the floor. It used to be quite a houseful . . . But we had ever such a lot of trouble over this house and the noise and everything, people coming in at all hours of the day and night, climbing in the windows and things like that, so we just stopped them all coming round in the end.'

Jenny is very critical of the low status, unskilled employment available locally and has so far only managed to find temporary work on the YOP. Jenny thinks of herself as an intelligent person. At school she was considered promising until she was dropped from most of the O-level groups through truculent behaviour. Towards the time of leaving, school just seemed to become more and more irrelevant:

'I just didn't like it. I just hated it. Hated the teachers, everything. They just don't teach you anything you need to know about life at school. They just pump stuff into you. Couldn't do anything *you* want.'

The best thing about school, she recalls, were the opportunities to lark around and challenge the rules. She is equally critical of the YOPs. After having finished the first YOP course, she was unemployed for a few months and then joined another. However, she left that after just two weeks complaining of the irrelevant and patronizing content of the instruction.

'It was just sort of stupid things, like games about how you was to survive if you was stranded on the moon. As if I'm going to the bloody moon. What good's that going to do me? Here I am stranded in Sheerness for hours on end. It's all out of perspective, isn't it?'

Because she left this scheme, her supplementary benefits were suspended for six weeks. Whilst unemployed, Jenny applied for a number of jobs with her friend, at a cafe, a bingo hall, but none of these really aroused her interest and she rejected these jobs before they had a chance to reject her:

'Oh yes, what else did I do then? Oh yes, quite a few forms I sent in. I got a thing for Tesco's 'cause they said I could work at Tesco's. Gives me one of them big questionnaires, about four pages. It got so personal, I thought, ''Sod it! I'm not filling that in. I'm not telling them all what they want to know.'' They wanted to know everything, really things they didn't need to know.'

Jenny draws an equation between the amount of humiliation she is prepared to suffer and the level of financial reward a job offers. She wants a job, but one that will engage her interest, one she can commit herself to.

Jenny refuses to modify her appearance to fit either employer's expectations or conventional models of femininity. The world would have to take her on her own terms.

But how long could she go on like this? When asked to look ahead Jenny said:

'I don't know 'cause I never think about it. No, I don't think about the next week. I think, as far as I'm concerned, I think in terms of a couple of hours. Don't think about what you're going to be doing tomorrow, you might go out and get run over by a bus. Don't plan anything. I just think ''Well, if I'm here, I'll see what happens.'' '

Five Years Later
1984

Part Two continues with the lives of the same young people at twenty-one. In this section, their lives in work and out of work are explored along with their relationships with friends, parents, and partners. Chapter 6 concentrates upon their work trajectories whilst Chapter 7 concentrates upon their domestic life courses. In Chapter 8 there are some more case studies to illustrate the material in other chapters.

Only 84 out of the original 153 could be traced in 1984. Of these, 7 were still at college or university. Fifty-seven were interviewed in depth, and biographical details about a further 27 who were abroad or away at the time of the interview were collected from relatives. I interviewed only those who remained on the island, since I did not have the resources to travel all over the country trying to find the rest. This attrition of the sample may have influenced the results: perhaps those who were still on the island were the most disadvantaged, or the least occupationally mobile? Since the 1970s, opportunities elsewhere have dried up and the rest of England has begun to resemble Sheppey more in terms of the labour market for young people. It is arguable, therefore, that in times such as these, few would have been lost through geographical mobility and those who were left were more or less typical of young people in general. One advantage of this limited geographical context is that we know that they were still constrained by the community and labour market described in Chapter 2, and this is important from the point of view of the analysis to be presented here, for other aspects of the island – most notably the housing market – started to become more influential.

In this section I address other questions: to what extent was the experience of employment and unemployment different at twenty-one to sixteen? What effects did employment and unemployment have upon the domestic life course of young people?[1]

6

In and out of work

I have indicated that on first entering the labour market, young people were not fully incorporated as members of the work-force. First, some of their aspirations had been out of phase with labour market conditions, although some were still hoping to follow their hopes through in the long term. Second, there was considerable instability in their employment careers during the first year in the labour market. This was due partly to the fact that the jobs young people did were marginal and insecure, but also because a large number of young people were discontented with their jobs. Although they had been socialized to accept their positions within the social hierarchy, they were not yet fully 'reproduced' as workers and some of them rebelled against the situation in which they found themselves. What happened to them five years on?

In 1984 I asked everyone about the jobs they were currently doing and the results of this are given in *Table 2*. This shows the current occupations of respondents, if they had one, or their last occupation, if they were either unemployed or housewives. These jobs were classified according to broad categories of skill in order to be compatible with the classifications used in 1979. These classifications are used rather than the usual 'social class' because with such irregular employment patterns it was very difficult to assign a social class to many young adults. It can be seen that the patterns of employment were very diverse: whilst some had left school at the minimum age, others had gone on to college or university – one person had even done both!

The table shows that most of this sample of 21-year-olds in 1984

Table 2   *Most recent employment of young adults 1984*

	Men	*Women*	%
College/university	6	3	11
Supervisory	5	2	8
Clerical	—	9	11
Skilled manual – formal	5	5	12
Skilled manual – informal	6	—	7
Unskilled manual	18	13	37
Armed forces	4	3	8
Never worked	—	5	6

Source: Survey of Young Adults on Sheppey. Total = 84 (44 male, 40 female)

had become manual workers, the majority of them being unskilled (37 per cent). A substantial minority (8 per cent) had joined the armed forces, as this was one of the few ways of securing a regular job. Two had found managerial or professional training, both of them being male (classified under 'Supervisory' in *Table 2*), whilst 11 per cent of the sample, all of these being female, had found clerical jobs. It would appear that most young people had had to adjust to the kinds of jobs of which they had been very critical five years previously.

The downward mobility in aspirations noted already in 1979 was further confirmed in 1984, for roughly one-half of the fifty-seven interviewed in detail had been forced to accept jobs that were less skilled or lower in status to those for which they had aimed, or jobs of which they had been very critical. Their subjective perceptions had been forced to fit objective conditions. When I asked them whether they regretted not doing the jobs to which they were originally committed, many of them had forgotten what aspirations they had held:

Alan: 'Don't know, can't remember what I wanted to do. I'll do anything at all so long as it is working. I don't mind what I do.'

Others tried to channel their creativity into spare-time hobbies:

CW: 'Originally you wanted to be a landscape gardener. Do you still want to do that?'

Martin: 'I would like to as a hobby, you know, design other
people's gardens. Like I'm doing mine now. . . . It's not a
very big garden, the one we're getting, so we're gonna have
sort of big white tubs.'

CW: 'Yeah.'

Martin: 'But, um, I've lost contact with that sort of thing now.'

Whilst still others did regret not acquiring a skill of some sort,
they realized that it was by then too late to do anything about it:

CW: 'In 1979 you said you wanted to learn a skill, do you still
want to do that?'

Tony: 'Well, everyone would, wouldn't they, if they had a
chance?'

Terry: 'You get a skill behind you and you're better off, aren't
you? The money is better.'

CW: 'Is it the satisfaction too?'

Tony: 'Well, yeah, that as well. Because otherwise you're just
labouring, aren't you really? You're just one of the underdogs.'

Others had come to change their views for different reasons:

CW: 'Back in 1980 you said you wanted to be a self-employed
builder. Do you still want to do that?'

Gary: 'No. I don't know really, but I don't want to do that.'

CW: 'Why is that?'

Gary (He pauses for thought.): 'Well, I always wanted to follow in me dad's footsteps since I was a young lad. You know
me dad was a builder, so I thought I'd be builder like him
and take over the business when he packed it in. I suppose
as you get older your views change and what have you. So I
didn't want to do it anyway.'

Gary's father was now unemployed. He continued:

Gary: 'I'm hoping to do something more constructive really. I
like being outdoors. I don't like being in a factory. But I
could be a salesman, for example, and the chiropodist job
that came up, I would really like to have done that. Strange
ain't it? See, I've applied for jobs in a factory, but I don't
really want to work in one.'

Thus, by 1984 young men and women were more likely to be

resigned to their lot in life. Furthermore they were likely to tolerate the kinds of jobs that were available, rather than rejecting
them as they had done five years previously:

> Dennis: 'Oh, it's lousy pay. Well, they can hire whoever they
> like, can't they? They can kick you out and they know they
> can get someone off the dole queue, so they don't have to
> pay so much, do they? They can find anyone, can't they? It's
> so simple so they keep the prices down, it's as simple as
> that. You can't earn no more.'

Another noticeable change was that young men and women
had become increasingly instrumental in their orientations
towards work. They were instrumental in the sense that they
increasingly began to think that any job was better than no job,
and in the sense that a job that paid more was better than one that
paid less. On leaving school, many respondents had sought
some sort of satisfaction from their jobs and felt disappointed
when this was not forthcoming: they had emphasized the *intrin-
sic* satisfactions of work. However, as they grew older they
sought instead any job that was regular and paid well: now they
emphasized the *extrinsic* factors. For example, one lad who had
eulogized the satisfactions of craft work when he first left school,
had not altered his preference for craft work, but had changed his
reasons for preferring it.

> CW: 'What's the advantage of getting a trade then?'
> Dennis: 'It's just getting a job, and more money, 'n' it?'
> CW: 'And more enjoyment?'
> Dennis: 'It's not that so much, it's getting a job. They can pick
> up a labourer anywhere, they're two a penny. But if you've
> got a trade then you know you can do something. I can go to
> a firm and get a job.'

It was not so much that young people thought job satisfaction
was any less important, it was more the case that they saw less and
less possibility of finding it in the kinds of work that was available:

> Deb: 'Then I wrote off for a job in Israel. I've only just got the
> papers through for that, but I don't really like the sound of
> it. You don't get enough pay, you see, really, to pay your
> way. It's one of those – what are they called?'

CW: 'Kibbutz?'

Deb: 'Yeah, that's right, one of them. So you don't come back with anything, but I'll have to see how it goes, I suppose.'

Sue: 'It's an experience, that's the main thing, isn't it?'

Deb: 'Yeah, well, I would like an outdoor job really. They said you see you could do factory work there, and I thought, "Cor blimey! You go all those millions of miles and end up doing the same sort of thing to what you've done here!"'

However, as Deb illustrates, they still dreamed of escapes and alternatives.

Thus, whilst outdoor and casual work were still seen as preferable to factory work in many ways, young men also complained that it was irregular and unstable – the very things that had been considered advantages when they first left school. Hence, many sought security rather than excitement, and a regular wage rather than irregular work. Young people were 'settling down' to regular employment. What were the reasons for this?

The first reason, already mentioned by one respondent was the 'discipline' imposed by rising unemployment. Those in work were grateful to have jobs, and those out of work were happy to accept anything in order to avoid being unemployed.

CW: 'Then you got laid off (from her factory job).'

Deb: 'Yeah, yeah. You see, I think a lot of it was to do with the prisoners, 'cause they got prisoners to do it. See, it's free labour for them, isn't it? So they got rid of us instead . . . and also 'cause they ran out of contracts. They brought out those electronic typewriters and no one was buying the other ones.'

CW: 'And how did you find it there?'

Deb: 'Well, I get on with them all. They weren't, like, bitchy in there, but I always used to think they were a bit thick, you know, that they were stupider than me. It sounds really stuck-up, but a lot of them really were. But you learn to put up with it in the end.'

CW: 'Did you think of leaving?' (She had left a previous factory job.)

Deb: 'No. Well, I always said that I wouldn't leave that job unless I had another one to go to. I got stuck in a bit of a rut, I suppose, and just didn't bother.'

The second reason was because an increasing number of respondents had come to accept family responsibilities and were therefore no longer in a position to chop and change jobs:

CW: 'Would you take any job rather than be unemployed?'

Dennis: 'I'd do anything, anything. I've even been down the Council to see if I can sweep roads.'

CW: 'Have your expectations gone down then, do you think?'

Dennis: 'Yeah, it's a real crusher, especially if you're out of work two years like I was. In the end. You're so hopeful at first. When I first got unemployed, I can remember, it was when Thatcher first got in and you could see the jobs disappearing then. . . . Oh, it's a real killer being unemployed for two years. See, it's not just me now, it's them (indicating his girlfriend and child) I got to think of.'

Thus, for men with a house, a wife, or children the search for employment became more determined and they were grateful to accept anything that came their way in order to pay the bills and meet their responsibilities. Women in this position encouraged their men to hold down a steady job for similar reasons. Hence, although most young men thought of themselves as more settled at twenty-one than at sixteen, there was a distinction between those with domestic responsibilities and those without. Young men are usually discussed in relation to their work lives in the public sphere, but it can be seen that their domestic lives in the private sphere had an important influence upon their lives in other respects.

Young women's commitment to work should also be seen in terms of their domestic life course. Young women who committed themselves primarily to a domestic life either gave up employment or were happy to take any part-time job just in order to make ends meet – depending upon their circumstances. Young women who were single, or who did not prioritize a domestic career, [1] on the other hand, were equally as committed to employment as young men were, and suffered just as acutely through the absence of it. In general, then, whilst assuming domestic responsibilities served as a spur to the employment commitment of young men, these served to depress the aspirations of young women. They were more likely to accept part-time work and local wage rates. However, both young men and young women became more instrumental under these circumstances. They worked now in order to assemble and improve their homes. The real divergence between young men and young women therefore came when they moved towards a family of their own. The different kind of domestic career adopted by young women and the reasons for adopting it are further discussed in the next chapter. At this stage, however, it is important to note that the roles within the domestic sphere and roles within the labour market were interconnected for young adults of both genders.

The third reason was habituation. If a person was in a job for long enough, then they simply became accustomed to it, developing various techniques of survival in order to cope rather than wasting time wondering what they might have done otherwise:

> Deb: 'Well I went to work at F's factory, but I hated it there. I only lasted two months. The rest of the time I've been at L's factory. That was five years I was there before I was made redundant. They kept twelve girls on but I can't really see it picking up myself. They made everyone else redundant. But I wouldn't really want to go back there anyway. Well, it's a dead-end job, isn't it, factory work? I should have got out long ago.'

Some things had not changed, however. Self-employment and outdoor work were still regarded as an ideal that could lead potentially to more independence and freedom:

> Collin: 'You're your own boss, sort of thing. . . . If I was working nine to five, that would be it. But as it is, I can just go on and do other kinds of work, I can do any kind of work, I can fit the hours to suit me. See, you end up working a lot more really. I'm working Sunday, Saturday this week, bank holiday we are having off. . . . There's no set time, it varies all the time. . . . We don't rush about, you know, we do our time. That's the good part of it. It's not boring at all, it's not the same thing all the time, it's always different. Different places, different times of day.'

> Ray: 'My ambition has got to be to own your own company and not work for anyone else.'
> CW: 'What are the advantages of that then?'

Ray: 'Well, look, you can only get out of something what you put into it if. If you are working for somebody else there is a limit to what you can get out. With a company of your own, you see, as long as the economics are right, it's entirely down to you what you get out of it and what you put into it. You see what sort of success it is and I work hard. You see people around the streets, people I went to school with, and I see them all on the dole and what have you, sort of thing, and it's turned me off. I wouldn't want to be in that sort of position. So it's a question of either you sit around and stagnate or you go and do it – and I don't want to stagnate.'

Job turnover

Turning now to job turnover, I found that 35 per cent had held only one job since they left school, but that these tended to be either jobs they could not leave, such as the army, or in more skilled occupations, or those carrying more responsibility: it would appear that as in 1980, job satisfaction leds to greater job stability.

What were the reasons for leaving jobs? It was evident from the interviews that 'voluntary' job departures – which had accounted for roughly half the turnover in 1980 – declined as people grew older.[2] As we have seen, by 1984 young people had come to accept employment they might have resented five years previously. Indeed, they often regretted their earlier impetuous behaviour:

Penny: 'Mind you, six months after he left that place he regretted it, he regretted what he had done. He realized how hard jobs were to get.'

Dennis: 'Yeah. I thought, if only I'd held onto it till I got another job, instead of just on the spur of the moment, sort of thing, packing it in. I should have held on until I got another job at least, but I just didn't think of it then. There were jobs going before that job, so I though it was easier to get a job. Within three to four months you could see the jobs just dwindling away and then I was unemployed for two years.'

However, as we have seen, at least half of this turnover was due to unstable conditions of employment. *Figure 8* documents

Figure 8   Nature of work experience 1979–1874

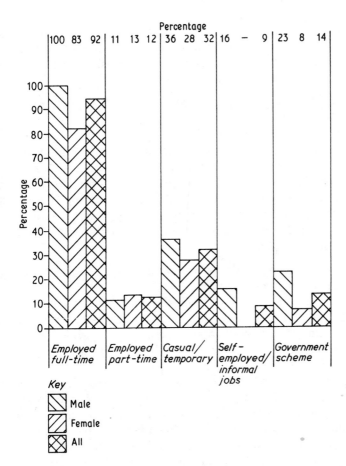

Key

▨ Male

▨ Female

▨ All

the different kinds of employment people had undertaken over the five-year period. It can be seen that although most had done full-time jobs at some point, many had been doing casual, temporary or 'self-employed' work (usually casual) and a further 14 per cent had been recruited onto temporary government schemes.

Thus, much of the work performed by young people could be said to be located within the 'secondary' labour market: that is, the sector providing temporary, low paid, and insecure jobs. The 8 per cent who had never worked full-time were those girls who had become housewives or mothers soon after leaving full-time education and these will be discussed more fully in the next chapter.

Whilst temporary and casual employment had been prized by young men when they first left school, it was evident that in the long term such jobs were unsatisfatory for providing a means of livelihood, especially as the labour market shrank:

> Dennis: 'I'm going for me subcontractor's ticket, going for a self-employed ticket.'
>
> CW: 'Does that make it more secure?'
>
> Dennis: 'Well, no, it's less secure actually. But the thing is, with construction sites now it's all subcontracting work and you need a ticket, that's the easiest way of getting on a site really if you have a ticket. And £3, £4 an hour, that's what you charge them. Well, that way, they don't have to bother with your tax and national insurance or nothing like that. They just give it to you.'

Those who had originally opted for such work found themselves trapped in it later.

It was evident that as they matured, young men and women adopted new styles of life, which in turn necessitated a regular income – something casual labouring could not provide. Thus, they looked for different qualities in their work, especially financial rewards and job security.

So far I have painted a rather gloomy picture of declining jobs and lowered expectations. This was the experience of the majority of the sample, with 51 per cent suffering downward mobility in relation to their aspirations during their first five years in the labour market. However, some did better than they had expected. There were five boys and four girls in this category. Two of the boys had become foremen or supervisors at the factories where they worked, and felt content with these careers. Promotion in most cases helped to foster greater commitment to the job. One young man had improved his position and his earnings substantially by judicious moves from one building contractor to another, until he had worked his way up to a position of site manager. Two other young men had left office or apprenticeship jobs to go to college and study – for a degree in one case and for theological qualifications in another. Those who had been upwardly mobile were noticeably more confident in their abilities to find reasonable jobs and to change their careers by their own efforts. They did not feel themselves to be at the mercy of the labour market or an unpredictable economic climate in the same way as those who had had to lower their expectations or had experienced substantial periods out of work. It also made them less tolerant of their less fortunate peers:

Ray: 'I mean, all these questions you keep asking me about unemployment, it must be really bad in the country at the moment for all these questions to be asked on unemployment. You see, they're taking it as a social thing on life, see. They say, "Oh, well people are unemployed, that's why they go around the streets bashing up the houses, bashing up old girls," that sort of thing, so it's all right because they're unemployed. I don't agree with it really, I think it's a bit of a grind all this stuff on unemployment.'

CW: 'But you're much better off than a lot of people of your age, aren't you?'

Ray: 'Yeah, but it's only because I've done it myself. I mean the government ain't giving me any money, or anything like that. I mean, it's purely because, I mean, I know this sounds big-headed, like blowing me own trumpet and everything, but it's purely because we done it, see we could have sat down and said, "Things'll come along, things'll come along." But then you don't get what you want, do you?'

Collin: ' 'Cause I wouldn't work in no factory. No, I'd just never work in a factory. I wouldn't go on the dole or nothing like that, but I wouldn't work in no factory. See there's always work if you want it, there's always work if you want it. . . . It's just like that I don't like sitting about. Not like a lot of me mates and that. You know, people who go around dressed like punks and Mohicans and all that sort of thing. I mean, how can you employ somebody like that? I wouldn't work with them myself. If I had to work with someone like that, and they turned up looking like a punk, I wouldn't have him. It's just pride, I suppose.'

Of the girls, two were now insurance clerks instead of working in shops. They were both now marrying young professional men and buying their own homes, looking forward to a privatized settled life. This was in contrast to their expectations five years before, when they had moved from job to job. Another girl had become a supervisor in a café after some years as a factory worker, and another had become a manageress of a wine store after some years of drifting in and out of work. Both of these had developed more settled life-styles and held longer-term plans as a result, both in relation to those of others in the sample, and in contrast to their own five years before:

> Tina: 'Well, I don't have much time really, because I've got too much to do, you see. I've got so much responsibility here with nine girls working for me at the moment . . . so I just work all day and when I get home all I want to do is to go to sleep. You don't get much time for anything else. It's a hard job, but I like it, I like the responsibility. I'd rather work for myself and be my own boss.'
>
> CW: 'What was the worst thing about being unemployed?'
>
> Tina: 'Well, probably not having enough money and just not working really. See, sometimes I think I'd rather not work, but I'd be so bored if I wasn't working, I'd be bored straight away. See, look at the moment, the job is my life really, everything is involved in the job, it's a twelve-hour day really.'

But these were the exception rather than the rule. By landing the right job at the right time, these young people discovered abilities in themselves they had never thought they possessed and gained considerable satisfaction from their employment as a result. What is striking when comparing this group with the rest, is how differently they approached their present lives and futures. Their self-confidence highlighted the sense of helplessness expressed by others in the sample. Their plans and expectations for the future contrasted with the more forlorn and tenuous hopes, or careful fatalism, held by others. This is illustrated in the case studies.

Informal and occasional work

Informal and occasional work had been important at the point of leaving school because it was a vehicle for learning skills and provided access to full-time employment. What was its role five years later? In 1984, respondents were asked in some detail about the kinds of informal and casual work they had carried out. The precise question was 'Do you have any extra sources of income?' and although few were actually doing any extra jobs at any given time, out of those who were interviewed in detail, a total of twenty-two, or 39 per cent, had done some informal or occasional work over the last five years. However, this sort of work did not provide a regular source of income, nor could jobs such as these constitute a livelihood. Many of these jobs were carried out in the form of 'favours' for friends, relatives, or neighbours, for which they might be paid wholly or partly in kind. One or two respondents, indeed, had established their own economic philosophy in this respect:

> Glen: 'So I'd rather, you know, I'd rather go round someone's house and do some wiring or something like that, and if they want to give me money I say, ''Nah, buy us a couple of pints later,'' which is better for me. . . . That's the easiest way to do it, you know, because that way you're not breaking any laws, you can't get done. 'Cause I've already checked up on that. . . . I'd rather have clothes, 'cause, you know, they won't give you a clothing grant, and it's clothes you need the most.'

These kinds of activities should therefore perhaps be seen as embedded in a whole range of social relationships and forms of social exchange (Pahl 1984; Wallace 1984). Thus, for example, one young man would help his widowed mother run her caravan site as a contribution towards his keep, and also out of a sense of loyalty and duty. Another girl, a housewife, would knit garments for neighbours in return for wool or a small additional charge. These were all part of on-going reciprocities.

Table 3 gives a breakdown of all the different kinds of jobs undertaken over the five-year period. It is evident that there is a clear division by gender with men in general doing more of it and finding the more lucrative occasional employment. Thus the divisions in the 'shadow' labour market reflect those in the formal one (Wallace and Pahl 1986). The most common form of additional work for women of this age group was to act as an

Table 3   *Extra sources of income*

Males		Females	
Bait digging	3	Knitting	1
Selling eels	1	Wedding catering	1
Painting and decorating	1	Agent	2
Building	5	Catalogue	1
Double glazing	1	Babysitting	1
Electrical	1	Hairdressing	1
Selling scrap	1	Apple picking	1
Doing up cars and motorbikes	1		
Helping on caravan site	1		

agent for a catalogue mail-order firm or for various home vending agencies, such as Avon or Tupperware.[3] For this they were often paid a small commission or were paid in goods. Mail-order sales appeared to be a fast-expanding means of purchasing goods, because with rising unemployment and irregular incomes, it was often the case that the only way a household could buy goods was to pay for them in small weekly instalments.

Young men's occasional work was often associated with the construction industry. Some respondents observed bitterly that this may have been a factor that contributed towards the erosion of wages in that industry. However, it was more often the case that this was undertaken for 'mates' as a favour, working on each other's homes. As such, it could also be a source of satisfaction:

> Glen: 'I like a challenge really, if you know what I mean. Like if someone says to me, like – it's like this car out there, like. If I sit and transform it into something different to what it looked like before, y'know, then I'm pleased with that. I can sit back and say, "I done that." '

This kind of work, sometimes associated with the 'black economy' has aroused considerable interest in the context of rising unemployment. For example, a group of economists at Liverpool have argued that the rate of unemployment could in fact be as much as 40 per cent lower if these kinds of jobs were to be taken into account.

'Yet if in the final analysis the size of the black economy is as substantial as many researchers suspect, this not only raises questions about output but also about our conception of unemployment, and with it other welfare considerations, not least poverty and inequality.'

(Mathews 1983: 267)

Others have argued that these jobs could be an alternative source of income and status during periods out of work (Henry 1982). However, the larger-scale survey in Sheppey found that only 4 per cent were working in this way at any one time and most of these were employed. [4] This was confirmed in the study of young adults, for whilst nearly two-thirds of the regularly employed respondents had undertaken extra jobs or had found extra sources of income at some point over the last five years, less than one-quarter of the long-term unemployed had done so – and this also included periods when they were employed.

The advantage of this survey, however, is that it is longitudinal rather than cross-sectional, thus we can see what role jobs 'on the side' have played over a period of time. It transpired that only a minority felt able to pursue such a career. The remainder either lacked the opportunity, as Miles (1983) has argued, or felt that it was immoral:

Andy: 'I wish I had (extra money). I wouldn't mind that. But it's illegal anyway, ain't it? It's not allowed by the Social.'

Gary: 'He said to me, "I'm afraid we can't offer you a full-time job, but if you carry on working part-time we'll give you a full-time job after Christmas." It was only a couple of days, so it weren't really worth signing off the dole. But I was right out up there in the open, and I thought, "If anyone sees me, I'm for it." So I was only up there for three days, 'cause I got so nervous, so I said, "No, sorry." '

It would appear, therefore, that the number of unemployed young adults engaging in informal jobs was very low at any given time, and certainly not of the dimensions estimated by the team at Liverpool. However, it would appear that informal jobs had different functions for school leavers than for older workers, and that they should perhaps be seen as part of the untidy patterns of job entry and departure spanning school and work, rather than as either a social malaise or a solution to the problem of unemployment.

Furthermore, it was evident that whilst some had developed an economic philosophy and a life-style that went with working in the informal sector, others had not. The former category – such as Glen cited earlier – had become adept at survival strategies and were explicit about this. These might be termed the 'swimmers'. These were often young adults who had been rebels at school and had been the most extensively involved in casual work even before they left. Others, however, like Gary and Andy cited above, did not develop survival strategies and did not have the inclination to do so. These might be termed 'sinkers'. They were the majority of the long-term unemployed, representing about nine out of ten of them in this sample.

Patterns of unemployment

In considering patterns of unemployment, the advantage of a longitudinal survey is that we can look at the cumulative effects. Although 17 per cent were actually unemployed at the time of interview, some of these were temporarily between jobs. However, others, including those who were employed at the time of interview, may have been unemployed for two years or more. Therefore it is more helpful to categorize the sample according to their *cumulative* experiences of unemployment in order to understand its consequences for life-styles and attitudes. These I have termed 'work trajectories' and they are illustrated in *Table 4*. It is evident that a clear pattern emerges.

There were three different work trajectories. The first category were the 'regularly employed', who had been continuously employed since leaving full-time education. The second category consists of those who had been unemployed for less than a year altogether – the 'occasionally unemployed' – who may have pursued a variety of jobs or government schemes and had periods in and out of casual and informal work. The final category consists of the 'long-term unemployed', or all those who had been unemployed for more than a year since leaving school. These were counted as a separate category, since research has indicated that adaptation to unemployment depends upon the length of time out of work (Jahoda 1982; Warr 1983). Many of these had been unemployed for as much as half of their first five years in the

Table 4   *Work trajectories 1984*

	%
Regularly employed	49
Occasionally unemployed	17
Long-term unemployed	33
Total number	72

Note: There were twelve in the 'other' category not included in this table. These were housewives who had never been employed and full-time students. Hence the total in this table is seventy-two.

labour market. Only the first group had followed conventional routes into work.

I have not included social class in this analysis since it was difficult to assign a social class to some of these respondents, given their irregular employment trajectories. However, measured against the social class of their fathers, it can be seen that the more regularly employed were more likely to come from higher social class families and the least regularly employed from semi- and unskilled manual working families (*Table 5*).

Table 5   *Social class* of origin by work trajectory (1984)*

	Middle class†	*Working class and clerical ‡*
Regularly employed	8	22
Occasionally unemployed	2	12
Long-term unemployed	1	23

Note: The social class of the father was used here rather than both parents because there was insufficient data about mother's occupation.

Key: * Measured by the social class of the father
        † Social classes 1 and 2
        ‡ Social classes 3, 4 and 5

Altogether, of those who had entered the labour market, roughly one-third had spent much of their time out of work, half had been regularly employed, and 17 per cent had been unemployed for less than a year as they moved between jobs or between schemes. A complicated employment career broken by periods of unemployment was the norm rather than the exception, as less than one-third had been regularly employed in just one job, and – as in 1980 – this was mostly because they had joined the army!

More males are long-term unemployed than females, but this is partly because 23 per cent of females had withdrawn from the labour market by becoming housewives. Those who are 'unemployment prone' are likely to be out of work for long periods of time.[5] In this way, there is an increasing divergence between the mainly employed and the mainly unemployed, both in terms of life-style and in terms of experience. Those who have never been threatened with unemployment find it difficult to understand its personal consequences. Those who have seldom worked regularly find it difficult to articulate the effects it has had upon them as they have never had any other experience. Hence it was often in the *way* in which the different groups spoke of their lives that we could see the contrast. This is best illustrated through the case studies.

The effects of unemployment were far more severely felt amongst young people interviewed at twenty-one than when they were interviewed at sixteen. This is partly because of the accumulated experience of unemployment: long-term unemployment was far worse than short-term unemployment, and many had been out of work for two or three years. The most tragic illustration of this was of a young man who had been admitted to a mental hospital after attempting suicide and drifting into drug-taking and minor delinquency. Since he had been a hardworking and conscientious pupil at school, his grandfather attributed this to the fact that he had been more than a year without work and had lost all sense of purpose and direction.

Another reason was because of the increasing divergence in incomes between the regularly employed and the mainly unemployed as they grew older. Most young worker's wages increased as they grew older so that the gap between wgaes and the single person's supplementary benefits allowance tended to widen as they moved through the age thresholds.

Moreover, young single women felt the consequences of unemployment just as keenly as young single men. In discussing unemployment, as with employment, young men and young women's responses depended upon their position in the domestic life course. For young men, holding domestic responsibilities made unemployment more serious. Young women, however needed to be divided between the single young women (for whom unemployment was in many ways a similar experience to that of single young men), those with domestic commitments that prevented them from working (such as children), and those with domestic commitments that encouraged them to seek jobs (such as home ownership but no children). These different kinds of domestic career are discussed later.

One difference between unemployed single women and single men was in the way they spent their time. Young women were expected to contribute to the housework and general well-being of the household whereas young men were not expected to do this to the same extent. As Deem (1982) has indicated, 'free time' is often built around male leisure patterns, which are in turn constructed around full employment.

> CW: 'And did you find you were doing more housework when you were unemployed?'
> Michelle: 'Oh yeah.'
> CW: 'Is that because your mum was working?'
> Michelle: 'Well, it wasn't that so much. She does – she did have a job, in between . . . because she gets just as bored as I do, doing nothing. But when I was working back at T's and me sister was working there too, then she wouldn't let us do things; you'd get up to go and do something, and she'd say, ''Oh, no, no, no – sit down. I'll do that.'' But you couldn't do that when she was just sitting around at the same time, could you? Oh, at the weekends, like, we'd help her out, but she wouldn't let you do it when you came home from work.'

Whilst some young women thought this was reasonable enough, others found domestic labour irksome and it could lead to arguments at home. What is clear, however, is that domestic labour operated as a constraint upon all young women in some way or other, whilst it was hardly mentioned at all by young men. The role it played in their lives is illustrated in Chapter 8.

The different ways in which young men and young women viewed employment and unemployment need to be seen in the context of the domestic life-cycle.

When asked what was the worst thing about being unemployed, the responses were fairly uniform:

Tony: 'The boredom, the sheer and utter boredom of it. It drives you round the twist.'

Darren: 'It's the days, you see, they just seem to drag. They drag on and on. And the boredom.'

Dennis: 'Not having anything to do and having no money to spend either.'

Andy: 'Time drags, you've got nothing to do. And the money, I suppose. It's so boring in this room, in here. Sometimes I sit up all night playing records, or I watch the telly, and there's only that really. And I keep looking at my watch and I think, "Is that all it is? My God! Surely it must be later than that?" Then I play some more records and look at my watch again and time really goes slowly. When I'm with my girlfriend I do meet other people, but it's only when I'm with her really.'

A number had taken tranquillizers or described themselves as 'depressed'.

As in 1980, the life of the unemployed was characterized by boredom, monotony, and lethargy: they were stuck in a kind of 'limbo' as Cooper Clarke (1983) has described it. The monotony and lethargy became worse the longer they were unemployed. Hence, looking back on their experiences of unemployment immediately after leaving school, many saw it as a kind of 'holiday' period:

Martin: 'Oh, I didn't mind then (being unemployed when he first left school). That was just a laugh. All me mates were out of work, we used to have a good laugh. Now though, I've got a kid to keep and a family, and I'd do anything, I think – yeah, anything to get a job. . . . It's not fair when you think of all the things they should be having . . . Nah, it's much worse now, you know. You notice the difference between you and your mates now.'

The work ethic

Many have hypothesized that the work ethic may be eroded with rising unemployment.[6] If this is the case we should expect this generation of young people to be evolving different attitudes towards work. It certainly appeared from their responses to unemployment in 1980 that this might be happening. For this reason I included several questions designed to test their commitment to the work ethic.

However, from the results, the work ethic appeared to be still strongly espoused by this sample of 21-year-olds, for 36 per cent of the fifty-three who answered this question said that they would work for less money than they could obtain 'on the dole' and eight out of ten would do any job rather than be unemployed. Indeed, many *had* worked for less money than the dole:

Andy: 'I'm not one of these blokes who don't like working. I've been to all the places really. I need to take my mind off things. It's not the money so much, just something to keep you occupied. Well, a lot of them, they don't pay much more than the dole anyway, do they? And by the time I've paid my rent (£60 a fortnight for a dingy bedsit) there wouldn't be much left anyway, would there? But I can't stand it on the dole. You don't go out at all. I just sit in this room all the time. I like work anyway. It gets me down being unemployed, you get depressed, you get tied down, and it leads to other things, don't it?'

CW: 'What sorts of other things?'

Andy: 'Well, you get moody. Don't go out so much. And I miss that, I used to go out a lot, I'm that sort of person. I'm not happy now, not at all. I want to get a job. I've changed you see, you can see I've changed and all my friends say I have changed. They say, "You're not like you used to be Andy." Everybody's noticed it. You see, I even take it out on my girlfriend sometimes – although I don't want to – but I can't help it.'

CW: 'Would you work for less than the dole?'

Michelle: 'Well, I did. . . . There isn't any job that I wouldn't do if I was out of work. See, look, when I've been made unemployed, I think, ah, next week I'll be unemployed, I'll have a rest, but give me about two days and then I think, "Oh God, I'm unemployed" and then I get really, really depressed. I get that bad.'

CW: 'And would you work for less money than you got on the dole?'

Mandy: 'Well, I did, didn't I? When I started working here (in a wine shop) I was working for less than I got on the dole. Because I hated signing on, I really hated it. You see, as a nanny (the job she most wanted to do) it's less than what you get on the dole. You only get about £30 as a nanny. It's not very good money at all.'

CW: 'Would you rather do any job than be unemployed?

Mandy: 'I don't think there's any job I wouldn't do – I've done most of them anyway. If there was two jobs standing side by side, like – a factory job and a shop job – then obviously I'd rather go for the shop job, but if there was nothing else then I'd do the factory one.'

Young adults were overwhelmingly committed to the work ethic, especially those who had been longest unemployed.[7] Those who were not prepared to do any job rather than be unemployed, or to work for less money than the dole either said this because their domestic circumstances would not permit them to do so (for example, if they had families to support), or because they already had 'good' jobs and could afford to be more choosy.

CW (to a girl who has just been made redundant from her regular job): 'Would you work for less money than you got on the dole?'

Deb: 'Well, no, it's the principle of it really, isn't it? I mean why should I work and get less money than what I would for doing nothing?'

CW: 'Would you get any job rather than be unemployed then?'

Deb: 'Well, no, not really. I'd rather drag it out for a while until something I did want to do came along. But if nothing had come along, say, by winter time, and I still didn't have a job, I probably would take anything by then.'

There was also a principle of a 'fair day's work for a fair day's pay', which was adhered to by some, and was being threatened by the numbers seeking work:

Terry: 'I don't mind working, you see. I don't mind working as long as you are working for the money you get. If you get a decent whack, otherwise it's just a rip-off, isn't it?'

Tony: 'Well, yeah, if you're unemployed it's not your fault, is it? So why should you be punished?'

Respondents were evenly divided as to whether the unemployed should be made to work in return for benefits. Whilst some thought this was a good idea, this prompted a tirade against government schemes from others who regarded them as 'slave labour'.

However, young adults were also swift to point to the distinction between the 'deserving' and the 'undeserving' unemployed in this respect. [8]

> Andy: 'Some of them are lazy, of course. Most of them are. They just don't want to work. They would rather get £100 from doing nothing on the dole than get £100 from working. Me, I'd rather work. Just to take my mind off things.'

> Sharon: 'I mean half of them, half of them are on dope because they've got nothing else to do, you know. They just wander about the streets, get drunk, 'cause they got nothing else to do with themselves. Like, I respect Kevin (her brother) because he won't go and sign on. That's what I liked about him, he's got self-respect . . . and I respect him for that. Whereas Barry (her ex-husband) never had no inclination to do anything, sort of thing. He just had it up in his head like, but he just couldn't be bothered really.'

Andy, who is quoted here, had himself been the victim of long-term unemployment. Naturally, people never included themselves amongst the undeserving unemployed!

The loss of the latent functions of work

So far I have indicated that unemployment was more severely felt by people at twenty-one than at sixteen. Let us now return to Jahoda's latent functions of work in order to illustrate this more systematically. Was the loss of the five latent functions of work more keenly felt at twenty-one than in 1980 when they had had little work experience to lose?

The respondents were divided according to their length of time out of work using the variable 'work trajectory'. Only the thirty-four with experiences of unemployment were asked these questions, and of these nineteen had been out of work for a year or more. The rest had experienced only short periods out of work, many of them when they first left school. Below I consider the loss of three of the latent functions of employment and their negative side: loss of identity, loss of a time structure, and loss of social contacts. The remaining two functions, loss of collective purpose and transcendent goals, proved too difficult to operationalize precisely using these data.

The loss of identity – stigma

Of those who had been unemployed, only half said that they had felt embarrassed or ashamed about being out of work. The long-term unemployed were disproportionately represented in this figure, being twice as likely to feel that they suffered from a negative status than other categories.[9]

The loss of time structure – purposelessness

I tested this idea of loss of a time structure by asking respondents what time they got up in the morning – did they spend half the day in bed? This was thought to be evidence of general purposelessness by many. I also asked respondents to explain what they did with their days by asking them to describe to me a typical day.

Not surprisingly, the unemployed tended to get up later. Two-thirds of these respondents got up after 9 a.m., although this did not seem to be associated with the length of time out of work. However, the long-term unemployed were more likely to complain of a feeling of purposelessness in this respect, and to say that they had trouble filling their day.[10]

> CW: 'And were you getting up later?'
> Sue: 'Well, not a lot later, 'cause my mum used to come and get us all out of bed. She used to hate us staying in bed. So I did get up later, but not that much later than when I was going to school. Maybe about nine o'clock. On Mondays you used to get in to sign on for the dole about half nine but other than that there wasn't much point in getting up really but I used to get up anyway.'
> CW: 'Describe to me a typical day.'
> Sue: 'Well, I'd get up, help me mum with the housework, then

sit down and watch afternoon television all afternoon. That's all I did, that was my day.'

CW: 'Did you go out at all?'

Sue: 'No, well I didn't have any money to go out, like I used to know some of my school friends then and I used to go round their house for the afternoon if I could, just to get out really.'

CW: 'Did you have trouble filling your time?'

Gary: 'Well, yeah. You get into a sort of routine. Getting up in the morning, going down town visiting the Job Centre, then it's dinner time. Then you have to fill the rest of the afternoon. I normally just sit around and play records then. Tuesdays evenings is band day, that's sort of the main event of the week to look forward to.'

It was evident that events took on a new significance in this aimless continuum of time. Going shopping with 'mum' or a band practice became high points around which the rest of the week was organized. Whereas on first becoming unemployed, young adults would do their hobbies *more*, find other things to do or regard it as a liberation from the tedious routines of working, the long-term unemployed by contrast, all did their hobbies *less* and found that time 'dragged'.[11]

CW: 'And do you find yourself getting up later?'

Deb: 'Well, I do, yes. I mean, I always set the alarm clock for nine o'clock, so I'm always up by nine o'clock, but, you see, when you've got nothing to do and the weather is like this, it's very difficult to get up, isn't it? Because you can't think of a reason to get up. I always think, "Well, why am I bothering to get up?" I've only got to have my breakfast and read the paper and then I'm going to be bored. But I suppose because I've seen Lorraine Moss, she got really lazy, and she started getting up in the afternoon and thought, 'Well, I'm not going to get like that,'' so I sort of make myself get up at nine o'clock.'

CW: 'Describe to me a typical day then.'

Deb: 'Well, it's different really. I go shopping with my mum a lot and I've been to the Job Centre. I've been going off looking for jobs, another day I'll just stay in for the whole day and watch telly or something like that. But I'm getting out more in the evenings now, 'cause you can't really stay on in day and night, so I go out round me friend's house, and that's more or less it really.'

CW: 'And do you have trouble filling your time now you're unemployed?'

Deb: 'Well, the first week I was unemployed, it was great, it was like a holiday. I found lots of things to do, you know all those things you don't normally do, but the second week I just got totally bored. See, I'd like to do my artwork really (she paints). I like doing art, it was the only thing I was good at at school, but it's too expensive. I can't afford it when I'm unemployed, can I?'

However, even with the long-term unemployed we need to make a distinction between 'sinkers' and 'swimmers' in terms of their use of time. Whilst the sinkers found time hung heavily upon them, the swimmers organized their time carefully to avoid getting bored. Having a variety of odd jobs to do helped to structure time in this way, and indeed one complained that he never had enough time to do all things that he wanted!

Glen: 'I get up in the morning, I go out, go and get the papers. Normally go down town if there's any shopping to do (for his mother or his girlfriend's parents). And then the rest of the day I might spend out on the car or doing up the back garden here (his girlfriend's father's flat). Or I go up me mum's and do some jobs round there. Doing all jobs round the house, or the flat.'

CW: 'Do you have trouble filling your time?'

Glen: 'I don't get bored if that's what you mean.'

The loss of social contacts – isolation

Respondents with some experience of unemployment were asked whether they saw their friends more, less, or the same. They were also asked if they felt more cut off or isolated as a result of being unemployed. Whilst those who had had only brief experiences of unemployment felt that they saw their friends the same or more even than before, those who were long-term unemployed were more likely to say that they saw their friends less. [12]

CW: Did you ever feel lonely when you were unemployed?'

Michelle: 'Oh, lonely, yeah. All me friends were working. You see, you think to yourself, "Oh, I'll do something different." So you get up, clear up, clean yourself up, and you say, "Right, who can I see now?" And you go through your friends and you'd say, "He's working, he's working, he's working." So you sit back down again.'

CW: 'And do you find you're getting isolated?'

Deb: 'Oh yeah, definitely. That's one thing I have noticed, especially with not seeing this bloke any more either. That was always something to look forward to. And in the factory, that's one thing about the factory, there's lots of people to talk to, and I'm just getting really fed up with mum now. Standing around in the kitchen all the time.'

As Dennis explains, it was more difficult to see friends when they did not have the resources to go out to the usual places. Access to leisure cost money.

CW: 'And do you see your friends more, or less, or the same when you are unemployed?'

Dennis: 'Now I see less of them. 'Cause you can't go out, you see, you can't go out with them. If you go out you've got to have some money with you in your pocket, to do something or other. And you know if you ain't got no money you just can't go out. You're stuck indoors doing nothing.'

Perhaps under these circumstances, it is not surprising that the long-term unemployed tended to associate more and more with other unemployed friends. [13] Short spells of unemployment, on the other hand, made little difference to patterns of sociability. The long-term unemployed were both more likely to feel that they were treated differently by other people and that they in turn behaved differently towards others:

Andy: 'I treat people the same as they treat me. My mate who lives up the road, he's unemployed, and he knows what it is like. He understands because he gets the same. He knows what I'm going through. Other people don't understand. All they can see is how I've changed.'

Conclusions

It is evident that long-term unemployment affected people far worse than short-term unemployment and this is borne out by responses to the loss of the latent functions of work.

There did not seem to be much evidence of an erosion of the work ethic in the long term despite superficial appearances. Short spells of unemployment did little to affect young adults' attitudes and behaviour, but long spells of unemployment served as an employment 'discipline'.

It is evident that young people had a different response to work at twenty-one to that expressed at sixteen. They were more prepared to work under the prevailing conditions, they had 'settled down' to employment. Unemployment was similarly a different experience five years later. However, experiences of employment, casual work, and unemployment now need to be distinguished by a person's stage in the domestic life course as well as by their gender. These domestic careers are explored in the next chapter.

In the Introduction I argued that unemployment may lead to a 'fracture' in the reproduction of work role. After five years young people had 'settled down' to meet the demands of employment to a far greater extent than they had just after leaving school. Hence this fracture that appeared to be taking place at the immediate work/school interface had become a process of adjustment later on.

7
In and out of the family

Many of the assumptions surrounding the transition to marriage and parenthood are predicated upon full employment. During the 1950s and 1960s, as the age of majority fell, many young people were beginning to start families by the age of twenty-one. This involved getting married, leaving home, and then having children. Although many poorer families had to continue to live with one or other parent until they secured housing of their own, it was assumed that this would lead before long to the establishment of an independent family unit. This in turn implied a whole range of shifts in the relationships with parents.

With the rising unemployment of the 1980s, it is important to ask how unemployment has affected the so-called 'normal' patterns of life-course transition and the attitudes towards marriage and parenthood. Is having a baby an alternative career to having a job for young men and women, or do having a job and a family go together?

What are the 'normal' patterns of family formation? In one sense there is no such thing as a 'normal' family, since family forms are continuously evolving (Eversley and Bonnerjea 1982). However, we could argue that the *ideology* of the family remains fairly constant.[1] For the sake of contrast, we can compare the patterns of family formation found in this sample of young adults with that which appeared from a variety of surveys to be 'normal' in the so-called affluent 1950s and 1960s.[2]

Leonard (1980) has argued that young people are able to embark on marriage at an earlier age due to their relatively high incomes during a period of affluence and full employment:

'Hence it is with the advent of full employment, family planning and social security in very recent times that the penniless
homeless match between young people which we know today
became a widespread phenomenon in Britain.'

(Leonard 1980: 80)

Leonard goes on to explain that the 'normal' pattern implied
that getting married and obtaining a home of one's own was the
only means by which young people in Swansea were able to
exert their social, psychological, and financial independence
from the home. Thus, marriage and parenthood were of central
importance to the lives of young adults.

These patterns differed between social classes. I have divided
young adults into three groups for this purpose, for transitions
into marriage follow the transitions into work (Wallace 1987).
These I have termed 'domestic orientations' derived from Ashton
and Field's (1976) model of 'career orientation'. The model presented here is derived from evidence obtained from surveys carried
out before the late 1970s and the advent of mass unemployment.

The first group are the young adults with 'extended domestic
orientations'. An OPCS survey of family formation found 10 per
cent of those in social classes 1 and 2 married in their teens as
against 41 per cent in social classes 4 and 5 (Dunnell 1976). This
was because professional and managerial occupations required a
period in higher education and training that might involve
moving around the country. Middle-class children therefore
might have left home at eighteen, but they got married and
bought homes much later. The second group are those with
'medium-term domestic orientations' and these are likely to be in
white collar and skilled manual jobs, and were likely to stay with
parents until they got married, and then marry in their early
twenties or late teens when training was completed. This was
reflected in patterns of shorter-term planning. The third group
are the unskilled and semi-skilled manual workers with 'short-
term domestic orientations' who earn relatively more money on
leaving school than do the other two groups and are correspond-
ingly likely to start families earlier. One report has argued that
one difference between classes in this respect was that middle-
class couples are able to defer marriage and family building until
they have the resources to do so because they are confident of

rising salaries later in life. Working-class couples, on the other hand, were less likely to achieve a range of consumer goals, which made deferring families in this way irrelevant.[3]

There were social class differences in the transition to parenthood too. It has been argued that working-class girls were more 'at risk' from unwanted pregnancies, which would in turn precipitate an unplanned wedding:[4] 'This research has shown that forced marriage is still the most likely consequence of pre-marital pregnancy for a working class girl' (Schofield 1973: 152).

A note of moral censure often creeps into the accounts of those who consider the so-called 'problem' of early marriage and pregnancy that is thought to affect the under-educated and deviant working-class young girl in particular. There are calls for more education for these 'irresponsible' young mothers-to-be in order to solve the problem of 'premature' transition. Hence sexual behaviour, like other aspects of working-class youth's life-styles, is rendered problematical. However, one piece of research has indicated that the way in which young women may decide to present their situation to professionals, such as doctors, may be different from the way in which they themselves view their pregnancy (MacIntyre 1985). This is based upon a realistic appraisal of the negative labelling they are likely to suffer. Hence, the idea of what constitutes 'planning', and what is 'premature' or not, varies between social groups and can be related to economic and social circumstances.

This also has implications for housing careers, as delayed marriage and childbirth were associated with becoming an owner-occupier (Dunnell 1976). Indeed, Ineichin (1977, 1981) concludes that working-class styles of transition can suck young adults into the 'vortex of disadvantage', with pregnancy, young marriage, and rented accommodation all serving to contribute towards cumulative disadvantages throughout life. However, as we have seen, there is little evidence that such young adults would have enjoyed a more advantageous life in any case and it would be better to conceptualize such domestic careers as determined *by* rather than *determining* economic circumstances. It is perhaps more appropriate to assume that their actions are based upon a fairly realistic understanding of these economic circumstances.

New domestic careers

The first fact that struck me as standing out in considering this research is that the domestic careers of young adults did not fit the tidy 'single at home' or 'married and left home' model described previously. Rather, there was a great variety of domestic situations. I have divided the domestic status of young people into four main categories spread across two dimensions: the degree of dependence or independence from the natal home, and whether they lived as couples or as single people. The results are presented in *Table 6*.

Table 6   *Domestic career by sex*

	Male	*Female*	*%*
Single living at home	17	9	35
Single not living at home	6	8	19
Cohabiting couples	7	5	16
Married couples	3	14	23
Irregular couples	4	1	7

Notes: 1. 'Irregular couples' include two single parents, one couple who are married and living with parents, and two couples who were cohabiting and living with parents.
2. Excludes nine away at college/university and one in a special home

There were twice as many young men as young women who were still single and living at home. The 19 per cent of the sample who were single but had left home (not including those away at college) included those in the army or in nurse training, as well as those living in flats and bedsits. Of the couples living away from home (39 per cent altogether) twelve were cohabiting and seventeen were married, so traditional marriage was certainly not the only way of establishing a household. Moreover, most of the married couples had cohabited before getting married, so that cohabitation was often a transitional stage between the family of origin and that of destination. Indeed, only one couple stated emphatically that they were going to live together only *after* they had got married! The five couples who continued to live at home represented a small but significant category, for a number of the couples who were living away from home had started life in this way. They tended to live at different relative's houses at different points of the week as they could not afford a place of their own. This category also includes two young adults – one male and one female – who had children but continued to live with their own parents rather than with the other parent of their child.

Altogether, then, there was a variety of domestic states that involved various degrees of dependency upon the natal home, and various kinds of home destination. Only about one-fifth had got married by the time they were twenty-one, although the majority had by that time left home. This is in contrast to the findings of Leonard (1980) and others writing in previous decades who found that the majority of young people in similar socioeconomic groups as these left home in order to get married.

How did unemployment affect domestic careers? *Tables 7* and *8* indicate the intersection of domestic and employment careers for single people and couples respectively. I have classified the couples according to whether one, none, or both of the partners are working, and according to the sex of the working partner.[5] This was in order to gauge the impact of working and nonworking partners upon domestic careers amongst this age group.

Table 7 *Domestic careers by work trajectory for single people (1984)*

	Long-term unemployed	Occasionally unemployed	Regularly employed	
Single at home	8	5	13	26
Single not at home	3	2	9	14
Total				40

Note: This does not include young adults who were away at college or university and thus had no employment status, or one who was in a special home.

It can be seen that the majority of those who left home were regularly employed, especially amongst the single people. Why was this? First, this was because unemployment created a greater dependence upon parents, as I shall demonstrate later. Second, employment perhaps provided the confidence with which to pursue plans and alternative life-styles. This was despite the fact

Table 8   *Domestic careers by work trajectories for couples (1984)*

	Both partners regularly employed	Man regularly employed, woman unemployed	Both partners unemployed	Woman employed, man unemployed	Non-couples	Totals (34)
Married couples	8	8	—	2	—	18
Cohabiting couples	7	1	4	2	—	14
Non-couples	—	—	—	—	2	2

Note: Non-couples here means single parents

that with supplementary benefits it was still possible for a young person to leave home if they were unemployed. Due to new social security arrangements this will become increasingly difficult in future for the present government are attempting to fulfil their intention to make unemployed young people primarily the responsibility of parents. There was an interesting contrast between young men and young women in this respect. The young men had most often left home in order to join the army or the navy, or, if they were unemployed, it was due to family arguments that could be a result of their lack of employment. Girls, by contrast, often sought their own flats or bedsits without becoming part of a couple and many of the girls still left at home expressed a desire to do this too.

This is understandable if we take into consideration the role of male and female offspring within the home. Male youth were not expected to contribute towards domestic work but could come and go as they pleased whilst they lived at home. As many informed me, they would have to be mad to leave. Where else could they have their clothes washed and ironed and food provided for between £10 and £15 per week? Girls, on the other hand, experienced the natal home differently. Their behaviour was much more closely controlled by parents and they were also expected to contribute towards domestic work. It is clear from the case studies that young women organized their lives around domestic work. For them there was some incentive to live independently as it was more fulfilling to be able to do domestic work in their own home rather than for their parents: it provided them with an adult domestic status. However, on the whole they managed to have their own flats and bedsits whilst remaining on good terms with parents. The kind of self-confidence needed to make plans of this kind was often acquired through having earned a living already for five years as these two young women illustrate:

> Deb: 'And I wouldn't mind sharing a house with a few girls as long as I had a room to myself, and as long as I knew the girls, like.'
> Anne: 'Yeah, and I think it's nice that a girl can set herself up in her own place without having to be married, sort of thing.'
> Deb: 'Yes, I like that place, like that place in West Ally. It was one of these great big houses all cut up into different rooms. They shared the kitchen and bathroom and that, but it was really nice that was, I'd live to live there. And most girls, you know, they're used to sharing anyway, because they've either shared with their sister or their brother or their mum, you know, so people don't mind sharing things that way.'
> Anne: 'But if I could get enough money, a decent wage and that, I'd like to buy me own place, get a mortgage and buy a flat of me own, 'cause then you wouldn't have to rely on a bloke, would you? 'Cause I think these days people depend on men too much to give them things. See, you get into a routine, you depend on them and then when they leave you it all goes to them.'

Thus, for girls, living independently was seen as an ideal – one which they could fulfil with the right job and enough money – whereas for boys it was mostly forced upon them by circumstances. This determined independence on the part of the girls was often justified in terms of their experiences of divorce between their parents or of unemployed or fickle boyfriends. Under these circumstances, men just could not be relied upon as 'breadwinners'. As one girl put it:

> Anne: 'Like me mum always says to me, she says, "Don't you give up your car and you always put so much of your money away, so you've always got some behind you." 'Cause it's

what she's learned you see . . . 'cause she's been through it
all, so you find out from experience, and this is why she
always wants me to get something behind me.'

Turning now to couples (*Table 8*), it can be seen that those
couples where the male partner was in a regular job tended to get
married, whilst those without jobs continued cohabiting. The
exceptions were one young man who had been long-term unemployed but married as soon as he had a regular job and a young
woman who married before her husband had become long-term
unemployed. There were several reasons for this. First, young
adults did not like to get married unless they could do so properly, with a real wedding and the accoutrements of a real home
– and perhaps even their own house. They could not acquire
these things without a regular job and so they tended to postpone getting married until such things were available.

The second reason was that parents did not approve of their
daughters marrying an unemployed man and discouraged them
from doing so. This caused problems for the young couples in
this position and one solution was to cohabit:

Sarah: 'You see, the way my mum saw it was that she never
  had a bad life when she got married, but when she had visions
  of Martin like not ever being employed, and she didn't want
  to see her daughter in that situation where she's with someone who's not employed. And you see he's got no financial
  background. None at all. None. And in her eyes she could
  see us really struggling to bring up a child and have a place
  of our own, like, and he'd be unemployed all the time.
  When I was pregnant, that's when it looked like he wasn't
  ever going to get a job, didn't it? And then he got a job and
  she was over the moon and started talking to him again.'

The third reason was that the young men themselves felt that
in order to be heads of household they also had to be bread-
winners, as Sarah's cohabiting partner, Martin, explains:

Martin: 'Well, we will be getting married next year, but no, I
  wouldn't get married if I were unemployed.'
CW: 'Why is that?'
Martin: 'Well, as far as I'm concerned, marriage isn't just a
  question of popping down the registry office, get a piece of

paper, and that's it, sort of thing. Well, when you're on the dole, that's all you can afford to do.'

CW: 'And you want a proper wedding?'

Martin: 'The proper thing.'

CW: 'In a church?'

Martin: 'Oh yeah, yeah, so we can be proper man and wife.' (He then goes on to relate stories of magnificent weddings and receptions laid on by relatives.)

Cohabiting was also thought to provide a way of getting to know a potential partner without the kind of irrevocable commitment necessitated by marriage. In this way, it provided an ideal prelude to marriage.

Ron: 'They keep saying that married life changes you. They start arguing more. Women especially, they think they've got you.'

Tracy (Andy's cohabiting partner): 'Yeah, it's more hard to get out.'

Ron: 'Hard to get out. . . . What's the point of getting married to someone if you haven't lived with them? You don't know what they're like, do yer?'

Finally the couples living at home did so because they could not find jobs and earn enough money to move out. This sometimes caused some tension, for many of those couples who were long-term unemployed had left home and had begun in this way but left after family disagreements:

Ron: 'We was living at her mum's house and it was getting on top of us. We decided to get a place. After we got engaged we decided to buy a place if I got a job. But I didn't get a job, so I just stayed at her mum's house and I just wanted to get out after Christmas.'

The experience of another young couple was as follows:

Martin: 'You see, we were seeing each other every day anyway. Yeah, you see, we were staying round her mum's house, up her sister's, up her aunt's, we were just all over the place. So we thought we might as well live together. It was two days there, two days up her mum's, two days round her sister's. We were all planned out all week. Plus then of

course we got Amy (their daughter) so obviously we had to
be together.'

Hence, it can be seen that work trajectories played a very
important part in domestic careers.

However, movement from one domestic status to another did
not only involve moving in with a partner, it often meant children too. Thirteen young adults had children and the majority
were living with the parent of their child. *Table 9* indicates the
distribution of children.

Table 9   *Domestic circumstances of those with children*

Single at home	2
Cohabiting	2
Married	9

Young women who had children mostly got married, although
they might have cohabited until then. Children were thus a way
of bringing forward a marriage that was planned in any case.

> Chrissie: 'As soon as we had this place (the house where they
> had been cohabiting) it was obvious we were going to get
> married eventually anyway. We just married a bit sooner
> than we had to really.'

Indeed, unmarried motherhood was considered as an acceptable alternative for many of those unemployed couples who
were likely to embark upon it. Rather than being stigmatizing,
living together and raising children either singly or in couples
was one of a range of possibilities. When asked what they felt
about such arrangements, most young adults responded that
'It's up to them' (i.e. to the people concerned) even if they did
not plan to do this themselves. Tracy and Andy, an unemployed
cohabiting couple, explained their plans like this:

> CW: 'Would you get married before you had children?'
> Tracy: 'Oh, I don't see as how it makes much difference really.
> I mean me brother's not married and he's got two children
> and they're in his name as well.'
> Andy: 'Yeah, well it's OK if you've got a decent job.'

Tracy: 'We'd like to really – '

Andy: 'Oh, I'd like to.'

Tracy: 'Yeah, get married first, but we haven't got the money to get married.'

CW: 'But what if you had children?'

Tracy: 'I don't know, we'd think about it. It would all depend if we had enough money. You see, we're happy now really.'

Some waited until the child was born to see how they would manage with their new partners, arguing that an unplanned pregnancy should not precipitate a hasty marriage. Abortions were nearly universally disapproved of, and very few said they would use this as a form of family planning. However, these pregnancies were not necessarily 'unplanned' – young adults were well informed about contraception.[6] Rather, pregnancy was seen as a hazard within all relationships, a contingency that should not necessarily force an unsuitable couple together. This certainly appeared to be different to ideas expressed in Schofield's (1973) study. Perhaps one factor that has changed is the decoupling of sex and marriage. Recent surveys indicate that young adults expect to have sexual relationships with at least one partner before they get married, and so it is no longer necessary for most couples to get married in order to pursue independent sexual activity.[7] However, this was still only considered appropriate within the confines of a 'steady' monogamous relationship. Whilst hardly being the basis for a 'permissive' society, it did mean that there was scope for a range of relationships apart from marriage. Having a child brought more independence for the mother or the couple, especially for the unemployed couples who would otherwise have found it difficult to set up an independent home.

Martin: 'He got engaged on the Saturday and found out she was pregnant on the Wednesday! That happened to us. We got engaged first and then found out she was pregnant the same week. But with an engagement you see it makes it a little more respectable, don't it? We discussed all this anyway, we discussed it. We decided that if she'd fallen pregnant at what? sixteen, seventeen, we wouldn't of had it because it would have spoilt our lives, sort of thing.'

CW: 'Yes.'

Martin: 'See, we thought if she fell pregnant when she was nineteen, and we decided that well, at that age we could accept it, sort of thing. We discussed quite a few things like that, the future and everything.'

For a young woman without a regular job it was often the only way of gaining any independent status either outside or inside the natal home. This point is disputed. Burrage (1986), Campbell (1984), and Willis (1984a, b) found in their research that unemployed girls were likely to become pregnant, as this provided them with a source of status, and in some circumstances, a better chance of local authority housing. Griffin (1985), on the other hand, has argued that girls did not see motherhood as an alternative status to unemployment, but rather as a long-term inevitability, one that was not necessarily welcomed. It was evident from my resopndents that this was not an actively planned alternative to unemployment, but rather that they turned to this domestic career when others appeared to be out of reach:

CW: 'Are you trying for a baby then?'
Tracy: 'Well, it's not so much that we have actually been trying but I was on the pill before Christmas and I just stopped taking it. Well, after Christmas I suppose we started trying.'
CW: 'Do you think if you found a job you'd change your mind?'
Tracy: 'Oh, I don't think so. No, there again, I suppose if I had a good career job, you know, that was leading me somewhere I would've put that first. But I wouldn't change it if I had just an ordinary job. You know, the sort of thing that's not leading anywhere. Round in circles.'

Like Griffin's young women, Those on Sheppey did not necessarily have a glamorized view of motherhood. Indeed, when they were sixteen, many were very critical of marriage, motherhood, and 'domestic careers'. Some still felt this way at twenty-one.

Anne: 'Well, yes, I mean this is what we've noticed about girls on the island, they're so narrow minded. There's two ways about them really. Either they're in and out of everybody's bed, you know, it's one after the other, or else they meet one bloke when they leave school or when they're at school and that's it, they settle down with him, and there's only ever him, then they get married and they've got a kid on the way, and that's it, isn't it? And I just think that there's so much more in this world that you can do really. That's why I don't really want to settle down yet, because I think, "Well, I might miss out," you know. There must be more things to do. I mean, there might be things I want to do. I mean, I wish I was born in London really, because the people down here, they're so narrow minded. At least you have a more exciting time in London. I mean, I've only been finding my feet these last couple of years really, and I think I could have found them a lot sooner if I'd been in London. We got 'Stage Three' (a discotheque) and at least you meet Londoners there. Okay, so like Sue said, they're only trying to get you into bed all the time, but at least you can go away and visit them. And everybody knows all your past here. Nothing is private. There's always someone lurking round the corner waiting to tell them all about you, you know. Everything you've done.'

Nevertheless, many of those who had been outspoken opponents of domestic careers for women in 1980 had children and husbands by the time they were twenty-one. What had happened? One explanation is that the possibility of a good job and some independence of life-style would have perhaps provided an alternative. However, this alternative was beginning to seem more and more remote as they grew older. In this respect, motherhood seemed to offer more status than either a low-status jor or unemployment, but less status than a 'good' job. It would appear that marriage, motherhood, and domesticity often 'caught up' with girls, despite some initial resistance, rather than being an actively espoused status. This ambivalence perhaps reflects the kind of status full-time wives and mothers hold in our society – elevated as an 'ideal' pursuit for girls on the one hand and seen as 'lower status' on the other. Moreover, many girls held examples of their own mothers – struggling on low incomes, divorced, or downtrodden – as negative role models in their minds. Hence the many writers who have studied girls' careers and have concluded that marriage and motherhood are main preoccupations are not necessarily wrong – it is just that the acceptance of these roles is problematical.

Such accidental pregnancies as did happen were less a result of irresponsibility as a result of an uncertain economic future (Jenkins 1983). There was really no point in planning a family when there was no certainty of a job, and the solution was either not to have children or to 'allow them to happen'.

CW: 'Would you have children if you were unemployed?'
Martin (Laughter.): 'We got one!'
CW: 'But did it influence your decision at all?'
Martin: 'Well, it stops you from making any plans you see, it completely stops you from planning ahead. You just think day by day. You just try and survive. You can't plan anything.'

Two respondents, however, had had children but never lived with the partners. One girl (whose son was taken into care) lived with her mother, and one young man claimed that family responsibilities might hinder his career as a rock star! This underlines the fact that children were considered a woman's responsibility once they had been born. They determined her life prospects from then on. For young men, there may have been moral sanctions against them abandoning the mother, but they still had more choice as to whether to take responsibility.

Certainly, the Isle of Sheppey was no different from the rest of Britain in terms of unmarried parenting. The number of illegitimate children has tripled to 17 per cent of all births between 1961 and 1984 (Social Trends 16) and children are more likely to be registered in the father's name as part of some kind of non-married stable relationship. The fact these forms of familial transition were becoming normal rather than deviant or stigmatized was reflected in the attitudes of my respondents. This leads us to question accepted definitions of 'legitimacy' and 'illegitimacy' since these do not fit the current practices, in the same way as 'marriage' no longer serves to define a heterosexual cohabiting partnership and the 'nuclear family' no longer describes the domestic circumstances of many people in Britain, who are as likely to be single or single parents as to be in a conventional family.

Where the girls needed assistance, this was normally provided by the girl's mother. Nearly all the girls who had children before they were living with their partners lived at home with their mother, and those who broke up with their partners also depended upon 'mum' for help. 'Mum' was particularly important as a stable figure, because as many young adults had experienced divorce in their own families, 'dad' was often an absent partner. 'Mums', and later 'nans', were therefore the bedrock of the domestic world particularly for the daughter (Binns and Mars 1984). However, two of the girls who became pregnant soon after leaving school by young men of whom the parents did not approve, were refused support and ostracized by their parents, so the relationship was not always a harmonious one.

If we now relate employment status to child-rearing, (*Table 10*) the results are interesting although the cell sizes are too small to draw any definition conclusions.

Table 10   *Work trajectories and sex of those with children*

	Male	Female	All
Regularly employed	2	3	5
Occasionally or long-term unemployed	2	4	6
Never worked	—	2	2
Total			13

When the sample as a whole were asked their attitudes to marriage, children and unemployment, slightly more (47 per cent) said they would not marry if they were unemployed, than those who would (35 per cent). However, a strong maority (72 per cent) said they would not have children as against the 16 per cent who said they would have children whilst they were unemployed. Hence, unemployment would appear to inhibit 'normal' family transitions in principle. However, in practice, *Table 10* shows that those with irregular employment careers were just as likely to have had children by the time they were twenty-one as those with regular jobs. This would confirm the idea that the unemployed tended to 'drift' into parenthood, although they would not necessarily plan to have children 'on the dole'. Indeed, both employed and unemployed respondents held strong opinions on the question of children and unemployment as this young unemployed dependent couple illustrated:

CW: 'And would you have children if you were unemployed?'
Ian: 'No.'
CW: 'Why is that?'
Ian: 'I mean, you've got enough on your plate to find yourself a job without an extra mouth to feed.'
Mandy: 'And it's not really fair on the child anyway, is it?'
Ian: 'Plus, I'd have to be mum all day with her at work!'

And this employed couple confirmed this:

CW: 'Would you have had children if Stephen (her husband) was unemployed?'
Marie: 'No, it wouldn't be fair.'
CW: 'Not fair on who?'
Marie: 'Not fair on us and not fair on the children 'cause you don't get a lot of money when you're unemployed considering the amount of stuff a baby needs.'

Thus, whilst the long-term unemployed couples would prefer to have waited until they had a job and a home they also realized that this might be a remote possibility that would lead us to question whether the idea of 'planning' was an appropriate one to use here.

This point was made more clearly when I asked respondents what they hoped to do in the future. Regularly employed and regularly unemployed couples all hoped for a very 'conventional' future with a family, children, a regular job for the head of household and home of their own. As two of the long term unemployed expressed it:

CW: 'And what do you think you will be doing when you are fifty?'
Ian (Thinks.): 'Well, I suppose I'd have my own house, car, couple of kids, sort of thing, not be unemployed I hope, not changing my car every year for a new model, nothing like that, just an ordinary, average Mr Jones really.'

CW: 'What do you think you will be doing in five years' time?'
Andy: (Pause.): 'I reckon if I had a decent job I'd want a nice house and a decent job, then I'd start saving up, something to look forward to. Otherwise you haven't got much to look forward to, have you? Yeah, yeah, when you come back in

five years' time I'll have me house, I'll have a decent job, a little kid to cause me lot of trouble. I should think we'll be married by that time too.'

Those who were already married with houses were planning their second and third houses in the future and planned their child-bearing strategies around these housing strategies:

CW: 'And what are you planning to do next?'
Elaine: 'Yeah, well, I'm going to stay here, you see, for about five years and then we're going to have children, but we want to get our house sorted out before that.'

A home of one's own?

How did work careers affect housing careers? *Tables 11 and 12* indicate the interaction of tenure and the employment status of the household.

There is a clear association between having a regular job and becoming an owner occupier amongst the couples. Local authority accommodation (becoming increasingly scarce) or the private sector was the only alternative for those without regular jobs. Those with regular jobs may begin in the privately rented sector before acquiring their own homes, but most people saved for their own home by staying with their parents until they had found a house. This link between owner-occupation and employment status was well recognized by respondents themselves:

Richard: ' . . . if you get married before you've got a job you're not going to have much of a wedding day, are you? You're not even going to have much of a good life after that. Or if you're in a council house, for example, if you're in a council house and you've got food and that, you've got to find the money to support the marriage. There's food, there's electrical items, there's gas and there's rent. *And* you have to save up for a house. And where would you get the money from? An' it might be a little while before you move into the house, so you've got to think of that. You've got to get your mortgage together. How would you do it if you were unemployed?'

Table 11   *Tenure by work trajectories: singles (1984)*

	Regularly employed	Occasionally unemployed	Long-term unemployed
Owner-occupied	—	—	—
Local authority rented	—	—	1
Privately rented	3	1	2
Tied accommodation	7	—	—
At home*	13	4	9

* i.e. the parental home

Table 12   *Tenure by work trajectory: couples*

	Both partners employed	Man employed woman unemployed	Both partners unemployed	Woman employed man unemployed	Non-couples
Owner-occupied	11	4	—	—	—
Local authority rented	—	1	1	1	—
Privately rented	2	2	2	1	—
Tied accommodation	2	2	—	—	—
At home	—	—	1	2	2
Total (34)	15	9	4	4	2

Note: In this case non-couples were the two single parents which have been included here rather than with the singles

Although most respondents subscribed to the idea of the 'male bread-winner' and this was reflected in their decisions to get married, it can be seen that those households who managed to purchase a house were mostly ones where both partners were working (*Table 12*). Unemployed couples and individuals of course found it impossible to buy a home of their own, and the exceptions in these tables are the ones who had been unemployed but had found regular jobs at the time that I interviewed them.

Marie: 'If we'd had this place and was living here when he got unemployed, that's different. But if I was pregnant and living apart and he was unemployed, then no, I wouldn't have got married. We would just have carried along together as we were until he found a job, but I always said to him I'd never get married until we had a house anyway.'

However, there were differences for the women between different kinds of domestic career. Those women who had children generally gave up work whilst the children were small and this resulted in a 'traditional' division of labour that was sex segregated. However, those who got married and carried on working together with their husbands towards consumer goods were if anything more committed to employment as a means of achieving their goals. Hence there was a real difference in life-style and affluence between those homes with two full-time earners who were relatively affluent, and those with only one full-time earner or no full-time earner. [8]

Couples who were able to buy property were already considering their second home. Two were buying land to build their own houses. They tended to see their futures in terms of a progressional housing career involving a move every five years or so. They hoped to improve their life-style by aiming for a better house, in a better area, with a bigger garden and other assets. Employment was just a means to this end, the ultimate goal being a status based upon residence.

Not surprisingly, tenure was also associated with domestic career. *Table 13* indicates that all of those who became owner-occupiers were independent couples, whilst single young people were more likely to be found in the privately rented sector or still at home. This was partly due to the need for two incomes but it was also due to the fact that a family of one's own was ideally associated with a home of one's own. A 'home' in this sense meant more than just a dwelling. It symbolized the status of the family itself. This is illustrated by the fact that marriage was associated with owner-ocupation – more owner-occupiers were married than other categories (*Table 14*).

This emphasis upon owner-occupation as part of a life strategy was partly a consequence of the local housing market: there were more owner-occupiers in this locality than in Great Britain as a

Table 13 Domestic career by tenure

Domestic career	Owner occupier	Local authority rented	Privately rented	Tied accommodation	Living with parents	Totals
Single at home	—	—	—	—	26	26
Single not at home	—	1	6	7	—	14
Couples not at home	15	3	7	4	—	29
Couples at home	—	—	—	—	5	5
Totals	15	4	13	11	31	74

Note: This excludes the nine young adults at college/university and one in a special home

Table 14 Tenure by marital status: couples

	Married	Cohabiting	Non-couples
Owner-occupied	10	5	—
Local authority rented	2	1	—
Privately rented	2	5	—
Tied accommodation	3	1	—
At home	1	2	2
Totals (34)	18	14	2

whole.[9] However, I would suggest that with present government policy, this might be a pattern other areas are moving towards. The extension of mortgages to younger people, to cohabitees, and to working-class couples during the 1970s may have made this more of a possibility for those who are regularly employed. Thus, employment careers were more important than social class in this respect. Owner-occupation has been absorbed into the ideology of the family in the 1970s.

New patterns of transition?

The tables so far give us a cross-sectional view of the lives of 21-year-olds, but little idea of the *process* of family formation, for this takes place over a period of time. Each young adult may pass through several of the stages mentioned so far. This process is illustrated more clearly in the case studies.

It is evident that in the 1980s there are complex and multi-stage transitions with a number of intervening stages between family of origin and that of destination. These stages can be taken in a number of different orders, with some moving from home to family of destination, some cohabiting or having children first, some preferring to live in single person's accommodation, either after an argument with parents or by preference. There appeared to be more variation in this respect than there were in more 'traditional' forms of family formation.

A further difference between the employed and the unemployed young adults is that the former tended to have a wider range of hobbies, and were able to accumulate consumer goods such as motorbikes, cars, stereos, and so on. This helped them to approach the future with confidence, full of hopes and plans. As with the married unemployed, the unmarried unemployed tended to have the same dreams and aspirations, but with no practical means of achieving them. Male youth in particular had a tendency to resort to fantasized goals and alternatives – such as becoming rock stars.

On a more positive note, it appeared that for the affluent employed there was the possibility of a considerable diversity in life-style – certainly more than has been noted in other studies such as that by Leonard (1980). Young men and women appeared to have more choice as to what sorts of lives they wanted to lead than they had had ten years earlier and young women in particular sought more freedom of movement and residence. However, more choice was available to those on a regular income.

Relationships

It is evident from the preceding discussion that employment and unemployment had an effect upon personal relationships. In the case of couples, one or two adapted their relationships to the man's unemployment, so that he participated more in domestic duties. This was particularly the case where the female partner was in regular employment and had effectively become the 'bread-winner' of the household, or where they were both working. Employment gave women a position of power from which to renegotiate the domestic division of labour. However, whilst some households adopted this more flexible approach, others held to the 'traditional' division of labour, and rather than unemployment serving to encourage men to do more housework, they did less. This was more systematically documented in the 1981 SCPR survey (Pahl 1984). Those young women with children were more likely to find themselves doing the bulk of the housework. Others described the way in which their partners had been a moral support to them both whilst they were unemployed and in their work as well.

> Mandy: 'One thing (about being married) is there's always someone to lean on. I mean, he's always morally supporting me and that. He helped me a lot in my job. I don't think I would have got on so far as I had if it hadn't been for him. 'Cause I never thought I could run a shop. It's really Mick pushing me that's done it. If I'd been on my own I don't think I would have had the confidence really.'

Whilst unemployment had brought some couples together in adversity, for other couples it was a source of tension, and in one case this resulted in the man deserting his wife, as is illustrated in the case study. Indeed it is perhaps pertinent that the two violent relationships amongst those whom I interviewed were ones where the male partner was suffering from unemployment.

Unemployment could operate to inhibit courting relationships too. One young unemployed man was distressed because he thought that his lack of employment would drive away his new girlfriend:

> Andy: 'I don't get out much now, and it's getting me down . . . I take it out on my girlfriend and I don't want to. I don't want to lose her, but I find myself doing it. She is very understanding, but you see she don't really understand. She knows I want a job, and she knows I wouldn't be like this if I could help it.'

Moreover, an unemployed young man could likewise appear less attractive to a young woman who wants to do more than sit indoors most nights of the week, although young women were concerned to point out that they were more interested in the man's character:

> CW: 'Would it put you off if you found out he was unemployed?'
>
> Anne; 'Well, my boyfriend, he has been unemployed for two years, and, like, we've written off all the time to get jobs but he's unemployed in winter mainly 'cause he's got a summer job. Each day we write off, and it's always the same – you never get any answer from anyone. See, but I wouldn't marry him 'cause my wage isn't enough. But if I was earning the same wage as a bloke then it would be OK, see.'
>
> Sue: 'Yes, 'cause you, say, meet a bloke and you say, "What do you do?" and if he says he is unemployed, I think to myself, "Oh God, this one's a bit of a waste of time." But say if you were going out together and he was made redundant, then that's different really, isn't it? But I think it would put me off to begin with.'
>
> Anne: 'Well, as you get older you see, you start to think about things like that. You start to think of things more in those terms. You think to yourself, it isn't much fun really, is it? Because I mean you find every night you are sitting in and then you find that you're doing all the sitting in, 'cause as soon as he gets any money he's out with his mates. I mean, this is what I had for the first year. All through the winter I was sitting in watching the telly or the video, and then when it come to Wednesday, and he had a bit of money, it was "Ta-ta then" – he was off playing pool with his mates!'

The patterns of dependency between parents and children were complex. I have already mentioned that parents continued to provide indirect financial subsidy to children through the low level of 'keep' they charged. Their children, however, mostly perceived this as 'fair'. Parents also subsidized young adults in other ways, for example by giving them an occasional couple of pounds to go out drinking, buying an item of clothing, or giving them cigarettes. For unemployed young people living at home, this could be the difference between survival and destitution. Those who did not have such advantages often had to make do without proper food or heating in order to make ends meet. Hence, the patterns of 'spoiling' continued to be one way in which parents cemented the bonds of dependency with their children.

In addition, parents often took over the management of a young person's income. In addition to 'keep' they might give money for the mother to pay life insurance or to put in a building society. Many parents also deducted money for clothing catalogues or Christmas clubs. Thus, responsibility for maintenance was taken out of their hands. Moreover, parents would use this dependency as moral leverage in persuading young people to 'settle down' to employment. However, in households where parents too had been struck by unemployment, there were more problems. Parents could no longer afford to subsidize their cildren's life-styles, as we saw with Sally in Chapter 5.

Despite this economic interdependence between parents and children, most young adults did not like to feel that they were dependent upon parents and others:

> CW: 'Do you mind getting help from people?'
> Michelle: 'Yeah, funny enough, I did. I hate being – I hate having to lend money, sort of thing. And I think I would've got more depressed if people hadn't been so much help. Like, I'd probably have locked myself in my bedroom and never come out again.'

> CW: 'And when you were unemployed – did you feel more dependent on your family?'
> Martin: 'I felt a burden on everybody. I felt like a leech on mankind.'

As in Leonard's study, parents often charged less in the way of 'keep' if their children were getting married in order to enable them to save for their own home.

> Jane: 'We got loans now and then and bits and pieces of bedding and all that. Things that, you know, when my mum's throwing something out we get our share. She divides it up between all of us.'
>
> Richard: 'Yeah, well she might have paid it at the time, but we pay it all back in the end. That's the only way you can do it, isn't it?'

Hence, even once children had left home, this occasional but steady help continued as the unemployed couple quoted below demonstrate:

> Dennis: 'Well, she gave all of us £30 when we first got out own place, you know, to get things for the house and stuff to help us move in, she gave everyone that. My mum used to pay for things, but we always paid her back. Like for Amy's christening, you see, she paid for the cake, and she paid for a few things, but we paid her back. . . . We've never had something for nothing though. She doesn't really give us money, but she helps us out food-wise. Like when we were on the dole. We wouldn't have money off her, but we used to go down there, like once a week, and she'd give us a couple of tins of this or a couple of that, sort of thing.'

Having children or getting married was something in which the whole community could participate. They supplied household goods, usually second-hand, as well as baby clothes and equipment. The social networks of senior women in the community were an enormous resource in this respect and this is what made it possible for the young single mothers, in particular, to cope. Everyone was prepared to 'chip in' if it was to set up a young couple in their own home or to help with a first baby.

Young people could usually rely upon parents for moral and financial support, and this was often the first place where they turned in emergencies. Hence, the young woman described previously who had been deserted by her husband turned immediately to her mother.

Thus children were tied to parents throughout the life-cycle, although they were tied in different ways at different periods.

The transition to adulthood involved a change in relationships with parents, but it did not involve severing links.

However, leaving school and starting work did result in some shifts in their relationship with parents. Although most people argued that they had become more independent from parents,[10] many of them were perhaps not as independent as they liked to think because of this hidden subsidy. Those who had gone away to college or university had a rather different relationship with parents.

Thus parents supported children out of a sense of moral obligation and children routinely underestimated the extent of this support, thinking that it was fair and economical.

Conclusions

It is evident from the data discussed so far that patterns of transitions in the life course had changed by 1984, when compared to previous decades. However, it would be wrong to attribute these changes to unemployment alone. Some were a product of changes in family formation and in life-styles generally. Unemployment merely encouraged young men and women to choose some pathways rather than others and perhaps to postpone what they would consider to be 'ideal' transitions. There still appeared to be variations in transition patterns between classes, but these had changed in content. Although the sons and daughters of the middle class may still defer the transition to family of destination until they have completed higher education, many of the affluent white-collar and manual workers were able to save for homes and accumulate consumer goods too, particularly if there were two earners. Indeed, the accumulation of these consumption goals appeared to be a major focus for life plans. It was access to employment rather than the kind of job the young adult undertook that was significant in this respect, and so unemployment could be said to be creating and increasing the divisions within social classes 3, 4, and 5. It is no longer possible to use class alone as the determining variable for social destinations.[11]

Moreover, it was evident that the 'planning' for a domestic career was dependent upon financial security rather than individual 'irresponsibility' or lack of an education. These findings would support those of Jenkins (1983) and Jones *et al*. (1981) in this respect. It is also arguable that some changes are due to shifts in social beliefs more generally. It was more generally acceptable to live together without being married, to have children either as a single person or as part of some other relationship, to live alone or in collective households. These forms of behaviour – perhaps more typical of the 'avante-garde' middle class in the past – have become more generally acceptable: many parents observed that it had been very different for them at the same age. Nevertheless, marriage and children, along with home ownership, remained an ideal for the future, so that the ideology remained intact even when family practices had changed. It is evident that the 'privatized nuclear family' survived as an ideology, just as 'full employment' (for men) was an ideology and served to shape young people's experiences, even when it did not exist in practice.

This flexibility in social relationships did not necessarily undermine relationships between parents and children, which remained strong even at twenty-one. Mothers especially were important sources of stability in this respect.

Employment was thus of equal importance to single young men and young women as a source of status, identity, and income in order to enable them to consume or save. However, for married men and women the pressures were different. They became more instrumentally oriented, putting their money towards the home. In most cases it was equally important for the man and the woman to work in order to ensure a mutually desirable life-style, but this depended upon their stage in the life course and upon whether or not they had children.

For couples with children, there was more pressure for the man to find a job in order to support his family, pressure from his own internal values, whereby he saw himself primarily as a 'bread-winner', pressure from his wife or girlfriend to provide for their family, and pressure from in-laws and extended family. This had implications for work trajectories, as we have seen in Chapter 6.

Were new norms being developed in response to unemployment? Certainly a higher proportion of young people cohabited before marriage in this unemployment-stricken community than the 24 per cent cited for 18–34 year-olds in the General Household Survey. [12] This may reflect the inadequacy of traditional means of data collection and recording, or it may mean that the younger group in this age band are more likely to cohabit than the older ones. It may also mean that many cohabitants do not get married at all! It would therefore perhaps be more accurate to say that evolving norms were adapted to new conditions.

Many of the trends discussed here – such as 'home-making' cannot be directly quantified. However, the contrasts between employed and unemployed young people and between singles and couples should be evident from the case studies in the next chapter.

Is there a fracture in the reproduction of the family, as I hypothesized in Chapter 1? To answer this we need to look at different levels of reproduction. The reproduction of the *ideology* of the family seemed uninterrupted and was perhaps reinforced by the extension of home ownership to younger working-class couples – no one could afford a house if they were not in a couple relationship! However, in practice, unemployment led people to postpone marriage, so in this sense there was a fracture. Moreover, new kinds of interstitial stages between family of origin and that of destination seemed to be emerging.

8
Some case studies

Sharon

I traced Sharon through her sister, who was now living in their mother's old house, Sharon's widowed mother having moved into a flat for old people. Sharon had become pregnant soon after leaving school by her boyfriend Barry, after a one-year courtship. She had had her baby whilst living with her mother, arguing that she would wait and see how their relationship developed before deciding to get married. In practice, however, they got married a few months after the baby was born and moved into Barry's parents' small flat with Barry's parents. Barry was eighteen and had been unemployed for most of his brief career since leaving school. He was known locally for drunkenness and getting into fights – fights in which he often came off the worst. His unemployment and the overcrowded conditions in which they lived meant that the marriage did not get off to a good start. They tried to improve things by renting a flat, and were offered a council house in a run-down area when Sharon had a second child. However, their relationship continued to deteriorate and when I interviewed Sharon she had been separated one year and was waiting for a divorce. During the interview she showed with obvious pride the improvements she had made on her home. She managed to attend to the noisily expressed needs of two small children and one large dog whilst talking to me.

CW: 'And where are you working now?'
Sharon: 'Up at Mace's as a shop assistant . . . but I lost my job on Monday. They wanted me to do more hours. They wanted

me to do another two days a week and I said I couldn't do it because it was too much with the children. And because anything I earn over £15 the Social stop me, so it wasn't worth it and I packed it in.'

CW: 'And did Barry ever get a job?'

Sharon: 'Yeah, he did have work last year, in fact that's the reason he left me. . . . He was working on the side and the Social Security caught him and they stopped all our money. He left me with a £20 electric bill, £200 rent arrears. He was leaving me on the Friday and I didn't believe he would go and he went on the Saturday morning and he said I wasn't going to get no money. But on the Wednesday – we usually get our money fortnightly – and it never turned up. And I went over to the Social Security and they said that the money had been stopped because they had caught him working on the side and they had already told him he wasn't going to get none. He told me that we wasn't going to get any and I didn't believe him. I didn't think he would walk out and leave me with all that. . . . He just cleared off and left me with that, and it was three weeks before I got any money. My mum come down and she kept me. But we had only been separated five weeks before I went and got meself a job. The day I left work this Monday I had worked a whole year without having a week off.

I know why (we broke up). Because I always put my family before I did him. And when we had the children, as Stevie grew older, I was more for him than I was for Barry. And I was a terrible wife anyway, I think. . . . It wasn't till just before Christmas, I sat here one day and I had a really good think and I thought to myself I was too young to get married, but I didn't realize it at the time. Everyone kept saying it wouldn't work, it wouldn't work, and I just had to prove them wrong, but in the end it got so much I thought it's not worth keep trying to prove everyone wrong, so it just happened. I could see it was going to happen anyway. It did happen the first year. We split up, but I went back. And he used to beat me up and everything. One time he just literally kicked me round the room. . . . I could've got the divorce then and there but I didn't know if I still wanted to go through with it, because in a way I still wanted him back. I still wanted him back until about a month ago in fact. . . . We had been married five months when he first hit me. When we was going out together he hit me once and then he hit me when his mum was there once, but she stopped him. He didn't hit me a lot, but as time went by it was getting worse. When he did hit me he was drunk and it hurt more. He never hit me on the face, it was always on the body so my face would never show a mark. He was always drunk when he done it, but he couldn't remember the next day. And I'd show him and say, "Do you know where I got that from?" and he'd say, "No" and I'd say, "I got it from you." The last time he kicked me in the stomach and kicked me in the back and hit me head against a brick wall.'

Sharon has pulled herself together, however, since Barry left. She has got herself out of debt and even managed to buy a few items for the house.

'Put it like this. I've done more in this past year on me own than I did all the time we was living here before. . . . I don't get much money, but I get more than what I had when he was living here. Anyone will say that. When we first moved here we was given a lot of things, but I've replaced them now with brand new. When we first moved here we was in a lot of debt too, and I sorted all that out.'

However, living as a single woman in a rough neighbourhood had its problems too.

Sharon: 'Before Christmas I was broken into three weeks running. First time I was here on my own and I was upstairs, but they didn't get nothing that time. The next time they broke in during the day and the meters were all done. They took £40 out of the meters, and I had to pay all that back. They went through all the drawers upstairs, kids' toys all over the place. Ripped up letters, ripped up photos. Then the third time it was a Peeping Tom hanging round here all the time. It made me feel so creepy I wouldn't go out. But then I got the dog and we ain't had no trouble since then.'

CW: 'Would you consider getting married again?'

Sharon: 'I don't think I would. I would live with someone instead. But I think, like, with a relationship, you have to to take them steady, not rush at it all in one. I mean, when I first got married to Barry I thought it was going to be a big white wedding, all this, but it didn't work out like that, like a fairy-tale story, it never does. . . . I'm much better off now. Financially, I'm much better off. [1] I mean, I used to pay the rent, the electric and plus I had to pay his fines and all. And he was working on the side and he said he was earning between £60 and £80 per week, he was always going around bragging about it, but I never see a penny of that. . . . It went all on the pub and on the (fruit) machines and you know, that really annoyed me. When the Social found out, they stopped the money, but they was depriving the children, not him, because he could earn money. He was going out the next week and bragging about the fact that he had all this money, and all of us was sitting here with no food and nothing. . . . If it hadn't been for my mum this past year I don't know what I would have done.

'The first six weeks after he left, I would never go out. Sort of really let myself go. Couldn't be bothered to dress the kids, you know, the house looked like a sty, you know, and all my friends, sort of they'd come back and say, "What do you expect," sort of thing. "You know what he was like." And then one day me mum said to me, "Look," she said, "Come on, buck yourself up," she said, "Go out and do yourself up now," and she offered to buy me some new clothes. Then one of my friends came down and said, "I'm going looking for a job, why don't you come along?" So then I found a job working in this fish bar for £1 an hour. Then once I started earning I never looked back. My friend she split up with her feller, so we used to go out on a Friday night, and I began to realize what I had missed out on. I mean, I went on out for an occasional drink with Barry, but I really started to enjoy myself. . . . Now I look around and I think with this room, that everything has come out of my own money. I mean, it's nothing fantastic or anything, but at least it's mine, you know.

'I mean, I've been out, you know, and the kids they have never wanted clothes, they got so many clothes. Like, when I was at school I had my sister's clothes, and I swore that just because we was on our own we would never have second-hand clothes. Everything I bought was brand new.

'I mean, Barry resents this really, 'cause I changed when he left. I'm more independent now. Like when they took us to court, they said that he had to pay £30 a week, 'cause he said he had all this money, but he never paid me a penny of it. Well, when he went to court, he called me a slut in court and all this, he called me a whore – and he wasn't drunk, you know. He said, "You have effing well got all that you want. You've got the kids and the house and you've got your money, and you're not going to get a penny out of me." And then he walked out, and the court was packed. And I mean, I didn't want nothing for me, I just wanted for the children what was their right, I didn't want nothing.'

CW: 'Where is he living now?'

Sharon: 'At his mum's. He started off living up the beach (i.e. living rough) and then he went back to his mum's. I think he was living with a girl for a while and then that didn't work out, so he went back to his mum's again.

'Sometimes I think I would like to have him back. I get so very depressed here and very, very lonely and sometimes it gets on top of me. Like the kids argue, and I take it out on them. I don't hit them, but I shout at them, especially since I lost me job, 'cause that used to get me out, you know. The only thing that saved me was my job.

'I used to go round and talk to me mum all the time, but I've been trying to get more independence from my family. I mean, I used to go and tell my mother things, when I should have been telling Barry, so I'm trying to do things on my own now, because I got very dependent on her, especially when I was splitting up with Barry. I have tried since then to try and live my own life more. Because she's got her life and I've got mine. She's too involved, sort of thing, otherwise. I was starting to rely on her again and I didn't want that. I mean I like to feel that I can go up there and treat her, sort of, like a mum, sort of thing, that I can turn to when I need help, but I like to have my own life as well.

'I've been seeing more people my own age recently too. I mean, there's my friend next door. I tell her everything, and she, like me, will just sit there and listen, and she'll give advice, tell me what she thinks, and sometimes she'll just sit there and nod, but it's enough for me just to get it off my chest, sort of thing. But I still talk to me mum and I talk to my sister as well a lot.

'I think I'll take up evening classes next. I've always wanted to learn to type and perhaps be a secretary. I said that when I was at school, and I still say it. When I was living at Barry's parent's house I booked up evening classes and I never told no one in case they just thought it was silly. Evening classes in English. And I told Barry he would have to start babysitting on Tuesday nights and I told him it was because I was going to start English classes. Well, he just laughed, and my mother-in-law said, "What the hell do you want to do English classes for?" And I said, "It's 'cause I want to learn", and she says – 'cause she really talks cockney – "There's nothing wrong with the way we talk," she said, and I said, "It's not 'cause I want to talk different, it's just that I want to improve my outlook." She said, "Well, there's no need to posh yourself up, 'cause you'll be getting too good for us," and I couldn't get home to her why I wanted to do it. If ever I wanted to improve myself, she was always against it, whatever it was.

'I mean, I want to do something with my life, before I get too old. I mean, I was talking to my sister-in-law and she's been married twelve years now, and she was moaning about her husband – who's worse than what Barry was – and I said to her, "But after twelve years you're still sitting around moaning about it," and I said to myself, "OK, so I put up with it for three years, but there's no way I was going to put up with it more than that. I can see myself in ten years' time, and by that time I would like to look back and say, "Well, at least I done something with my life." There's no way I would want to end up like her, but now I've got my independence, and I've been out to work.

'But, like, when I was with Barry all I wanted to do was to settle down and have a happy marriage, that came first. All my friends, when I used to look round at them, I always thought that they all had happy marriages and that, but now I've split up with Barry, they come round to moan about their husbands . . . and I always say, "Well you're much better off on your own," but you see you can't have everything. I mean, I get really lonely here on my own.

'The kids have suffered from it – well, the eldest has, anyway. I mean he's been shifted around so much now from one place to another place. I mean, he still asks for Barry, says, ''I want to see daddy,'' and all this, but I don't tell him anything to turn him against his father. But, I mean, he saw it all, saw all the arguments even though he was only young. He's seen so much in a short time. Like every time we used to argue, Barry used to hit me and he would cry, ''Don't hit mummy any more,'' and Barry would still be hitting me and he'd say, ''Don't hit mummy, don't hit mummy.'''

'I can always find jobs in any case. I suppose I'll find something else. Like in that fish bar, the hours were terrible, the money was bad too, but I can always find part-time work. Like cleaning jobs, especially in the summer. I mean, if you don't mind what you do, there's always things, aren't there? I mean, I done Tupperware, Avon, cleaning jobs, shops, all sort of things. . . . I feel as though I always have to have a job, you know, besides being at home. . . . Otherwise I feel too tied down. If I have a job I got something else to occupy me, and at least I'm meeting people, and I've got a different life. I'm not talking about babies all the time.

I think these government schemes are a good idea actually. I mean, if I was younger I would have been happy to work on a scheme rather than do nothing. The youngsters, they get so bored, really, they don't know what to do with themselves. I mean, my brother's only eighteen, he's so young and yet half his friends are on dope, they've got nothing else to do, you see. I mean, Fred, he does work, he won't sign on, and I respect him for that. He just doesn't want to be unemployed and that's one of the things I like about him.

'I still read, I still read a lot. I read love stories mainly, but occasionally I read history books.'

Michelle

Michelle lives in a house that she shares with her brother and a couple of his friends. She works as a scrap metal sorter, but her main preoccupation is with biking. I traced Michelle through her mother's address, where I had last interviewed her in 1980. We sit in the living room, which is dominated by a large pool table.

Young men in oil-stained jeans move in and out, casually playing pool whilst the interview is taking place. In the hallway and other downstairs room there are various motorbikes in various states of dismemberment.

Michelle: 'I'm single. I'm single – and I'm staying that way! I moved in here, what? two months ago. . . . It's not exactly ours, you see. It's complicated. You see, there's this bloke, Jake, and he went up to London, so he didn't want it, so we said we would have it whilst he was away. . . . There's me brother here and there's him (indicating one of the pool players). Originally it was his sister's, but she moved out with her boyfriend, 'cause he had a house. Then me brother, he met a girl and so he moved out. And then I was trying to find a place so they said, "Why don't you move in with us?" So I moved in and then my other brother joined us. Otherwise I would've had to go on the Council's list.

There are some disadvantages to it – like my brother! . . . Yeah, I do find that I am looking after them. I do all the cooking and cleaning and that sort of thing. But that's all right. If I want anything done, I just say, "Do that!" and they say, "No", so I say, "Look, I done this, I done that, that, that, that and the other thing," so then they say, "Oh all right then." On Friday he (her brother) gets his own tea, 'cause I do the shopping. This sounds terrible, doesn't it? See, the thing is, he hasn't got an idea in his head, he doesn't know how to look after himself. He does need me. But it works out all right. If I want to do something, I just go and do it, sort of thing. . . .

'At the moment I work over in Medway in a scrap metal business. You get the metal from other places and it's all mixed metal what has been dumped. You get it up on your bench and you go through it, and there's so many tons of zinc, so many tons of copper, brass, wire, iron, rolledaly, castaly, what we call "dirty stuff", that's got nuts and bolts in it. And dirt – there's plenty of dirt. You have to sort it all out. People think it's a factory, but it's just a great bit corrugated iron shed, sort of thing. There's no heating. In winter it's freezing and a few times we've had to give up 'cause our hands all froze up.

'There's mainly women up there more than blokes. You need blokes to do all the heavy stuff. Lift these forty-five gallon tins and things like that, but the women do the actual sorting . . . I been there a year now. . . . It's piece-work. At other places the sorters come out with a hundred pounds a week apparently, but I've come out with a hundred – what? – once since I been there. A bad week would be sixty and a good week would be over ninety. But with it being piece-work, you can leave when you like. Like me mum, she has over twenty-four cats to look after, so she doesn't get there till about nine and then we all leave about four, so it's not bad really.

'We all work there. It was Sid – what lives with me mum – Sid was out of work and she kept sending him out to look for work, and he came home one day, and he said, "Do you want a job?" and I said, "Yes, course I do," and he said, "Well, It's a bit dirty but it's a proper job." He said, "I've got to get a gang together first," 'cause in our job you can't get the money on your own, you have to do it in gangs. So he got my little brother, he had just finished school then. And he got my bigger brother – he's left now, he's a bit of a snob and he said it was too dirty for him. And there was me mum who was working down the dry cleaners then – and that's the whole family. . . .

'Originally, when I first left school, I wanted to go on one of those government training schemes. I wanted to go to college, but they wouldn't let me. They said, "What would you like to do, Michelle?" And I said, "I want to be a mechanic," and they said, "Oh no, no, you just think you're interested in that but you won't like it once you start," and I said, "I would you know," and they said, "Well, there ain't any places for you anyway." So I got put on a retail distribution scheme, as they called it. After that I was nearly a year out of work.

Then I got a job down T's as a cashier, but it was only temporary, like, but they were going to make me full-time. Then they laid me off. Then they took me on again. Then they laid me off, then I went back part-time, and so it went on. For three years I was backwards and forwards there. It worked out I was paid £1 worse than I would've been on the dole. I was getting £23 at work and £24 on the dole. After five months of it, I went back and said, "What about that job you promised me," and they said, "What job? We didn't promise you anything," and that had been going on for five months, and I hadn't been giving me mum any petrol money and she had been buying me a meal down there, and I weren't giving her anything, like, so I said that in that case I would go back on the dole.

'I worked part-time at a chemist in between, but Sid was working on the new T's and so he got me an application form for there. I liked the people there, I just didn't like the management. They didn't have the faintest idea of what they were doing. So you didn't have any respect for them. It seemed all wrong to me. One time, you know – and it only happened twice – I had been out drinking till seven in the morning and me mum said, "Why don't you stop at home?" but I said, "No, I've got to go into work," so I went in and I was ten minutes late. The shop hadn't even opened. And they said, "Oh, Mr Smith wants to see you." He's the manager, like, and he said to me when I got up there, "You're continually coming in late" – and it was twice in three years – "Do you want to work or don't you, Miss James? You don't seem to be sincere about this job," and I felt really bad, so I went down and sat on me till, and then I was so mad I packed up me machine, turned the light off, went back up there and said, "What about the full-time job you said you was going to give me?" and he said, "I suppose you are doing this so that you get your dole money straight away, is that it?" and I said, "Well, I'd be better off on the dole anyway!" and that was it, I left.

'I thought to myself, "I could do that manager's job better than him." Because they didn't know what they were doing half the time. You see they're all off with each other, and arguing with each other. That's how I got into trouble, that's why he didn't like me. You see, how you got promoted in that place, all the supervisors had affairs with the manager, sort of thing. And they used to knock off all the shop girls and all – it was a right scandal in there. And one time, like, the assistant manager had been chasing me apparently. I didn't know, I just got a Christmas card off him. And then one day he asked me out, and I said, "No." They all told me in the shop, "Don't tell anyone you're going out with someone, 'cause he'll give you some really bad jobs," 'cause he could do that, 'cause he was the assistant manager. So I said, "No. Why should I?" Then he asked me again and I told him I was going out with someone and he took me off the tills and gave me some really grotty job to do. In the warehouse. He thought that was highly amusing. Then the supervisor didn't like me after that, 'cause she thought I was after him. That was what it was like in there. So you didn't get the supervisor's job 'cause you were good at the job, sort of thing. . . .

'You see, I'm just one of those people, I like to take pride in what I'm doing. So like, they put me on the wines and spirits and I wanted to find out everything about it. I was only there to stack the shelves, but I wanted to know a bit more about it. So when the manageress came along, she used to say, "What are you doing? Reading?" And I said to her, "What if someone was to come along and they wanted to know about the wines, I could tell them." and she said, "All you need to tell them is, 'That is red and that is white.' " You see? It's silly, isn't it? I used to read all about it. I knew what all the different lagers were and I knew the difference between a claret and a chateau some-thing or other. I used to know what was an eight-year-old whisky as opposed to a ten-year-old whisky, and all this. 'Cause I used to take pride in what I was doing. Even if I was only stacking shelves. But that didn't get you nowhere in that place. They weren't interested in that.

'And then I was out of work after that. I hate being out of work, I really do, and it's not that I want a particularly well-paid job or anything like that. I mean, I wouldn't have stuck at T's that long if that was the case, would I? It's just that me mum has always brought me up to work. You're lazy if you don't work.

'Me mum gave up work when me mum and dad broke up. She said she was giving up to look after us. That was all right for two months and then she couldn't find nothing to do with herself and so she had to go back to work. I mean, even me brother, you can see sometimes he hates it over there, he gets really fed up, but if he had no job, in a month he'd be tearing his hair out. . . . You've got to imagine seven tons of metal in front of you and this tiny little 'ole appearing. It takes ages and you lose heart, but I suppose it's no worse than any other job. . . . At least with piece-work you haven't got no one hanging over you, coming up and saying, "You're not working fast enough," sort of thing, "You can go for your tea break now." You just get on with it.

Then I done apple picking in the summer months. That was in between T's. Used to get £28 a week for that. I said to my mum the other day, I was saying about all the things I would like to do, and I said, "What I'd really like to do is get a skill," and she says, "Yeah, but think of all the things you've done. You're a jack-of-all-trades really". So I said, "Yeah, yeah, but I'm not skilled in any of them." That's why I wanted to be a mechanic.

'It's my main interest really, bikes. My main hobby. A couple of months ago, I was with a boy, you see, and I'd go on about bikes and he hated it, 'cause he couldn't ride a bike or drive a car or nothing. He said to me, "Why do you have to keep going on about bikes all the time?" It really used to get on his nerves. And it got on *my* nerves, 'cause it got on *his* nerves, sort of thing. But the boyfriend I used to go out with before that, we used to natter on about bikes all the time. He'd done up his bike so he got another fifteen mile an hour out of it and it would do a hundred and twenty top end. I used to *love* riding that. When he got a bit drunk I used to say, "I'll drive you home" . . . So on these occasions, he would give me a pair of waterproofs and his leather jacket and trainers – 'cause I only had a skirt on. One time he had a mate with him. His mate said, "She don't ride a bike!" and he said, "Yes she does, you just watch," and it was a beautiful bike, a beautiful bike, but the clutch was slipping, so I really had to whack the throttle down hard to get it going and I was going away and I was bombing down the road and his friend come out and says, "Cor blimey! She terrifies me!" and Michael told me afterwards that his friend just couldn't believe that I rode a motorbike.

'You see, most of me friends are boys. No one understands it. The girls say to me, "How come you know all these blokes?" Like you go in the pub or something and it's "Hello", 'Hello'. That causes some arguments, I can tell you. And I says, "Well, it's because we like the same things, you know." And you know how girls are, many girls, they say, "Look at my new nail-varnish," "Oh, isn't my hair really beautiful," and this and that. I'd rather just put a lid on and go ride a bike. . . .

'When I was at school and this Youth Opportunities thing come up, I thought, "Great! Great!" I can do my mechanic's job, you know, but girls didn't do that sort of thing. I thought, "Right, if anyone can do it, equal rights and all that," I thought, "I can get in there." 'Cause a garage wouldn't take me on. But I got talked out of that. After that I went mainly for shop work, but really, you know, I would have been much happier working in a garage. I went round every single factory, all over the industrial estates, all round Sittingbourne, but it was only in the shops that I got any interviews. But if someone now said to me, "You can be a mechanic but you'll have to take fifty pounds a week," rather than the seventies and eighties that I'm getting now, I'd do it. Yeah, I would definitely do that. . . .

'Now I think, you know, this Youth Opportunities thing, it's a fiddle really. They're just cheap labour. See, that way, they get lots of people working and it's cheaper for them. When I was at T's, we got laid off and they took on all these Youth Opportunities people. For every two that got laid off, three Youth Opportunities kids got taken on. They laid off about fifteen altogether. They kept on all the older people, people that had been there years and years and got rid of the newer ones like me. . . .

'Hobbies? Bikes mainly. . . . My brother is getting a scrambler and we'll go over the mud flats on that. And there's drinking. We go over Sittingbourne to the troublemakers' pub. But you've got to be in the mood for that. Like, everyone gets really drunk and there's fights there, guaranteed fights there at a weekend. You've got to have the stomach for it. Like, a lot of girls won't go, because they're scared they might get their hair spoilt.'

CW: 'And would you get married if you were unemployed?'

Michelle: 'I wouldn't get married any time. I think, you see, that once you get married, it's for a life, you see, and seeing as I've never met anyone that I would want to spend the rest of me life with, that's out. See, like most people, they get a slip of paper saying they're married, but I'd want it written in blood, that he'd be with me for ever, and all that. . . . I've got a very high regard for marriage, and I think if you get married, you should do it in a church, have a honeymoon and all that stuff.'

One of the pool players interrupts:

'I can't see that it makes much difference actually. I mean, nobody's asked me, but if you're employed, unemployed, or whatever, it shouldn't make no difference.'

CW: 'And would you have children if you were unemployed?'

Michelle: 'No, I think children basically cost too much. If you can avoid getting pregnant when you're on the dole it's better. . . . I just think that babies should have everything they want, everything in life, but I'm a romantic at heart, I suppose.'

CW: 'Why did you decide to leave home?'

Michelle: 'Well, really, I just kind of wanted a place of my own really. It's been more or less the last year that I was thinking of it, I got the idea into my head, and I thought, right, That's what I'm going to do. And after that I couldn't think of anything else.

'The worst thing about being unemployed is not having a job, especially if you want to work. I know a couple of people round here and they're quite happy on the dole, but I *want* to work . . . I got depressed. Like, you see, say me mum was in the kitchen making the tea, I'd go in there in the kitchen and I'd lean against the door, and I'd say, "You know, I wouldn't really mind if one of those great big articulated trucks come and run me over." It wouldn't have bothered me. I used to spend most of my time up in my bedroom, with me telly. I'd come down, get me tea, go up in me bedroom with it, bring down the plate later, and then I'd go up there again. I suppose I spent eighteen out of twenty-four hours a day up there in my bedroom.

'Me mum used to say to me, "Oh you'll get a job, don't worry," and try to buck me up a bit. And if I bought something, like, she would pay for it, and I didn't have to pay her back straight away. Then I used to have to beg her to take the money back later. And I always used to like, look to her for ideas. You know, I used to say, "Are you going out in the car?" when she had a car. I'd say, "What are you doing?" Are you going shopping tonight?" and that sort of thing.

'I do get treated like one of the lads when we go out. It can get quite hectic sometimes. Like I like talking about bikes. But sometimes we go out and I'm all cleaned up, like, and someone will say, "Oh, she's a bit of all right" and I hate being called "A bit of all right", anything like that, "Oh, she's tasty," sort of thing. And I think, if you want to say something why not say it to me? It's not as though I ain't got a tongue in my head. It insults you, don't it? And you're supposed to just sit there and say nothing. That's why I get on with blokes better I think. I mean, I think I'm equal. That's why I learned to ride a bike. Someone said, "Oh she'll never ride a bike," and I thought, "How dare you!" and so I learned to ride a bike, so now, when Terry's mates say I should be tied to a kitchen sink, he tells 'em, "I tell you, you get her on the road, and she'll outride you!" So I prefer that. You see, when I'm cleaned up and I'm going out somewhere with Terry, I spend hours getting ready and people say, "Oh, she looks better than she does," and they compare you and all this, judging you against the others. And I want to go home and do it all again! That's why I'd rather ride a bike. . . .

'It's your standards, your standards and morals and stuff, I suppose. Things like you don't go out with people and let them buy all the drinks, sort of thing; never owe people money, 'cause it's not nice for them waiting on you for the money. And always work, 'cause you know you're doing something. And respect for other people's things, and having a sense of personal pride. All those things I got off me mum.

'But marriage and stuff – I don't know where I got that from. 'Cause mum and dad are divorced – I don't even know my dad really – and that put me off marriage. I don't think you should have children unless you can give them the things they need.

'See, I've always been brought up to think you're as good as the next person. You're as good as anyone else. Even when you're in a rotten job and your house isn't a palace, you've still got your self-respect. See, when someone says you're bad at tht, I know I'm not as bad as other people are, I know I'm better at some things and worse at others, and I think, "Right, that's it," I have to have a go at it. So I take pride in myself you see.'

Martin

I interviewed Martin in his mother's house. He brought his fiancée, Sarah, a trainee dental nurse along with him.

Martin had been unemployed for around two years altogether. After leaving school with a handful of CSEs, he worked at odd building jobs for a while in order to support his widowed mother. However, he did not make enough money from them and eventually had to sign on. At present he works in a factory and has just bought a house. He is planning to move there once he and Sarah are married. He still does jobs around the home for his mother and is still very close to her – the house is just round the corner from where she lives.

'So, um, I saw someone I know down the road, doing some roofing jobs and I got talking talking to him and then through that conversation, his guvnor gave me the job. He must have taken a liking to me. . . . I had that for about three months and then, um, in that time the Council houses opposite were being redone . . . so I kept going over there and asking for a job because that's what I had decided I wanted to do. Go into the building game. Eventually, they turned round and said ''Yeah'' so I left my roofing job and worked on a building site for six months. . . . But then the building company went through a difficult time and started laying people off, and I was one of the first ones to go.

'But I had a good recommendation from them in any case, so with that I went back to roofing again. But I was having the same trouble as before. Not working every day of the week. Sometimes I'd only get £14 for the week, you know, and that was less than what I could've got on the dole. . . . So I had to pack that in, 'cause I couldn't afford the housekeeping. Then I was on the dole for a long time and I went back round all the different firms I had been to before . . . all the shops, as many shops as I could. Prop Corrugated about three times, and different building firms, all the building firms all over the island. Adverts. Just about anything.'

Martin was unemployed for two years on and off in this way.

CW: 'Did you feel embarrassed about being unemployed?'
Martin: 'Well, the first day I walked in there and claimed the dole, I thought the whole world was waiting outside for me, saying, ''Oh look, there's Martin.'' and I was really ashamed, and when I was in the queue I felt really, really

bad. Sort of had me shoulders up like this and hope no one there knows me, and things like that, you know. It's all so bad. I really, I just can't explain how bad I felt. I mean, I'd spent all my savings just to try and stay *off* the dole. No, even after a while, you know, I just didn't like it. When I used to walk down the road I used to think, ''What are these people going to think of me, a man who can't do a day's work.'' I just felt really bad. I used to try acting like the school kids so that they would think I had just come out of school, you know. I always used to walk with me head down.

CW: 'How did you spend your time?'

Martin: 'I used to go round the factories and I used to do a bit here. Was that floor up last time you came? From the floor up, hallway, knocked that down, rebuilt it again . . . that's how I used to spend my time.'

CW: 'And did people treat you differently?'

Martin: 'Uh, no, because I think I had a strong enough character to put over to them, looking back on it now, that I wasn't just some sort of lazy good-for-nothing person on the dole doing nothing, you know, that's it. . . . I mean going on the dole has made me sort of respect tax. I don't think I'd ever blame getting taxed. . . . so being on the dole in a way has made me a lot better.'

Martin eventually found a job in a local factory.

'And then I saw Mr Smith again, and, uh, he had a word with one of the foremen and I started there at L's on a government scheme. . . . They gave me a packing job to do to begin with and they said, ''We'll give you this and then we'll move you round like we've got to for the government training scheme.'' Then I done that for a fortnight and then the foreman come up to me and said, ''Would you like to go on the marshalling?'' and I thought, ''No one likes working there, so it must be a grotty job – but if I don't take it I might lose out,'' so I thought I'd take it.'

However, he did not find it easy to settle down to factory culture.

Martin: 'Where I am at the moment it's more or less the same. You got people who've grown up to be bullies, and have got an image to keep. Yeah, no respect for anyone. They shout, bawl, and swear in front of all the women, you know, they come out with really bad things. But since then I've tried to keep myself to myself. I just don't go down the canteen. Perhaps if I had gone in there with, you know, with big heavy Doc Martin's and threatened to kick the foreman in the teeth I'd've got on better . . . '

CW: 'Then you met Sarah?'

Martin: 'It was at a fête, wasn't it?'

Sarah: 'At a fête, yeah.'

Martin: 'Fête along the road.'

Sarah: 'Late in June.'

Martin: 'Sarah walked over – '

Sarah: ' 'Cause I knew some of his friends.'

Martin: ' – to where we were, and I saw Sarah and I thought ''mm''.'

Sarah: 'Not as ''mm'' as I thought about him though. Be truthful!'

Martin: 'I mean, when I started going out with Sarah, the stick I got for that was unbelievable. . . . Very nasty names. I mean they all thought, ''He don't deserve a girlfriend.'' I'm not – I shouldn't have one, like . . . so I got a lot of stick for that. They tried to talk me out of getting married and all sorts. But they had a tendency to push me into it more, if you see what I mean. I don't listen to them, I just think of what I've achieved since I met Sarah, you know, and it helps me to ignore them. . . . Like one bloke, he used to be a right drunken idiot, going round picking fights with people, causing trouble. What got up his nose was that I'm like I am. I'm twenty-one, I've got myself a girlfriend who's very talented in all sorts of things, I've got myself a house, and I'm going to get married.'

He has been engaged to Sarah for a year and they are preparing to get married and move to their house.

CW: 'And are you going to continue at L's?'

Martin: 'For the time being, yeah. Because, uh, with the house and everything, to move now, I mean, to change jobs would be a really dodgy crisis. For the moment, you see if you're buying a house, you see you can't. . . . If I could get a better job, I would, but I've just got to stay there through thick and thin at the moment really. . . . But I'm looking for tomorrow, you know, looking to see what there is perhaps for the next house, you know, got plans for that.'

CW: 'Your next house?'

Martin: 'Yeah, and another one later on.'

Sarah: 'We don't want to stay in that house too long. . . . We like it, it's a lovely little house. But we've got ambitions and really we'd love a country cottage but we'd never be able to afford one. But we're going to try to aim towards it.'

Martin: 'Yeah, we're going to try to climb up . . . '

CW: 'And are you planning to have children later?'

Sarah: 'In about six years . . . '

Martin: 'Yeah, 'cause I don't want to be, you don't want to be silly like some people, you know. Sort of have a lot of things to pay out for and then find they can't pay for it. Want a bit of money behind so we can say, "Oh, we can afford to have a child now," or something like that . . . '

CW: 'Would you work for less money than the dole?'

Martin: 'Yeah, well, I have done. But not now, I couldn't. I couldn't afford to. With the house and everything, it would be impractical. But I just don't think it's right. I mean, I know some people just claim for this, claim for that, when I think they haven't got a right to. You know, if it wasn't for people claiming for things they didn't have to claim, you know – even though they're bringing in money on the side – that money could go to a hospital or to handicapped people. The elderly, something like that. So why should I be a burden on the country if I can do a job? When I get my money I think, "Well, that's mine, I've worked for that." . . . '

CW: 'And would you have got married when you were unemployed?'

Martin: 'Nah. Because it isn't right. Because then you would have to claim. That isn't right. Plus that, um, you've got to look on the sensible side of it. What life can you lead on the dole? Because for us, anyway, I want the best. For Sarah, like, you know, and for myself.'

Sarah: 'We doubt if we'd have got married even if I hadn't had a job. Me dad said, "Look," he said, "I'm sorry to say this, but I don't think it's right you should get married if you haven't got a job Sarah." 'Cause we just wouldn't have been able to manage and we thought we could. But now, even now we worry, don't we?'

Martin: 'Yeah, yeah.'

Sarah: 'We're not going to have hardly anything left to save once we've paid the bills and everything.'

Martin: 'But once we've got the costly things out the way, you know, they say the first two or three years are the worst. Then we'll be able to put a bit of money away. . . . '

CW: 'And how about when you were unemployed, did you depend on people?'

Martin: 'I felt a burden on everybody. I felt like a leech on mankind. I felt really bad. . . . '

CW: 'And what do you normally do with your money?'

Martin: 'Now I spend it on things for the house, you know, bits and pieces. . . . But before I used to spend it on my guitar, I used to drink a lot. . . . Go out with me mates. I was always the quiet one, I used to sit in the corner quietly getting drunk. . . . But when I stopped doing that, when I stopped going out and that, the money I saved was tremendous. . . . '

CW: 'So you're living round your parents' houses now?'

Martin: 'Yeah, its cheaper that way if we stay like this.'

Sarah: 'That's what we're worried about. I mean, you afford the mortgage and those sort of things for the house, but you're worried about saving for the wedding. We don't expect to leave the parents to put much towards what it costs. I mean, my father's retired and me mum don't earn much, you know.'

CW: 'And what do you think you will be doing when you're fifty then?'

Martin: 'I'd better not be working at L's, that's for sure. Well, by then I would like to have a nice house. You know, the sort of house that's a home. Not just a house, but a home. . . . By then, the mortgage will be paid for. But I want to pay the mortgage as soon as possible anyway. I don't want to spend the next twenty-five years paying the mortgage back. I mean, you look at all the men of fifty, they're dropping like flies down our place, and most of them have got mortgages and things. I mean I want to actually own our house, if you see what I mean. . . .

'It's people at work. They constantly take the mick out of

you. Getting married or anything I do. I mean, me and Sarah, they tried to talk me out of getting married in anyway they could at all. You know, I mean, a couple of days before I actually signed for the house, I went into the office to see the foreman. I went in there, and he calle me a rather rude name and told me there was no way I was going to make it. And they say to me, ''Oh you're never going to do this,'' and all the things they said I was never going to do – I've gone out and done! So when I turn around and they take the mickey out of me, they say, ''Oh you'll be washing screaming kids' nappies out and that,'' all this sort of thing.

'But look at them! I feel rather proud sometimes. I feel, I think at least I'm not going to turn out like they are. You know, when Sarah came along, my life just changed completely. Just before she came along, they was really taking the mickey out of me for not having a girlfriend and that, you know. Not doing this and not doing that. Then Sarah came along and it kind of shook them up. It changed my life completely. They changed their attitudes completely. . . . I became a lot more confident. A lot more really, I suppose. It's a bit awkward for me to explain, you see, but she came along just at the right time.'

CW: 'You were a bit down?'

Martin: 'Yeah, very, very. I was really down. I was really down in my job. I was really down in my social life. I was beginning to get very, very down. . . . Yeah, I mean, whereas I used to look at life the day before or at that moment, when I did look at the future it was always – it seemed to be fine, or I thought, ''What has the world got to offer me?'' You know. But it's different now, you know. . . . You see, perhaps later in life I could put some money into a business, something like that. I mean I never thought of myself as doing that, putting money into a business! But now I can. It's strange, you know. That got up a lot of people's noses at work and that's another reason why they got at me. I've done a lot more. I tell you. I tell them, ''You're just living in a council house. You're going to be living there for the rest of your life. You've been living there for twenty years already. You've got no hope of getting out of there, you know!'' That might sound a bit pig-headed as a way of looking at it but that's the

way they look at me. I've got to look at it like that, otherwise
I would just crack up, I think. And I have done on a few occa-
sions, you know. I've been on tablets and all sorts of things.
Now I'm beginning to walk with my head up.'

Sarah: 'We've been lucky, you know, since the beginning of
this year – since we met. We've been lucky getting this
house. Bits of furniture, I mean, it's a lovely little place. . . . '

Martin: 'Well, you see, it's been like that. It's been like a fairy
story, a real fairy story.'

Collin

Collin lives with his widowed mother, who runs a guest house in
Sheerness. He joined the navy initially, but left that and now
works in his uncle's removal business. He has not been out of
work so far because his sister, who works in one of the local Job
Centres, is always able to get him work if necessary.

Collin: 'So I left the navy. I was seven weeks in that. . . . I just
didn't get on with it really. . . . I was in the sea cadets for years,
and me dad was in the Merchant Navy and his dad was in the
Royal Navy, so I always wanted to do it, 'cause I've always liked
boats and that sort of thing and I've been brought up to it really.
So they went up the Careers Office, me dad and me uncle
and they sorted it all out up there, and I think they like put a
word in for me to help me out a bit. But then you realize after
a while that just 'cause your dad wants to do it, it's not necessarily the thing for you. You know, when you're a lad you
think you want to be everything your dad does. . . .

'Then I went on one of them job schemes (i.e. a YOP). Up
the lifeboat station. Did that about three or four months and
then I went with the work team. Done a bit of painting and
decorating and stuff like that. Queenborough Church Hall,
that kind of thing, done them up. . . .

'Then me uncle come in here one day, and he asked me if I
wanted to go with him, like, so I said, "Yeah". . . . I work
with him and his son. They do it together, removals. Self-
employed, like. Buy all me own stamps and things.

'And I help me mum. Do all the decorating around the
house and stuff, 'cause me dad died. . . . I keep going all the

time, don't like sitting around. There's no set time in removals. One week we're up in Birmingham, then it's Bristol, other weeks we're down here again. Don't rush about too much, you know, we take our time. See, that's the good part about it. It's not boring at all, it's not the same thing all the time. It's always different – different places, different times of day.

'You work when it suits you. See, tomorrow I don't start until one o'clock. I'll still be up at seven though.

'Yeah, see it's better for you (being self-employed). You see, because if I want to go off and do another job before one o'clock, I can just go and do it. But if I'm with a firm, I just couldn't do it. It's less aggravation, sort of thing.

''Cause I wouldn't work in no factory. No, I'd never work in a factory. I wouldn't go on the dole or nothing, but I wouldn't work in no factory. See, there's always work if you want it, there is *always* work if you want it. . . . It's repetitive (in a factory). I mean, me uncle and me dad went down there to the mill, years ago. Me uncle lasted half a day and me dad was out after six months. They came along one night and found him sleeping and said, ''You're sacked,'' and he said, ''No I ain't – I'm leaving!''

'But I wouldn't have gone on the dole because I don't like sitting around. Like, I wouldn't go down there. Like one of me mates, he went down there and I went with him one time, to sign on, you know, and he said, ''Coming in?'' and I said, ''No. I'm not coming in there, I'll wait outside, like.'' I didn't want anyone to see me.

'I can do any extra work I want at the moment. I'll do any extra jobs at all, 'cause I don't like sitting around. With being self-employed I can just go and do it. Like, I work on a caravan site sometimes, do caravans up, put the fence up, cut the grass. If something comes along, I'll do it. I wouldn't mind having another job really, 'cause we get a fair bit of free time on the removals. I could work on something else. It's all extra money, and every little bit helps. I don't like sitting around, you see. If there's something to do, I'll do it.'

CW: 'Didn't your mum miss you when you were in the navy?'

Collin: 'Well, at the time she was glad to see the back of me. . . . I was out every night, stuff like that. Well, I still am out every night, it's just that I do a bit more work around the house now. I used to go out on me motorbike and stuff like that when I first come out the navy.'

CW: 'What pastimes do you have?'

Collin: 'Well, me motorbike, then I've just taken up photography. I got a camera from me sister for me birthday, so I got a tripod, a flashgun, a couple of lenses, you know. Then I go out shooting twice a week. Target shooting. Then I go boating, always liked that. Messing around in boats. Fishing, swimming, camping. Oh, and I grow vegetables. Vegetables and flowers. I'll do practically anything. I used to go screaming round the streets on me bike, you know, racing, but I got too old for that. That was when I was seventeen, eighteen, I suppose. . . .

'Then I got a car, paid half with me mum. But she mostly uses that. I still prefer to use me bike mainly.

'I wouldn't get married at all. Full stop. What do I want to keep someone for? I mean, get married and you can only keep one happy. Stay single and you can keep more than one happy, I say! It's all right taking them out, but not living with them. I mean, I nearly got caught one time. We had been going out three years and she wanted me to get engaged, this was the idea. But I wasn't having that, so I ditched 'er. See, that's what stopped me racing about on a bike all of a sudden, it was when I was with her. You see, women, that's what they're like. She doesn't like bikes and she wanted me to go round in the car all the time. . . . I wouldn't have kids neither. You can't catch me, you know!'

CW: 'How about if you were unemployed?'

Collin: 'No, no, definitely not. You see, you get married, you get kids, and that's more you have to worry about when you're on the dole. You see, they take advantage of you, they take you for granted after a while. I don't mind taking them out, but nothing much else. You feel obligated all the time. It's "Don't do this, don't do that." I don't want to get engaged or nothing like that. I mean, that's the first part of the knot, isn't it? I'm too busy working.

I never have money off me mum. I never need any. It's pride, I suppose. But I earn enough to get by. If I can't afford something, I save up for it until I can. I don't owe nothing on

HP or anything like that. If I want something, I save for it. Yeah, 'cause when me mates are there they say, "Race you," sort of thing, "My bike's faster than yours, I'll beat you with it," and I say, "Yeah, but my bike's paid for." See, I'll get a new bike soon, and that's two and a half grand, so I'm saving for that. I've had that one – what? – two years or something now, and I want a bigger one, 400, 500 cc, sort of thing.'

CW: 'What do you think you will be doing when you're fifty?'

Collin: 'Trouble is, you retire and that's it really. Me uncle's still working and he's in his sixties. You've got to keep going, otherwise you get fat and lazy. I don't want to move, I'm happy here. I've got no neighbours, nobody to scream at you. See, in winter you can make as much noise as you like up here, and in summer there's only the holidaymakers, and I can tell them to get lost. . . . If I found a little bungalow up in Minster with its own patch of land, I might move, but only then.'

CW: 'Are any of your friends unemployed?'

Collin: 'No. See, I don't like lazy people, people who just sit around all day. People who stay in bed till eleven and then say they're feeling tired. I just don't like that.

'I mean life could be better. I mean I could win half a million on the pools! That's what life's about really, ain't it? Money. Money is the main thing. As long as you've got stuff in the bank, that's it, isn't it?

'I mean, I don't go out drinking or nothing like that, just two or three times a week, that's all. I don't go out racing like we used to with my mates, every night nearly. We used to go out racing all the time. 'Cause lots of me mates were unemployed anyway, or they were on government schemes. Or they were just starting work so we didn't have the money really to go out drinking. We all had bikes and we just used to race around on them.

'Yeah, you see, some people, they go out drinking, getting stoned and all that sort of stuff, but it's not for me. There's no point in me making money so I can give it all to the barmaid, is there? Smoking, that sort of thing. I don't do any of that. I just keep my money and spend it on things I want.'

Dennis and Penny

Dennis and Penny have been living together in a council house just across the road from Penny's mother for six months. Penny gave up her factory job to care for their daughter Amy, aged two, and Dennis has had a variety of jobs but has spent at least half his time unemployed since leaving school. Penny now works part-time at the local pub.

Dennis: 'At the moment, I just have a casual job, till it finishes, like, then they lay me off again. Before that I was working with her brother up in Birmingham doing the bridges. . . . The hourly rate is £1.84. It's really poxy money, the things we have to do, like, but we get a bonus every week, but even that's low on a site like that. You see they're just not paying out the money any more. . . .

'I managed to save quite a lot when I was up in Birmingham for three months. I used to only spend £30 or £40 a week and the rest I used to save up, so it was £1,000 after a while. All the money was all planned out. We were going to buy a car and I was going to learn to drive, pop over to Holland for a weekend and everything else. Then of course this house came along so all the plans went. See we've done all this up. Like some of it is new, like that table over there, but quite a lot I've been doing up.

'When I left school I went on a government scheme to begin with, then I finished that a month later and I got into building the sea defences at Sheerness. Then I left that job and went into R's import firm, undersealing cars. Then I worked there for – what? – three months, until, uh, I got the sack from that, 'cause I wasn't turning up for work. I didn't get on with the bosses at all down there. They tried to sack me twice before, that's how it was between me and the bosses down there. Well, then I was out of work for nearly two years, nearly two years I couldn't find nothing at all. Then I got a job over at Sittingbourne laying pipes. That lasted about three months. My jobs always seem to last three months! And, uh, then I was on the dole for about a year, then I got a job with her brother up at Potters Bar, then I went for three months to Birmingham, then Lincoln. Then I had a couple more days work from him, but they've closed down now, out of business, so there ain't no more work down there. Then I've been out of work since last October – six months – till I got this job.

'I'm going for me subcontractor's ticket. You send away the tax form and some photographs and you get a little ticket back. See, these things are worth a lot of money now – they'll fetch £4,000 on the black market. If I get it is another thing. See, it's so hard to get these days, there's so much competition for it.

'That other job I got, I got from a bloke down the pub one night. Some bloke come in and said if there was anyone wanted work. So she said, ''Yeah, he'll have it.'' So I went over there and got it. Laying gas pipes. That other job I got off her brother Paul who was the foreman and pushed for me.

I've applied for hundreds of jobs, thousands. I just keep applying, applying, applying. Any job, even sweeping the roads. The times I've tried. I even went over Freshbakes – even there – but I didn't hear from them. I've been round all the factories, all the factories on the island and the ones over Sittingbourne. I've tried all the fire service stations, because I've been trying to get into the fire service (as a part-time volunteer) ever since I left school. But you have to live three minutes away and I live the wrong side of the traffic lights. You see, you can get a transfer after a year, and once you're in the fire service you've got a job for life.'

Penny: 'Because he wants to be a local hero, that's why. He fancies himself going in and climbing in windows and saving people. That sort of thing. You know, going into burning houses. That's his little fantasy, isn't it, dear?'

Dennis: 'Oh, I go round all the building sites, all the time, every time I see a building site I go and ask. I got offered a job as a tea boy, but that was about all. I've been round all the shops, all of them. I went down me brother-in-law's firm, but he wouldn't have me because I didn't spell Sheppey right! Yeah, left one of the "e's" out! I even went down the council after a road sweeper's job, and that's a very poor job really. Six days a week for £70 and no bonuses or overtime or nothing. I even wanted to do that. I've been for so many jobs it's unbelievable.'

CW: 'In 1979 you said you wanted to be a plumber's apprentice.'

Dennis: 'Oh yeah, I'd like plumbing but I'm too old for an apprenticeship now. Like I've worked with a bloke plumbing and I can plumb a bathroom and that, but there are no apprenticeships going at all really. Plus, you've got to have O-levels before they'd even consider you now, which I wouldn't take anyway. Me and four other blokes got expelled from school for having a go at the teacher. And, uh, they asked me to go back 'cause they said I had to be at school. So I said, "You won't get me back there!" And in the end they had me working with all the maintenance blokes which kept me back at school.

'You see, it's really wrong not having a trade because that's what you need nowadays to get a job. See, there's this bloke I'm working with – who I was working with in Birmingham – and he's a driver, a digger driver, a diesel driver. He's got everything. He can do the lot and he's got so many jobs to offer, and of course they offered him a job full-time. 'Cause, you see, he can drive their diggers and stuff, and he's a general handyman, he's handy to have around. . . . He said he would try to get me in there and teach me to drive a digger, or perhaps a crane. So that's something to look forward to, because it pays more money with a trade. Perhaps he can teach me that lot.'

CW: 'What are the advantages of getting a trade?'

Dennis: 'It's being able to get a job, just being able to get a job. The money's more and that.'

CW: 'Is it the enjoyment?'

Dennis: 'It's not that so much, it's just getting a job. You see, they can pick up a labourer any day, they're ten to the dozen. Anyone can be a labourer. But it's better to have a trade. That way they know you can do something. I can always go up to a firm and say I can do pipe laying, but no one wants to know. Anyone can do that. You're just classed as a labourer. You see, it's as simple as that. . . . See, a labourer ain't just a labourer no more. Not nowadays. You can't just pick up a shovel no more and be a labourer. A labourer has got to be able to do everything. They call him a "skilled labourer" because he can do so many jobs, like, a handyman, like. . . . And you've got to have many years of experience – even as a_ labourer! That's how tight it gets.

That's why it's best to have one of the top trades on the building site. 'Cause you can really earn the money if you're a driver. . . . But the money is not going out for labourers now, in fact it's gone right down to the lowest it's ever been, 'cause there's so many of 'em, they can choose anyone, can't they? The money's gone right down. See about three years ago, you could claim about £7, £8 an hour but now you can just claim £3 an hour. That's how bad it's got. You see, 'cause there's so many unemployed now. . . . See I just can't live on £40 a week now, it's not possible with Penn and the kid. See, the rent's what – £22 a week.'

CW: What do you think of these government schemes then?'

Dennis: 'Well, I think they're better really, than being unemployed, because that way people appreciate their money at the end of the week instead of just sitting there. . . . Sitting around doing nothing, like. Yeah, because, you see, there's some people never look for jobs. They can't be bothered, and it's not right, you see.'

Penny: 'Yeah, they sit around for years doing nothing, and they're all right like that.'

Dennis: 'Yeah, plus it would give them more incentive to go out and look for work. Some people haven't got the incentive now, they think to themselves, "Oh God! There's three million unemployed, how am I ever going to get a job?" But if they're doing something, learning something, then they're not doing nothing. It gives them encouragement if they've got the foresight enough to get some kind of skill. You know, they've got something to look forward to, instead of just having nothing.

'You see, with unemployment, it stops you from making any plans, it completely stops you from planning ahead. You just think day by day. You try and survive and you can't plan anything.'

Penny: 'Well, the first time we tried to make plans to go on holiday, you see, we tried to go up to Cornwall for a couple of weeks' camping. Well, that got wrecked 'cause he lost his job.'

CW: 'Why did you decide to live together?'

Dennis: 'Well, you see, we were seeing each other every day anyway. Yeah, you see, we was staying up her mum's house, up her sister's, up her aunt's, we were just all over the place – so we thought we might as well live together. It was two days here, two days there. . . . We were all planned out all week. Plus, then we got Amy, so obviously we had to be together.

'Me mum still gives us things, but we have to pay them back. Like for Amy's christening, she paid for the cake, and she paid for a few other things. Plus she takes Penn down to Sittingbourne shopping now and then. . . . We've never had something for nothing. She doesn't really give us money, and we wouldn't ask for it anyway, but she helps us out sometimes with food. When we was on the dole we used to go down there and she'd give us a couple of tins of this, a couple of tins of that, that sort of thing.

'Me brother-in-law would always lend us money. Say, like, I'm going out tonight, he'd always lend me a couple of quid for drinks, sort of thing. Mind you, her brother has been really good to us. Bought us drinks. He earns a lot of money though. Pulls two £50 notes out of his pocket and I thought "Blimey!" I've never even seen a £50 note in all me life and he's got two of them!

'I left home really when I was seventeen. I lived with me brother Gary for about six months, I lived with me sister until we got this house. I didn't get on with me mum for the first two or three years after I left home, but since we had the baby she wants to see her every week, so we go down there every week. But when I left home we weren't on good terms at all – in fact I was virtually kicked out! Because I stopped going down the car sealing place. She got me that job and me rent money was meant to be going up to £15 a week 'cause I was earning quite a bit down there. And she started asking £15 a week off me, then of course I lost the job and I was only getting £18 a week dole money, so I said "No". So she said, "If you won't give me any money you can leave then." So I left. She was angry with me 'cause I jacked in the job, sort of thing.'

CW: 'Did it get you down ever, being unemployed?'

Penny: 'Yeah, you always used to get annoyed, 'cause I had the money, didn't you? We used to go out and I always used to pay and it got to you a bit, didn't it? And, see, I used to give him the money so that he could buy drinks but people still know anyway, don't they? Because you can't hide it, can ya? But since we've had this place we haven't gone out much anyway.'

Dennis: 'Well, it does play on your mind, you get depressed. . . . I just got really down. You know, like not bothering to go out looking for jobs, not looking after yourself, not washing, not shaving, and the things like that. You know, just generally having no respect for yourself. And, luckily enough, I haven't been that bad, I've always thought, you know, ''Oh sod it! You've got to go out''. But I haven't got so low, sort of thing, I haven't got so low. I've always managed to pull myself back out of it. I always pulled out of it after a couple of months.'

Penny: 'Mind you, if we hadn't had this place it would have been worse. . . . When we was decorating, you could see there was always things to do and it wasn't so bad, but when we finished this room, we didn't have the money to venture anywhere else.'

Dennis: 'Yeah, I spent three months, slogging away, seven days a week, and all I got out of it was a stereo, the rest went on the house.'

Penny: 'Yeah, but we had the pleasure of doing it. £1,000 just went in two weeks, but we had a lot of bills to pay off and all. There was Amy's pushchair, and £50 savings for Amy's future.'

CW: 'Describe to me a typical day when you were unemployed?'

Dennis: 'Well, I'd get up around ten, and, uh, if I could afford it, go out and get a paper. Then I'd sit down and read the paper for about an hour. Then I'd go down town to Sheerness for a couple of hours. Go down the Job Centre. . . . But that wasn't much cop anyway. . . . It was really a very boring day. Dinner at five o'clock, sit down and watch telly, not doing nothing. . . . You can't go out, you see, because if you go out with other people you have to have some money in your pocket, so you're stuck indoors. Without money, you can't do nothing. . . . So much time to fill when you're unemployed.'

Penny: 'But we had one good day, before Christmas, didn't

we? We finished off three bottles of sherry in one day. Me, you, and your mum. . . .

'You see, my mum, she's on social security at the moment and she helped me out when I was short, so I help her out now. So we work out our meals together, so it all goes round. See, even though he's unemployed, I'm here all day as well. He used to get on my nerves sitting around all day. We used to argue quite a bit then, didn't we? But we haven't argued for ages now, have we, darling?'

Dennis: 'Yeah, you see it's because I'm sitting around here all day. That's what caused the arguments. You get depressed, you get depressed every couple of months, like, but it depends on how you take it. You can go very deep into depression. 'Cause there's so many application forms I've filled in I've never even had a reply. . . .

Cause you don't feel like doing nothing. Honest you don't. Well, I didn't anyway. No get up and go, sort of thing. It's great when you are first unemployed, a few lie-ins, sort of thing, but it gets worse. . . . And people used to moan at me all the time, it's unbelievable. . . . '

Penny: 'Yeah, 'cause we find it really embarrassing, you see. Sometimes you find it embarrassing because we do like to pay our own way and people say, "We'll buy you a drink, don't worry about getting one back." But it's embarrassing. You don't say anything, but you can see it in their eyes, you can see what they're thinking.'

CW: 'Or you think you can.'

Dennis: 'Exactly, exactly, that's the right way of putting it, 'cause they might not be thinking that at all, but you think they are. You're feeling it yourself, sort of thing.

'My parents think it's about time we got married. They think we should have got married when she fell pregnant, sort of thing, but there was no way that we were going to get married then, not for the wrong reason.'

Penny: 'But my mum didn't speak to you for three months, did she?'

Dennis: 'No, your mum thought I was never good enough for her. She kept on thinking Penny was going to marry a prince or something. . . . It got to the stage where I'd go in the pub and if her mum and her brother were sitting there they'd get up and walk over and sit on the other side of the pub. It really got to a stage where I thought, "Oh sod it! We're finished then". If it had gone on another month it would have got to that stage.'

Penny: 'Well we don't like living in a council house really. You see, we've talked about getting our own house, haven't we? We've looked at loads of houses for sale and that but we're not very good at saving, you see. If you're gong to go for your own house, you really need £100 a week or so to cover your expenses, and you need £1,500 to put down before that. But after we've married we'll do that. After all, we've been together nine years now, haven't we? You see, it really frightened me, the idea of getting married, frightened me, 'cause so many people say it changes your relationship, you know. We're getting on just fine as we are, we get on OK. But there's more to life than that. See, marriage isn't just a piece of paper, is it? You've got a hold over someone, you've got a bit more responsibility for someone.'

Dennis: 'Yeah, you see, you can't just get up and go when you fancy it, like when you're living with someone. 'Cause it runs through my mind all the time, "Will getting married change our relationship" If it does, I'd rather not bother, sort of thing.'

Penny: 'See, we were engaged already. We planned to live together anyway, I mean it's not as though we've just been seeing each other a couple of months, we've been seeing each other since we were thirteen. . . . His mum was pleased, she started buying nappies and all this, but my mum weren't. She was very upset. And my dad said nothing. He knows that Dennis wouldn't leave me, so as long as he knew that, he was all right, my dad. My mum was the trouble. Going back to the unemployment thing again, she was thinking, "What sort of life is my daughter going to have?" See, so many of the girls round here move into a place with their fellers, get pregnant, and then the feller leaves. Well, it's not much of a life, is it?

'But we've never regretted it, never regretted having Amy. Dennis watched it all to the end, the birth, and he cried then, didn't you?

'But I'll go back to work once they're at school, 'cause I'll still be under thirty then, and I enjoyed my time in the factory. The girls there were a good laugh.'

CW: 'What do you think you'll be doing in five years' time?'

Dennis: 'Well, hopefully, digger driving. And were having another kiddy next year, and we're planning to get married in May.'

CW: 'What do you think you'll be doing when you're fifty?'

Dennis: 'Fifty? Blimey! Taking it easy by then hopefully. I mean, hopefully we'll be in our own home by then. If I get a full-time job – it's what really I want, a full-time job – instead of being in and out of work all the time, then I can go for my own house.'

Chrissie

Chrissie met her future husband Rog when she was fifteen. When she left school she worked alongside the rest of her family at a local factory until she was accepted onto a pre-nursing course at one of the local colleges. However, she left after a year to move in with Rog and to find a job so that they could save for a house. After moving there, she became pregnant and they married. She has done a variety of odd jobs since then and now has two children – Gary aged 3 and Dwain aged 1 year. Rog works at a local factory too and earns a good wage there. They live in their own home just down the road from where Chrissie was born.

Chrissie: 'We moved in straight away. The mortgage was too much apart because we had to pay £180 a month on this place, plus paying keep to my mum and we just couldn't do it. That's really why we lived together, because of the mortgage. Then we found out six months later that I was expecting Gary, so we was going to get married anyway, so we thought we'd better do it straight away before he was born, so it was a bit of a rush wedding, but rather a nice wedding. . . . We had a big church wedding, thanks to the Gas Board. If I hadn't had that job we wouldn't have had nothing, I don't think.

'I worked exactly a year for the Gas Board – I finished when I was four months' pregnant with Gary. Then when Gary was small I had a job doing the accounts for a local garage and then I worked as a barmaid for a while. But we're planning to have another baby now. I probably won't go back to work until they are at school. Rog doesn't believe in it, he thinks I should be at home. Besides, with three of them I wouldn't be able to manage. I'd do a part-time job, perhaps, as a barmaid. I've got an Avon round, I do that. you see, my mother always worked when I was small and I don't think I would. I wouldn't deprive them of me to be honest. I was always from aunt to aunt when I came home from school, or nan had us, and mum was never there, so unless we were really short of money or Roger was made redundant – God forbid! – then I wouldn't go back to work full-time. . . . '

CW: 'What do you want to do in the long term?'

Chrissie: 'I still want to be a nurse. I'm still mad on nurses programmes and films and books and I think that's what I'll do when they are grown up, I'm determined to. I shall go to night school first. . . . An SRN takes four years and then it's a long training. I suppose I would be thirty five by that time but I wouldn't mind doing midwifery. They can be very choosey now, but you see I passed the tests for Canterbury, Dartford and Gravesend College, before I even got all my O-levels and CSEs and they have hundreds of girls applying for that. It was quite a privilege really.

'I love kids, I've always wanted them. It's just that Gary came a bit at the wrong time really, but I don't regret having them. Carol helps me a lot. I look after her children if she goes out, and she looks after mine if I go shopping or anything. I'm always looking after someone or other. I'm a real agony aunt round here! Because they've all got funny husbands and I haven't. They are strict with them. They go out and they're allowed to go out and do what they want and the wives have to do what their husbands want too. I suppose they are the men in the house, but mine lets me do what I want really. . . . He's ever so good really. He just gets a bit humpy when I have friends round and he has to go out on night shift. . . . He's always helped with the baths, fed and changed the children. He's good with them, I'm lucky really.

'At the Gas Board I was a personal clerk. I used to take the phone calls, get the services officer's paperwork done, file, answer his rude letters so he never had to see them, and I used to work the switchboard – PMBX. I learned a lot there. I still do my dad's paperwork for him now. He brings it all round for me.

'I don't think I could go on the dole. Well, there's no need for me ever because Roger would keep me anyway, but if there was a job going I'd take it rather than be unemployed. Because let's face it, your money's going to go up anyway and there's more prospects in a job than what there is on the dole. But I didn't like factory work, because of some of the people you get down there. Perhaps I'm a bit of a snob, but they were a bit rough. Even though my step-dad's a factory worker and Rog is, but some of them – the language they use! The effing and blinding – especially the women – they just don't care. Horrible! And I said to Rog, I just couldn't take that. They called me stuck up. It was only because I spoke properly to begin with. I don't speak properly really, but when I was at the Gas Board I was very la-di-da, because I had to be. I was a bit of a different person then.

'I don't know what it is like for your husband to be unemployed, but Rog's brother was unemployed for two years and that was just awful, you know. He used to come round and just sit here. And there are so many men round here like that. You can see the unemployed ones. They've grown older. Yes, they look older. I mean, there's Bill Smith down the end and he's been unemployed five years and he looks years older. He's applied for job after job, but they told him at thirty-five that he is too old! If Rog ever left his job, I think we would sell up and leave here, because there's nothing here at all for the ones out of work.'

CW: 'What is your main pastime?'

Chrissie: 'Knitting. I do loads of knitting. I charge for it though. I used to do it for nothing, but then I thought I was a bit of a mug, you know, so now I charge for it. Like, I'm just doing an Aran sweater for my neighbour's mum and I'll charge her £7 for that, even though it's a lot of work. I knitted Carol thirteen baby coats and I charged £20 for that, although that was with bulk wool which I get from Rog's mate at work. Normally I charge about £3 for a cardigan, which is cheaper than you would get it in a shop.'

CW: 'Would you have got married if Rog was unemployed?'

Chrissie: 'No, even if I was pregnant, I don't think we'd have got married. If we had this place and we was living here and he got unemployed then yes, I expect we would've done, but if we was living apart we wouldn't. We would just have carried along together until he found a job. Because I always said to him that I'd never get married until we had a house anyway. As soon as we got this place it was obvious that we was going to get married eventually anyway, we just married a bit sooner than we had worked out really.'

CW: 'Would you have children if you were unemployed?'

Chrissie: 'No, because it wouldn't have been fair. Not fair on us and not fair on the children. Because you don't get a lot of money when you are unemployed, and the amount of stuff a baby needs. I mean, we must have spent – I mean the pram alone cost us £200. I always like the best for my kids and I'm quite proud of the fact that they always get the best. Now if I had a baby and they had everything second-hand and as they got older they had to go without things that other children had, I would never have brought a baby into the world with those prospects. I don't think it is fair. I've got high standards, and if I couldn't keep my standards I would start on Roger and it would go round in a circle.'

CW: 'Do you think people should get married when they are unemployed?'

Chrissie: 'If one's a wage-earner, yes. But if he's unemployed, what chance has a chap got of actually getting a house or even if you rent a flat and you go up to them and you say, "I'm unemployed," they wouldn't want to know. As for buying, they'd laugh in your face if you tried to buy a house. Then there's furniture to buy and everything else. A single bloke only gets about £25. You couldn't do it. I think it's silly. You start off on the wrong foot. You've got to have a good bank balance, I think, to get married, so you can get the things you want, your house together. So we had nice furniture when we moved in here. It was all new. We've just decided to replace it with something better. When I was at the Gas Board, I was earning £200 a month and Rog was getting £500 a month and all we had really was the mortgage to pay. We had a new kitchen, carpets and three-piece suite and then we went and bought a telly and video. We saved up a hell of a lot. Mind you, when we moved in here all we had was the downstairs furnished. The upstairs had a wardrobe and a bed and that was it.

'And we paid for the whole wedding ourselves. I mean, my friend bought my wedding dress for a present and I bought my own wedding cake. I paid for the photographer, and dad paid for the reception. We had a £120 overdraft after that lot. And we put £1,000 down on this, plus the solicitor's fees and things. My dad helped a lot. He helped to keep my head above water. He used to drive me to Rochester every day and wouldn't take any money off me for petrol, and he bought me lunch because I was so broke I couldn't even afford a lunch. But once we got the deposit saved up and the solicitor's fees, that was it, we was back to our own money again. But it was hard work.

'Rog wasn't so self-sufficient as me. He's always lived at his mum's and dad's before he moved here. He doesn't have much idea of what goes on in the house really, he leaves it all to me.'

CW: 'What do you think you will be doing in a few year's time?'

Chrissie: 'My friend and I were thinking of starting a play group down at the church hall because she's a nurse and I've had a year's pre-nursing course. . . . I don't think we will be living here. I'd like a nice semi with a garage, I can see that actually. Eventually, we're going to have to sell up to better ourselves. Because we just can't do any more with this place really. We've had the walls knocked down and the bathroom, and we could always get a third bedroom and it would be worth £19,000 and we only paid £14,000 for it. But we can't go any higher because of the area it's in.'

CW: What did people say when they found out you were pregnant?'

Chrissie: 'Mum was really pleased. She said, "Lovely, I want to be a grandma." I remember I came home from work and opened the front door and Rog was cooking fish fingers and chips and he said, 'Hello mum!'' and I said, "Whatever are we going to do?" And he said, "We haven't got to do nothing. We're quite happy as we are." I wasn't very happy about it, but it never crossed my mind to get rid of it. Mainly because of the way I found out about it. My whole family knew before I did, because my sister-in-law told them the results of the test.

'The one I was really worried about telling was my dad. Oh, that did worry me. The next day I got in the car to go to Rochester and I felt sick and he said, "Well, that's your own bloody fault, isn't it?" It was just the shock, I think. He thought I was a career woman. I don't think he ever thought I was going to get married to Roger, even though we had this place. But after a couple of weeks he came round. Nan started bringing baby clothes round. But of course I had trouble with me mum at the wedding because I wanted dad to give me away instead of me step-dad. She started walking past me in the street, but two weeks before the wedding we made it up.

'Once I was married people were more open about it, I think they were a bit embarrassed to be honest. My nan tried to ignore it at first. There was me out here and we went round to the greengrocer's and she asked me, "When's the baby due?" and I said, "September," and me nan looked the other way. My nan couldn't really accept it until it was born. . . . I suppose she's from a different age, I mean having to get married was a shame on her, I think. I felt sorry for her, but it's not unusual now, is it? She had a strict upbringing, I suppose. But as soon as Gary was born, she couldn't do enough for him. But when I was having the second one she used to ask me how I was feeling and whether I could feel it kicking and everything. She never did that with Gary.'

CW: 'What would have happened if you had had to bring up Gary on your own?'

Chrissie: 'I think me mum would have stuck by me, but I would have found it very difficult. But there are so many girls – my school friends – now doing it. But it would have meant that I would have had to go out to work and me mum look after the baby.'

CW: 'What advice would you give to a friend who was thinking of having children and whose husband was unemployed?'

Chrissie: 'I'd say, "Look, you've got plenty of time to have children." I mean, twenty-one isn't the age to start a family anyway. I'd say that it was best to wait a couple of years. I mean, there's a girl up the road, Lindsay, she's just had a baby and to me she's playing "mum". That's what a lot of them do. She's playing dolls, if you know what I mean. She wants a proper little girl. Dressing her up in frilly dresses and all this. And she gets no housework or anything done. But I would certainly advise people on the dole not to have children, because I don't think it's right, to be honest.'

CW: 'So has your life-style changed much, do you think?'

Chrissie: 'Yes, because when we had the first baby we could still go out to a certain extent because we used to go out all three of us in the car. Then when I had the second baby, I mean Dwain is still in the push-chair, so he can't walk far. But still, I don't have to walk far because all my friends are in the same road, they are all in the same situation. But my school friends, I don't see much of them any more. They're still the same as they were when they were still at school. And to be honest, they seem a bit immature because they have never had any responsibility. . . . And I've had responsibility, I've had it since I was seventeen. I mean, I talk to Anne and she says she's feeling a bit of an old maid, being left behind. But what else can I speak to them about apart from children? I mean that's what we all talk about together round here, or what they had for dinner. I mean, we very rarely go "out". We go out for a drink on a Saturday night when he's off or we might go and have a bottle of wine up Carol's. I prefer what money we've got to spend spent on this place, 'cause we're going to end up with more money in the long run if we sell it. We've got that to look forward to. All we can do now really is better ourselves. We'll have plenty of time to go out when these are grown up, 'cause when Gary's sixteen, I'll be thirty-four. They'll be the ones settling down and stuck indoors, and I'll be going round visiting them. First of all, that was the only thing that kept me going was thinking about that, because I did get a bit – felt a bit that I was left out when I first had Gary. Then I thought, "No, blow them. They're the ones missing out, not me." Because they don't know what it's like to have your own children to look after and play with. They'll know what it's like when they get there, but they'll just have to take my word for it at the moment.'

9
Conclusions

It would appear from the lives of young men and women discussed here, that unemployment at sixteen is a qualitatively different experience from unemployment at twenty-one.[1] There is a growing divergence between the mainly employed and the mainly unemployed as they enter early adulthood: in other words, a form of social polarization. In this study we can see the occurrence of polarization identified by Pahl (1984) and others as a *process* as well as a cross-sectional phenomenon at any given point in time. We can see the way in which divergences develop between people who left school at the same time, according to things which happen to them at critical points in their lives.

Responses to unemployment need to be seen in the context of responses to work. In general, there was a 'settling down' to employment and a sense of resignation towards the kinds of jobs available. This process is perhaps best illustrated in the case studies in Chapters 5 and 8. One of the striking factors conveyed by the general tone of these accounts was the way in which the long-term unemployed tended to see themselvs as helpless flotsam and jetsam washed around by the receding economic tide, whereas those with steady jobs or raised aspirations were more likely to approach their lives more positively, confident in their ability to change their lives and their situations if it was not to their liking. They had prospects, they had a future, and tended to see this future in terms of the acquisition of a house, a family, and various consumer goods rather than as a 'career' in any middle-class sense. To this extent, what seemed to be emerging were new divisions based upon whether young adults had access to a job or not, rather than the kinds of jobs they held. Hence, young people could leave school with the same hopes and expectations but end with very different careers. In this respect, it was the long-term cumulative experience of unemployment that was important.

Critics might ask: to what extent were these processes a result of social maturation, as I have argued, and to what extent were they the product of rising unemployment during the 1980s, which has perhaps led all sections of the population to cling to their jobs? Certainly, there are elements of both factors at work. Unfortunately, there are not many equivalent longitudinal studies either now or in times of full employment with which to compare this study.[2] However, one study does provide an appropriate comparison. Michael Carter re-interviewed a sample of school leavers in Sheffield after a period of five years. This was at a time of full employment when there were ample jobs for young people to take. He found that although most boys eventually entered the steel and related industries in the locality, they tended to reject these jobs when they first left school. Only later, with accumulating family responsibilities did the need for extra income lure them back:

'The occupational structure afforded the opportunities, but many boys reacted against the vastness, the noise and the dirt of the steel industry, and the move away from steel also represented a significant, if modest challenge to the dominance of the industry. Youth left their jobs almost as an act of defiance, a token that notwithstanding the constraints of the employment scene as it confronts young school leavers, they retained at least a modicum of free will and control over their lives. But the logic of the industrial structure is not to be defied and by the end of five years there was a move back to steel and engineering, with a third of the youth employed in it.'

(Carter 1975: 94)

Carter goes on to describe the kinds of pressures that pushed them back into steel: 'Marriage and impending marriage turn thoughts towards the need for a higher income with a wedding to be saved for and furniture to buy' (Carter 1975: 95).

Thus it would appear that 'settling down' is a process common to other groups of young people and that this has implications for their responses to unemployment. The domestic life course and the process of maturation should be seen as a crucial variable. Parker (1976) found this happening with respect to delinquent careers. His 'lads' stopped stealing car radios and found more reliable sources of income as they entered into relationships with girls.

It is perhaps important at this stage to situate the issues discussed so far within a broader theoretical framework. The transition from school to work should be set within the broader framework of social and cultural reproduction. The sociological problem is to explain how society reproduces itself from moment to moment and from generation to generation. How do we all come to fulfil our different roles with the appropriate beliefs, attitudes, and behaviour? This is especially problematical when some people benefit far less than others. Some of the school leavers interviewed in these surveys benefited very little from their employment. It was unfulfilling and badly paid. In this respect, the experiences of many of these school leavers was similar to that of all industrial workers;

> 'What constitutes the alienation of labour? Firstly, the fact that labour is external to the worker i.e. does not belong to his essential being; that he therefore does not conform himself in his work, but denies himself, feels miserable and not happy, does not develop free mental and physical energy, but mortifies his flesh and ruins his mind. Hence the worker feels himself only when he is not working; when he is working he does not feel himself. He is at home when he is not working, and not at home when he is working. His labour is therefore not voluntary but forced, it is *forced labour*. It is therefore not the satisfaction of a need but a mere means to satisfy needs outside himself.'
>
> (Marx 1975): 326)

However, in other respects their experiences were different from other industrial workers because they were encountering their condition for the first time, and their adjustment to, or rejection of, this was therefore problematical.

In addition, the economic slump meant that they were likely to find themselves out of work, on temporary schemes, on a lower income and excluded from the consumer roles and other kinds of status considered 'normal' for young people. How did they come to terms with this? Seen from this point of view, what needs explaining is how they ever accepted the jobs open to them rather than why they rejected them.

To return to my four hypotheses set out in Chapter 1. The first hypothesis was that there would be a fractured reproduction of work roles because 'traditional' work roles and training were no longer available and many young people did not find work. It was evident from the discussion in Chapter 3 that there was indeed a 'fracture' in this respect with some young people resisting employment, and many of them having to lower their expectations. However, young people still believed in the ideal of full (male) employment.

Second, it was hypothesized that there would be a discontinuity in youth cultures, with some young people being less affluent. In my discussion of the results presented in Chapter 4 it is evident that an 'anti-work ethic' and deliberately anti-respectable youth cultures were adopted by some. These provided alternative forms of status to that of the fully employed. However, these seemed to be transitory and fragile in character rather than a continuous feature of youth unemployment.

Third, it was hypothesized that the restructuring of the labour market had implications for the reproduction of gender roles and 'masculinity' and 'femininity' generally. This is discussed in Chapters 4, 6, and 7. From the evidence it would appear that we would need to look at the reproduction of gender roles on several levels – the economic, social, and symbolic, and also in terms of people's ideals and fantasies. Where the economic and social supports for gender identity were no longer available, fantasized roles could be used as a temporary substitute. However, the reproduction of gender roles was tied to the reproduction of the family as well as work roles and work cultures. This relates to my next hypothesis.

The fourth hypothesis was that there would be a discontinuity in the reproduction of the family. It would seem that new styles of living are emerging more generally and that the conventional family form is just one of these. However, most still held conventional marriage and the nuclear family as the ideal towards which they aspired and unemployment served to postpone this ideal. This is discussed more fully in Chapter 7.

It would appear, therefore, that there are important fractures in the process of social and cultural reproduction produced by the recent restructuring of employment. However, the ideology of full male employment and the ideology of the privatized nuclear family persisted even when these were not realizable in reality. Indeed, it could be argued that, at the symbolic and fantasy levels, they were reinforced.

Whilst the idea of 'social reproduction' helps us to situate the experiences of young people, this study would indicate that it would need to be modified. Young workers did not simply replace adult workers, as much literature has assumed – it was a far more slow and painful process. They were not automatically 'reproduced' by the time they left school, for it was only through other pressures that they came to accept the discipline of labour. Indeed, acquiring a family was a far more effective labour discipline than government schemes or vocational training ever could be.

Hence, the new model of social and cultural reproduction I am proposing is one where transitions into the family take place in parallel across three stages. This can be expressed diagrammatically thus:

Figure 9 The social reproduction of roles and relations

Parallel stages in the reproduction process

	I	II	III
Layers of reproduction	School $\rightarrow$	Entry into labour market $\rightarrow$	Full incorporation into labour force
	Family of origin $\rightarrow$	Courting $\rightarrow$	Family of destination

This takes place at different ages and is more or less compressed according to the social class, gender, and employment or unemployment experience of the person involved. In this way social reproduction is in fact a much longer-term process.

This in turn affects the way in which young adults themselves *perceive* their maturity or immaturity. Since these transitions constitute together the entry into adult citizenship in our society it is not surprising that girls (who do this younger) should feel themselves to be more mature than boys of the same age, and that minimum age school leavers (who make these transitions youngest) should feel themselves to be more mature than those staying on for more school or more training, and this could be a source of conflict between different groups. This situation will presumably be complicated by the introduction of youth training more universally.

Whilst hitherto sociologists have talked of the transition from school to work as though these were two distinct institutions and there was a clean break between them, it can be seen from this research that the transition stretched both before and after sixteen. Some had effectively left school much earlier, either in order to stay at home and do nothing: for them it was a transition from not much school to not much work. For others it was a transition from part-time jobs to full-time jobs. For yet others it was a transition from a variety of casual and informal 'odd jobs' to more of the same. It can be seen that many of these had left school in spirit before the official school-leaving age and had not necessarily entered full-time work afterwards. Some still continued to go from school to full-time work in the conventional way. Rather than being a 'smooth' transition it was a 'ragged' one.

Similarly, the transition from the natal home to that of destination is normally taken to mean from one family to another. Furthermore, the 'family' is normally taken to mean the nuclear family with a male (employed) head of household married to a dependent wife. This represented only a fraction of school leavers since they usually made such transitions in a far more complicated way. Leaving home generally meant living in bedsits and shared houses, moving in with boyfriends but not being married, having children and continuing to live alone, and so on. There were evidently new household styles or old ones becoming more acceptable.

It is often argued that there is now no longer much in the way of a 'transition from school to work' as such. It is more often a transition to further education, training and various schemes such as the YTS, with entry into work deferred to eighteen and beyond. Does this mean that many of the issues discussed here are no longer pertinent? Evidently, new styles of transition – some of them chosen – are evolving in the 1980s. 'Youth' itself is being defined as a longer period of dependency with new social security regulations raising the age of independence to twenty-five (Youthaid 1985). However, issues of gender, the family, and expectations of work and domestic roles are still crucial in the process. This study can only capture one moment in the intersection of history and biography, but any fragment of social time contains the vestiges of the past as well as the seeds of the future.

Looking at the problem from another direction it can be seen that the issue of social reproduction has perhaps been too narrowly focused upon school and employment. How do young people become women and men, mothers and fathers, wives and husbands, houseworkers and patriarchs? These broader issues need to be incorporated. Crucial modifications need to be made in the more general model of social reproduction.

Many have criticized this model for its masculine bias (Mac-Donald 1980). It is evident from a variety of studies that girls' experience of becoming a worker, becoming an adult, is very different from that of young men. It has been argued that one of the reasons for this is that domestic roles in the present and the future cast a long shadow over other aspects of young women's lives. Hence, their job prospects are inhibited and they see themselves as preoccupied to a large extent with their sexual status rather than employment or educational status. My interviews would indicate that this assumption of feminine status and domestic roles is likewise more fractured and contradictory than many have assumed. Young women did not uncritically accept their situation and were often torn between conflicting expectations.

Unfortunately, no black young people were interviewed in this survey as there were none on Sheppey. However, for experiences of black girls see Griffin (1985) and problems of race in the transition from school to work see Solomos (1986).

This focus on young women leads us to re-evaluate the role of the domestic sphere and domestic life courses, in relation to young men too, and hence in relation to life courses more generally. Experiences of employment and unemployment need to be seen in this context and the debates have perhaps focused too narrowly on transitions into work.

Finally, the process of life course development cannot be separated from the development of sexual identities and what it means to become a young man or a young women. None of my sample talked of homosexuality (except derisorily) and it can be seen that social maturation was couched very much in terms of heterosexual careers at work and in relations with partners and peers. A number of pressures forced young people to conform – employers, parents, and their own peers' expectations – so that a socialized heterosexual adult was produced. And yet, as we have seen, the fact that young people had their own ways of responding to such pressures means that change was always a possibility.

The research discussed here indicates that growing up in the 1980s is a different process to that in previous decades. However, it would appear that whilst models previously used to understand young people's behaviour need to be reassessed in the light of these changes, it would also appear that the models themselves need modifying in any case. Many pessimistic conclusions and results have been presented – the disillusionment, poverty, and purposelessness of many young people is sad to record and sad to read about. However, more optimistically, I have been privileged to document much creativity and critical awareness. Evidently, young adults do find alternatives in adversity. There is also evidence of change. New life-styles and attitudes are being explored at a personal level. Conceptions of what constitutes 'employment careers', 'marriage', and the 'family' will perhaps need to be rethought.

Appendix 1 School leavers' questionnaire 1979

Part 1 Basic information

NAME: NO.
DATE OF BIRTH: M   F
ADDRESS: MONTH OF
                                         LEAVING SCHOOL

FIRST JOB

Employer ....
Starting when ....
Nature of work ....
Pay expected ....
Know people working there ....
....
How found job ....
Why job chosen ....

Employer ....
Starting when ....
Nature of work ....
Pay expected ....
Know people working there ....
....
How found job ....
Why job chosen ....

LONG-TERM EMPLOYMENT GOAL

Employer ....
Starting when ....
Nature of work ....
Pay expected ....
Know people working there ....
....
How found job ....
Why job chosen ....

PAST JOBS

Pt/Ft	Employer	Dates	Occupation	Pay

FAMILY'S JOBS

Relation to ego	Pt/Ft	Employer	Occupation	Pay

Younger siblings ....

THOSE WITH NO FULL-TIME JOB ARRANGED

Are you going to claim supplementary benefit? ....
Do you mind being unemployed? ....
....
Do you intend going on a government training programme? ....
....
Are you looking for work? ....

How? ....
Are you waiting for work arranged? ....
How long do you think you will be unemployed? ....
....
Are you doing part time or casual work? ....

Pt/Ft	Employer	Occupation	How often	Pay
....	....	....	....	....
....	....	....	....	....
....	....	....	....	....
....	....	....	....	....
....	....	....	....	....

Part 2 Open-ended questions

PRESENT EMPLOYMENT

1. How long do you expect to remain with your first employer?
2. If you change jobs would you change
   (a) in order to find something better
   (b) for better pay
   (c) due to boredom
   (d) in order to seek self-employment
3. What do you consider most important in a job:
   . pay/conditions/mates/job satisfaction/career prospects? (probe)
4. What do you think of your first job?
5. Do you think it is difficult to find a job?
6. Is it as difficult as you expected?
7. What do you think of the pay? What do you think is the minimum wage you would accept? What do you think is a reasonable wage for a school leaver?
8. Is there any job you would not do?
9. Have you ever considered becoming self-employed?
   Why? (probe formal/informal)

UNEMPLOYMENT

1. What would your family think if you were on the dole?
2. Do you think you get enough money on supplementary benefit?
3. Would you go on supplementary benefit if
   (a) you were waiting for a suitable job
   (b) if no suitable job were available

PAST JOBS

1. What did you think of the pay/people/conditions in the jobs you have had in the past?
2. How did you discover them?
3. Do you think it was useful experience?
4. Why did you do work in the past?

SCHOOL

1. What did you think of school?
1. Did you have problems or difficulties in your school career?
3. Do you ever play truant? When? Why?
4. Do you think qualifications are important?
5. What do your parents think of school?

LEISURE

1. What do you do in your spare time?
2. Where do you go?
3. Who with?
4. How do you manage for pocket money? (probe, sources)
5. How do you spend your pocket money?

FRIENDS AND FAMILY

1. Who are your main friends and what are they going to do when they leave school?
2. How old are they?
3. Where do you usually meet them?
4. Do you have a boyfriend/girlfriend? How old are they? What does he/she do? How long have you been together?
5. Do you talk much about jobs with your friends?
6. Do you ask your friends about job vacancies? Has anyone asked you?
7. Do you ever talk about jobs with your parents?
8. Has anyone in your family tried to find jobs for you?
9. What do your parents want you to do?
10. Did you find the Careers Service helpful?

Appendix 2
1980 school leavers' questionnaire

Work history (ask all)

1. What has happened to you since you left school?
2. Describe the jobs, and how you found out about them.
3. What did you like/dislike about them?
4. Why did you leave?
5. How did you get on with the supervisors and foremen?
6. What other sources of finance do you have apart from your main job?
7. What did you want to do when you left school? Why have you changed your mind? What would you *really* like to do now?
8. Have any of your friends or family asked you to help them get a job?

Unemployment (ask only those who have been unemployed)

1. What did you/do you do with your time whilst you were/are unemployed?
2. What is/was the worst thing about being unemployed?
3. Does it/did it get you down at all?
4. Are you/were you looking for jobs? How? How often?
5. Do your/did your parents encourage you?
   Do they/did they find work for you?
6. Are most of your friends working or not working?
   Has it/did it make any difference to the people you go around with?
7. Does it/did it make you feel awkward, or embarrassed if you go and and someone asks you 'what are you doing'?
8. Do you/did you go out to the same places as when you were working? Do you/did you go as often?
9. Do you/did you miss the money?
10. (If unemployed at present) If I told you there were jobs going at .... (name a factory) at the moment would you go for them?

Family (ask all)

1. Are your dad and mum still working at the same places as last year?
2. Have you lived here all the time?
   Are you planning to move out?
3. Do your parents treat you differently since you left school?

Leisure (ask all)

1. Are you still going around with the same people as you did when you were at school?
2. Do you go around with any people from work?
3. Where do you meet your friends?
4. Are you married/courting/engaged?
5. How do you spend your spare time? (probe: pub, club, disco, etc.)
6. Have you any pastimes?
7. Do you go out more or less often than when you were at school?

Attitudes (ask all)

TO WORK

1. What is your idea of a good boss?
2. If you went in the Job Centre now, what sort of jobs would you look for?
3. What sort of things would you want to know about the job?
4. Have you ever considered being self-employed? Why?
5. What sorts of jobs would you not do?
6. If you were offered the chance to be a supervisor would you take it?
7. If they offered you training would you take it?
8. Attitudes to authority:
   (a) If they told you to . . . . . . (name menial job) what would you do?
   (b) If they told you to cut your hair/change your clothes what would you do?
   (c) Would you have done that at school?

UNEMPLOYMENT

1. If you were made unemployed, would you claim supplementary benefit or dole money?
2. Would you go to work if it paid the same as supplementary benefit or dole money?
3. Would you go to work if the only job available was . . . . . . (name the job they would not do)?
4. Do you think the dole money is enough?
5. If you were made redundant tomorrow, what would you do?

OTHER

1. What do you think you will be doing in five years' time?
2. What do you think you will be doing next year?
3. Who do you know that you would want to be like?
4. Who do you know that you would not like to be like?
5. Looking back at school, what do you think of it now?
6. How do you spend your money at the moment?

Appendix 3
Follow-up questionnaire of young people, Summer 1984

Part 1 General data (from relatives if necessary)

Name:
Address:
Case Number:

1. Marital status
2. Children (number and ages)
3. Living arrangements/housing
4. Employment at present:
   (a) Length of time employed.
   (b) Wages.
5. Employment of partner (where appropriate):
   (a) Length of time employed.
6. Employment and domestic chronology.
7. Unemployment:
   (a) Number of times.
   (b) Periods of unemployment.
   (c) Total time unemployed.
8. Jobs:
   (a) Number of jobs.
   (b) Reasons for leaving.
9. Number of applications.
10. Father's employment.

Part 2 Attitudes

ASK ALL

1. In 1979 you said that you were really looking for a job as a

   ....

   Do you still want to do that now?
   Do you have any regrets about not doing that?

2. The work ethic:
   (a) Would you work for less money than you get on the dole?
   (b) What jobs wouldn't you do?
   (c) Would you rather do any job than be unemployed?
   (d) How about benefit?
   (e) Some people say that the unemployed should be made to work for their money. Do you agree with that?
3. What pastimes do you have?
4. Marriage morality:
   (a) Would you/did you get married whilst unemployed?
   (b) Would you/did you have children when unemployed?
   (c) Do you think that it is right that people get married when they are unemployed?
   (d) Do you think it is right that people have children when they are unemployed?
5. Do you ever get money from:
   (a) Your parents?
   (b) Other members of the family?
6. How much do you give your mum?
7. Do you feel more dependent upon parents than when at school?
8. Do you have any extra ways of getting money apart from your main job?
9. Plans:
   (a) What do you think you will be doing in five years' time?
   (b) What do you think you will be doing when you are fifty?
10. Peers:
    (a) Are your friends still the same ones as when you were at school?
    (b) Are most of your friends employed/unemployed?
                     married/single?
11. Have you ever considered leaving home?

Part 3   Questions for those unemployed

1. (a) (status/identity)
   (a) Do you feel embarrassed or ashamed about being unemployed? How do you describe yourself in the pub?
   (b) (time structure)
       Do you find you are getting up later when unemployed?
       Describe to me a typical day:
   (c) (isolation)
       Do you feel that you see your friends more or less since being unemployed?
       Do you feel isolated?
   (d) (activity)
       Do you find you have trouble filling your time?
       Do you do your hobbies more or less?
   (e) Do you find other things to do when you're unemployed?
   (f) Do people behave differently towards you?

(g) Do you behave differently towards them?
(h) What is the worst thing about being unemployed?
(i) Are there any advantages?
2. Did your parents support you when you were unemployed? (probe)
(a) Financially.
(b) Morally.
3. Did you feel more dependent upon your parents when you were unemployed?
4. Did other members of your family support you? (probe)
(a) Financially.
(b) Morally.
5. Did your friends support you?
(a) Financially.
(b) Morally.
(c) In other ways.
6. Who do you think was the most help to you when you were unemployed?
7. Do you mind getting help when you are unemployed?

Part 4   Questions for those married/living as married

1. Why did you decide to get married?
2. Was it planned?
3. What did your parents say?
4. What did his/her parents say?
5. What did your friends say?
6. Are you planning to have children?
7. When are you planning to have children?
   (probe use of contraception)
8. (a) Would you think of having children before getting married?
   (b) Under what circumstances?
9. If one of your friends was thinking of getting married and they had no job, what advice would you give?
   Or the man/woman had no job?
10. Would you have got married if you had no job?
11. Do you think your employment/unemployment influenced your decision to get married or live together in any way?
12. Do you feel more or less dependent on your parents now?

Part 5   Questions for those with children

1. Why did you decide to have children?
2. Did you plan to have children?
3. In what way did you plan to have children?
4. If ...... had arrived at the wrong time, what would you have done?
5. What did your parents say?

6. What did his/her parents say?
7. What did your friends say?
8. Would you have had children *before* you got married?
9. If one of your friends was going to have children and had no job, what would you advise them?

IF UNEMPLOYED

10. Do you think your unemployment had any effect on your decision to have children?

OF WOMEN

11. (a) Would you want to go back to work?
    (b) Do you miss work?
    (c) Would you have children if your husband/boyfriend/you had no job?
12. Do you feel more or less dependent on your parents now?

Notes

Chapter 1

1. Willis (1981) has elaborated the distinction between cultural and social reproduction. Here, I am using definitions provided by the Centre for Contemporary Cultural Studies who argue that social reproduction is about the reproduction of the social relations of production (from Althusser 1971), whilst culture refers to the way in which people make sense of this through 'lived experience' (Hall and Jefferson 1976). Cultural reproduction refers to the ways in which such meanings are transmitted.
2. Meillasoux (1975) has addressed the role of the family in the process of social reproduction under differing social conditions. Edholm, Harris, and Young (1977) on the other hand have distinguished three meanings of the word 'reproduction': biological reproduction, the reproduction of the work-force using women's labour within the home, and the reproduction of social relationships – which also takes place through the family. Here I am referring only to the third meaning.
3. Studies of male youth cultures such as those contained in the Mungham and Pearson (1976) volume and the Hall and Jefferson (1976) volume have tended to adopt this perspective, and this has been part of the critical thrust of the oral history movement. More recently, however, some feminists such as Stanley and Wise (1983) have argued that qualitative research is the best method for contributing towards feminist theory and practice.
4. Out of this 1979 sample, fifty-three were Easter leavers and 100 were chosen randomly from the school register.
5. Other work is currently being carried out in this area. For example Burrage's (1986) work uses both official statistics and information gathered at medical centres in Liverpool to look at early pregnancy in the context of unemployment. Hutson and Jenkins (1986) are gathering information about young unemployed adults in Swansea.

Gill Jones at the University of Surrey is examining issues of youth and transitions through the General Household Survey.

Chapter 2

1. According to a propagandist historian Augustus Daly, whose book *History of the Isle of Sheppey* was first published in 1904.
2. From the 1981 census.
3. From the Chief Constable's Report for Kent 1982.
4. This survey was part of an ESRC project Grant No. G/00/23/0036. Results are provided in Pahl and Wilson (1984).
5. From Kent County Constabulary Statistics.
6. The history of the naval dockyard and its relationship to the town, based upon a detailed analysis of the 1851, 1861, and 1871 census, was carried out by Buck (1981).
7. From Sheppey School Report (1984) and interviews with senior staff.
8. The most popular amongst my sample were a typing and secretarial course for girls and a 'technical' course for boys. These courses were available at the school partly because there was no technical college within easy reach.
9. The local Careers Office held statistics going back to the early 1950s, so it was possible to compare these with 1979. However, we should be cautious in doing so, since the means of recording information had changed in the intervening period and Careers Office records were not complete either in the 1950s or in 1979.
10. Careers Office records appeared to indicate that about one-fifth of all young people on the island entered the dockyard in the 1950s (Wallace 1986).
11. See *A New Training Initiative*. Cmnd 8455. London: HMSO.
12. It was estimated by one MSC official that one WEP scheme trainee using employer's premises cost two-thirds of the price of one on a youth and community work scheme.
13. From a comparison of first job placements of Sheppey school leavers 1979–80, and those on YOP using Sheppey Careers Office statistics (see Wallace [1985] for further details).
14. Mode A originally replaced the WEEP scheme and Mode B the youth and community-type schemes. These divisions are again under revision at present.

Chapter 3

1. Willis (1977), for example, has excluded girls from the analysis, whilst Ashton and Field (1976) describe 'young workers' in an ungendered way.
2. Blackburn and Mann (1979) found that although working-class men had few real choices in the labour market, they nevertheless perceived themselves as choosing between jobs.

3. Jones *et al.* (1981) also constructed a hierarchy of work for boys and for girls in which clerical work came at the top for girls, and skilled work followed by 'outdoor work' for boys. Factory work was the least popular for both sexes. Phillips (1973) has also documented these negative job preferences.

4. Raffe (1984) in a larger scale survey of 2,929 school leavers in 1984 found that there were two tiers within the YTS in its first year of operation corresponding with the different motivations of different types of trainees.

5. Markall (1980) and Finn (1984) have noted in empirical studies how young people at the bottom of the school system often leave school earlier on the pretext that they are looking for work, or because they are doing odd jobs.

6. This is an extract from an interview carried out by R. E. Pahl in a piece of joint research carried out for the Department of Employment (Pahl and Wallace 1980).

7. This was lower than the rate of job departure reported in other studies. Maizels (1970), for example, found that one-half of job changes were voluntary, and Roberts, Duggan, and Noble (1982b) argued that some two-thirds of job departures were voluntary. Raffe (1984), however, argues that the rate of job changing has declined since the rise of unemployment in the 1980s.

8. I have called these 'odd jobs' since they spanned a wide range of activities including informal unpaid work, work for cash, illegal work, occasional jobs, seasonal work, helping relatives, and so on.

Chapter 4

1. Some of the publications by the Social and Applied Psychology Unit relevant to this area include: Banks and Jackson (1981), Jackson and Warr (1983), Jackson *et al.* (1983), Stafford (1982), Warr (1982). There is an overview of some of this literature provided by Warr (1983). The unit has undertaken a variety of large-scale surveys over a period of years, comparing different groups of unemployed and employed both cross-sectionally and longitudinally. They have measured psychological well-being through the use of established tests.

2. Donovan and Oddy (1982), Stokes (1981), Roberts, Duggan, and Noble (1981, 1982c) have all indicated that unemployed girls take on more domestic responsibilties. Furthermore, Breakwell (1984), Gurney (1980), Stokes (1981), and Warr and Parry (1982) have indicated that girls suffer fewer adverse social psychological effects than boys when they are unemployed.

3. The CND became a flourishing movement on the island during the course of my field-work. Some of its main recruits were the young unemployed.

4. In Gaskell's (1983) interview with school leavers, the same picture emerges. They did not whole-heartedly embrace traditional feminine roles at this stage of their lives.

Chapter 5

1. This interview was taken from the Department of Employment project rather than from the survey of 153 school leavers described here. The project allowed us to hold lengthy interviews with unemployed seventeen-year-olds and provided extended transcripts. Hence this was good material to use as case studies. The respondents were chosen as a cross-section of unemployed young people of this age group on Sheppey.

Part Two

1. Domestic 'life course' or 'domestic career' is used in preference to 'life-cycle' since Harris (1986) has demonstrated, the latter implies a static, orderly process. What is being described here is a less predictable process subject to a variety of contingencies and so a more open-ended terminology is required.

Chapter 6

1. 'Career' is used in this chapter to refer to the young person's movement through different kinds of work and different domestic stages. It is not intended as a linear concept in the same sense as a middle-class professional career. On account of this meaning of 'career' I have used the terms 'work trajectories' to refer to employment activities but 'domestic careers' or 'life courses' to refer to activities outside of employment.
2. Job turnover did appear to decline with age, but it is impossible to document this precisely on the basis of these data.
3. Taylor (1978) has documented the social relationships of Tupperware parties.
4. Similar results were found in a much larger survey conducted by the Economist Intelligence Unit in 1982.
5. These trends would correspond with Sinfield's (1981) argument that the 'unemployment prone' sections of the population are likely to spend substantial portions of their lives out of work, whilst others remain more or less permanently in work.
6. For example, the OECD in its report *Entry of Young People into Working Life* claimed that young people were losing the work ethic. Evidence for and against this is discussed by Jahoda (1982).
7. In response to the question 'Would you rather do any job than be unemployed?', 81 per cent of the regularly employed, 66 per cent of the occasionally unemployed and 80 per cent of the long-term unemployed said that they would.
8. Golding and Middleton (1982) discuss the way in which images of the deserving and undeserving poor are conjured up in the media and the way in which 'undeserving' comes to be attached to the unemployed, leading to 'moral panics' about scrounging.

9. In answer to the question 'Did you ever feel embarrassed or ashamed about being unemployed?' three of the six regularly employed who had been unemployed for only a few weeks after leaving school said 'yes'. All of the 4 occasionally unemployed said 'yes' and 12 of the 19 long-term unemployed said 'yes'.

10. All of the 6 regularly employed had got up after 9 a.m. when they were unemployed. Half of the 8 occasionally unemployed had done so, as against 13 of the 19 (68 per cent) long-term unemployed.

11. In answer to the question 'Did you have trouble filling your time?' half of the 4 regularly employed who answered the question said that they did, 3 out of 8 occasionally unemployed, and 11 of the 19 long-term unemployed. Similarly, when asked if they did their hobbies more, less or the same, the results were as follows:

	More	Less	Same	Don't know
Regularly employed	4	—	2	—
Occasionally unemployed	3	2	2	1
Long-term unemployed	5	7	6	—

12. In answer to the question 'Do you feel isolated?' only 1 of the regularly employed did, 3 of the occasionally unemployed, and 10 of the 19 longer-term unemployed said 'yes'. Answers to the question 'Did you see your friends more, less or the same?' were as follows:

	More	Less	Same	Other
Regularly employed	3	2	1	—
Occasionally unemployed	1	3	3	1
Long-term unemployed	2	11	5	—

13. In answer to the question, 'Are your friends mostly employed or unemployed?' the responses were as follows:

	Mostly employed	Mostly unemployed	Half and half	Other
Occasionally unemployed	8	—	1	3
Long-term unemployed	9	5	4	1

Chapter 7

1. It is arguable that the family should be analysed in terms of an ideology, since normative roles are subscribed to even when in practice few people are able to conform to them. Hence, Porter (1983) found that men still thought of themselves as the 'bread-winners' even when their wives were earning more.

2. The main studies to have been carried out in this field are: the Family Formation Survey (Dunnell 1976) which covered a random sample of 6,589 women between the ages of sixteen and forty-nine; the longitudinal survey conducted by Schofield (1973) who interviewed 376 young people at ages eighteen and twenty-five; the study of fifty weddings in Swansea conducted by Leonard (1980) in 1967; and the National Child Development Study (Fogelman 1983). Whilst the OPCS survey provides detailed data across a representative range of the population, the surveys of Leonard and Schofield, whilst less representative and wide-ranging, provide a source of more general interpretative comment.

3. However, in Dunnell's (1976) survey, working-class women were just as likely to want a home of their own along with a variety of consumer durables – they simply did not expect to get these things.

4. Schofield attributes this to the 'contraceptive gap' between starting sexual activity – which happens younger amongst working-class youth – and starting to use contraception regularly. Whilst this has often been attributed to so-called ignorance on the part of the young person, there is also evidence to suggest that girls do not take regular contraception for fear of being labelled as 'easy' (Lees 1986).

5. It should be noted that whilst an association between domestic and employment careers was evident, these data are not sufficient to suggest any particular direction of causality.

6. I asked what form of contraception was used at the time that respondents had children.

7. A survey of this kind was carried out for the *Sunday People* in 1985 by Public Opinion Surveys. In this survey 1,006 girls aged between fifteen and twenty were interviewed in England, Scotland, and Wales between the 9th and 11th of March 1985. The main finding was that although girls were more likely to engage in sexual activity than had been the case in previous years, they did so within very 'traditional' constraints of having a 'steady' boyfriend and this activity was sanctioned by ideas of romantic love.

8. This was confirmed in a more systematic measurement of the domestic division of labour on Sheppey conducted as part of the SCPR survey (R. E. Pahl 1984).

9. Tenure of Sheppey households compared to Great Britain as a whole in 1981:

	Sheppey %	GB %
Owner-occupied	69	56
Public rented	22	31
Private rented	6	13
Other	3	—
Totals	730	19.5 million

Source: SCPR 1 in 9 household survey, Isle of Sheppey. 1981 census.

10. In answer to the question 'Do you feel more independent from your parents now?' 49 said 'yes' and 6 said 'no'. Of those who had experienced unemployment, 21 felt that they were more dependent upon their parents when they were unemployed and 11 said that it made no difference.

11. Roberts (1985) has argued that employment and unemployment may be superseding class in importance as a variable in his discussion of new patterns of transition in the 1980s.

12. The General Household Survey indicates that pre-marital cohabitation is increasing. Twenty-four per cent of women aged 16–34 cohabited before they married in 1979–82 where marriage was the first for both partners. This rose to 65 per cent where partners had been married before. This had risen from 8 per cent and 42 per cent respectively in the 1970–74 period (Social Trends 1985: 35).

Chapter 8

1. Jan Pahl's research into battered wives and into the allocation of money in the household indicated that wives often felt better off on social security than they had with their husbands. Moreover, it is evident that benefits paid to the head of the household do not necessarily reach the rest of the family (J. Pahl 1980).

Chapter 9

1. To some extent these conclusions are borne out in the more quantitative studies of age-differential responses to unemployment (Warr and Jackson 1984).

2. Work is currently being carried out along these lines by Burrage (1986), Jones (1986) at the University of Surrey and Jenkins and Hutson (1986).

3. The importance of the Fowler Review of Social Security for young people is discussed by Youthaid (1985).

References

Abrams, M. (1961) *The Teenage Consumer*. London: London Press Exchange.

Althusser, L. (1971) Ideology and Ideological State Apparatuses. In *Lenin and Philosophy and Other Essays*. London: New Left Books.

Apple, M. (ed) (1982) *Cultural and Economic Reproduction. Essays on Class, Ideology and the State*. London: Routledge and Kegan Paul.

Ashton, D. N. and Field, D. (1976) *Young Workers*. London: Hutchinson.

Ashton, D. N. and McGuire, M. (1980) The Function of Academic and Non-Academic Criteria in Employer's Selection of Strategies. *British Journal of Guidance and Counselling* 8 (2): 146–57.

Ashton, D. N. and McGuire, M. (1981) Employers Perceptions and the Use of Educational Qualifications. *Educational Analysis* 3(2).

Ashton, D. N., McGuire, M., and Garland, V. (1982) *Youth in the Labour Market*. Department of Employment Research Paper No. 34. London: HMSO.

Banks, M. and Jackson, P. R. (1982) Unemployment and the Risk of Minor Psychiatric Disorder in Young People: Cross-Sectional and Longitudinal Evidence *Psychological Medicine* 12: 789–798.

Barratt, M. (1980) *Women's Oppression Today*. London: Verso.

Barratt, M., Corrigan, P., Kuhn, A., and Wolff, J. (eds.) (1979) *Ideology and Cultural Reproduction*. London: Croom Helm.

Barron, R. and Norris, E. M. (1976) Sexual Divisions in the Dual Labour Market. In D. L. Barker, and S. Allen (eds.) *Dependence and Exploitation in Work and Marriage*. London: Longman.

Bates, I., Clarke, J., Cohen, P., Finn, D., Moore, R., and Willis, P. (1984) *Schooling For The Dole*, London: Macmillan.

Baxter, J. L. (1975) The Chronic Job Changer: A Study of Youth Unemployment. *Social and Economic Administration* 9 (3): 184–206.

Bazalgette, J. (1975) *School Life and Work Life*. London: Hutchinson.

Binns, D. and Mars, G. (1984) Family, Community and Unemployment: A Study in Change, *Sociological Review* 32 (4): 662–95.

Blackburn, R. M. and Mann, M. (1979) *The Working Class in the Labour Market*. London: Macmillan.

Bloxham, S. (1983) Social Behaviour and the Young Unemployed. In R. Fiddy *In Place of Work*. Lewes: Falmer Press.

Bourdieu, P. and Passeron, J. C. (1977))*Reproduction in Education, Society and Culture*. London: and Beverley Hills: Sage.

Bowles, S. and Gintis, H. (1976) *Schooling in Capitalist America: Educational Reform and the Contradictions of Economic Life*. London: Routledge and Kegan Paul.

Brake, M. (1980) *The Sociology of Youth Culture and Youth Sub-Culture*. London: Routledge and Kegan Paul.

Breakwell, G. (1985) Young People in and Out of Work. In B. Roberts, R. Finnegan, and D. Gallie, *New Approaches to Economic Life*. Manchester: Manchester University Press.

Brown, P. (1984) Schooling and the School/Post School Transition: An Early Assessment. Paper presented to BSA Conference, University of Bradford.

Brown, P. (1987) It Is a Job Being Adult: The Social and Educational Consequences of Changing Labour Market Conditions for School Levers. In P. Brown and D. Ashton *Education and Economic Life*. Lewes: Falmer.

Browne, K. (1981) Schooling, Capitalism and the Mental-Manual Division of Labour. *Sociological Review* 29 (3): 445–73.

Buck, N. H. (1981) An Admiralty Dockyard in Sheerness in the Mid-Nineteenth Century. Aspects of the Social and Economic History of Sheerness. Final Report to the ESRC Grant no. HR/6939/1.

Burrage, H. (1986) Premature Pregnancy and Parenthood. A Working Paper on Socio-economic Variables Associated with the Fertility of Young People in the City. Paper Presented to the BSA Conference, University of Loughborough.

Campbell, B. (1984) *Wigan Pier Revisited*. London: Virago Press.

Carter, M. P. (1962) *Home, School and Work*, Oxford: Pergamon Press.

Carter, M. P. (1966) *Into Work*, Harmondsworth: Penguin.

Carter, M. P. (1975) Teenage Workers. A Second Chance at Eighteen? In P. Brannen, (ed.) *Entering the World of Work. Some Sociological Perspectives*. Department of Employment. London: HMSO.

Chief Constable's Report for Kent (1982).

Cherry, N. (1976) Persistent Job Changing – Is it a Problem? *Journal of Occupational Psychology* 49: 203–21.

Clarke, L. (1978) The Transition from School to Work: A Critical Review of the Literature. Report No. 49. Department of Education and Science ESD2.

Coffield, F., Borrill, C., and Marshall, S. (1986) *Growing up at the Margins*. Milton Keynes: Open University Press.

Cohen, P. (1985) Rethinking the Youth Question. Post-16 Education Centre Working Paper No. 3. London: Institute of Education.

Colledge, M. (1977) Young People and Work. *Employment Gazette*. December 1977: 1345–347.

Cooper Clarke, J. (1983) *Ten Years in an Open Necked Shirt*. Colchester: Arrow Books.

Corrigan, P. (1979) *Schooling the Smash Street Kids*. London: Macmillan.

Cowie, L. and Lees, S. (1981) Slags or Drags. *Feminist Review* No. 9: 17–31.

Daly, A. A. (1904) *History of the Isle of Sheppey*. Sheerness: Cassell.

Davies, L. (1973) Gender, Resistance and Power. In S. Walker and L. Barton, *Gender, Class and Education*. Lewes: Falmer.

Deem, R. (1978) *Women and Schooling* London: Routledge and Kegan Paul.

Deem, R. (1982) Women, Leisure and Inequality. *Leisure Studies* 1: 29–46.

Doeringer, P. B. and Piore, M. J. (1971) *Internal Labour Markets and Manpower Analysis*. Lexington: D. C. Heath.

Donovan, A. and Oddy M. (1982) Psychological Aspects of Unemployment: An Investigation into the Emotional and Social Adjustment of School Leavers. *Journal of Adolescence* 5: 15–30.

Dunnell, K. (1976) *Family Formation*. OPCS. London: HMSO.

Economist Intelligence Unit (1982) *Coping with Unemployment: The Effects on the Unemployed Themselves*. London: Economist Intelligence Unit.

Edholm, F., Harris, O., and Young, K. (1977) Conceptualising Women. *Critique of Anthropology* 3 (9/10): 101–29.

Employment Gazette, October 1984 and October 1975. London: Department of Employment.

Eversley, D. and Bonnerjea, L. (1982) Social Change and Indicators of Diversity. In R. N. Rappoport *et al.* (eds.) *Families in Britain*. London: Routledge and Kegan Paul.

Finn, D. (1982) Whose Needs? Schooling and the Needs of Industry. In T. Rees and P. Atkinson (eds.) *Youth Unemployment and State Intervention*. London: Routledge and Kegan Paul.

Finn, D. (1984) Leaving School and Growing Up: Work Experience in a Juvenile Labour Market. In I. Bates *et al.* (eds). *Schooling for the Dole?* London: Macmillan.

Fogelman, K. (1983) *Growing up in Great Britain*. Papers From the National Child Development Study. London:Macmillan.

Gaskell, J. (1983) The Reproduction of Family Life: Perspectives of Male and Female Adolescents. *British Journal of Sociology of Education* 4 (1): 19–38.

Gill, C. (1985) *Work, Unemployment and the New Technology*. Oxford: Polity Press.

Golding, P. and Middleton, S. (1982) *Images of Welfare*. Oxford: Blackwell.

Goldthorpe, J. *et al.* (1969) *The Affluent Worker in the Class Structure*. Cambridge: Cambridge University Press.

Gray, G., Smith, A. and Rutter, M. (1980) School Attendance and First Year of Employment. In L. Hersov and I. Berg (eds.) *Out of School*. London: Wiley and Sons.

Greenwood, W. (1969) *Love on the Dole*. Harmondsworth: Penguin.

Gregory, D. and Urry, J. (eds) (1984) *Social Relations and Spatial Structures*. London: Macmillan.

Griffin, C. (1985) *Typical Girls?* London: Routledge and Kegan Paul.

Griffiths, V. (1986) Adolescent Girls: Transition from Girlfriends to Boyfriends? Paper Presented at the BSA Conference, University of Loughborough.

Gurney, R. M. (1980) The Effect of Unemployment upon the Psycho-Social Development of School Leavers. *Journal of Occupational Psychology* 53: 205–13.

Hall, S. and Jefferson, T. (eds) (1976) *Resistance Through Ritual*. London: Hutchinson.

Harris, C. C. (1977) Changing Conceptions of the Relations Between Family and Societal Forms in Western Society. In R. Scase (ed.) *Industrial Society: Class, Cleavage and Control*. London: Routledge and Kegan Paul.

Harris, C. C. (1986) The Individual and Society: A Processual Approach. Plenary Paper Presented at the BSA Conference, University of Loughborough.

Hendry, L. and Raymond, M. (1983) Youth Unemployment, Leisure and Lifestyles: Some Educational Considerations. *Scottish Educational Review* 15, 1: 28–40.

Henry, S. (1982) The Working Unemployed: Perspectives on the Informal Economy and Unemployment. *Sociological Review* 30(3): 460–77.

Holland Report (1977) *Young People and Work*. London: Manpower Services Commission.

Hunt, P. (1980) *Gender and Class Consciousness*. London: Macmillan.

Hutson, S. and Jenkins, R. (1987) Coming of Age in South Wales. In Brown, P. and Ashton, D. N. (eds) *Education and Economic Life*. Lewes: Falmer Press.

Ineichen, B. (1977) Youthful Marriage: the Vortex of Disadvantage. In J. Peel and R Chester (eds.) *Equalities and Inequalities in Family Life*. London: Academic Press.

Ineichen, B. (1981) The Housing Decisions of Young People. *British Journal of Sociology* 32 (2): 252–58.

Jackson, P. and Warr, P. (1983) Unemployment and Psychological Ill-Health: The Moderating Role of Duration and Age. MRC/ESRC Social and Applied Psychology Unit, Memo No. 585.

Jackson, P., Stafford, E. M., Banks, M. H., and Warr, P. B. (1983) Unemployment and Psychological Distress in Young People: The Moderating Role of Employment Commitment. *Journal of Applied Psychology* 68 (3): 525–35.

Jahoda, M. (1982) Employment and Unemployment. *A Social Psychological Analysis*. Cambridge: Cambridge University Press.

Jenkins, R. (1982) Managers, Recruitment Practices and Black Workers. Working Papers in Ethnic Relations No. 18. ESRC Research Unit on Ethnic Relations: University of Aston.

Jenkins, R. (1983) *Lads, Citizens and Ordinary Kids. Working Class Youth Life-Styles in Belfast*. London: Routledge and Kegan Paul.

Jones, G. (1986) Youth in the Social Structure: Transitions to Adulthood and their Stratification by Class and Gender. PhD thesis, University of Surrey.

Jones, G. (1987) Leaving the Parental Home: An Analysis of Early Hosing Careers. *Journal of Social Policy* (forthcoming).

Jones, P. *et al.* (1981) *Out of School. A Case Study of the Role of Government Schemes at a Time of Growing Unemployment* MSC Special Programmes Occasional Paper No. 4. Sheffield: Manpower Services Commission.

Land, H. (1978) Who Cares for the Family? *Journal of Social Policy* 7 (3) pp. 257–86.

Lees, S. (1986) *Losing Out. Sexuality and Adolescent Girls.* London: Hutchinson.

Leonard, D. (1980) *Sex and Generation: A Study of Courtship and Weddings.* London: Tavistock.

MacDonald, M. (1980) Socio-Cultural Reproduction and Women's Education. In R. Deem, *Schooling for Women's Work.* London: Routledge and Kegan Paul.

MacIntyre, S. (1985) Gynaecologist/Woman Interaction. In C. Ungerson (ed.) *Women and Social Policy.* London: Macmillan.

McRobbie, A. (1978) Working Class Girls and the Culture of Femininity. In Women's Studies Group, Centre for Contemporary Cultural Studies, *Women Take Issue.* London: Hutchinson.

McRobbie, A. and Garber, J. (1976) Girls and Subcultures: An Exploration. In Hall, S. and Jefferson, T. *Resistance Through Rituals.* London: Hutchinson.

Maizels, J. (1970) *Adolescent Needs and the Transition from School to Work.* University of London: Athlone Press.

Makeham, P. (1980) Youth Unemployment. Department of Employment Research Paper No. 10, London: Department of Employment.

Markall, G. (1980) *The Best Years of Their Lives. Schooling, Work and Unemployment in Oldfield.* William Temple Foundation Occasional Paper No. 3.

Marx, K. (1975) Economic and Philosophical Manuscripts. In *Marx: Early Writings.* Harmondsworth: Penguin.

Mathews, K. (1983) National Income and the Black Economy. *Journal of Economic Affairs* 3 (4): 261–67.

Meillasoux, C. (1975) *Maidens, Meal and Money.* Cambridge: Cambridge University Press.

Miles, I. (1983) Adaptation to Unemployment. SPRU Occasional Paper No. 20, Sussex University.

Morris, L. (1985) Renegotiation of the Domestic Division of Labour in the Context of Male Redundancy. In Roberts, B., Finnegan, R., and Gallie, D. *New Approaches to Economic Life.* Manchester: Manchester University Press.

Mungham, G. and Pearson, G. (eds.) (1976) *Working Class Youth Culture.* London: Routledge and Kegan Paul.

National Youth Employment Council (1974) *Untrained, Unqualified and Unemployed.* Department of Employment. London: HMSO.

Newsom Report (1963) *Half Our Future.* Report of the Central Advisory Council for Education. London: HMSO.

Organisation for Economic Co-operation and Development (OECD) (1977) *Entry of Young People into Working Life.* Paris: OECD.

Orwell, G. (1937) *The Road to Wigan Pier.* Harmondsworth: Penguin (1977).

Pahl, J. (1980) Patterns of Money Management Within Marriage. *Journal of Social Policy* 9 (3): 313–35.

Pahl, R. E. (1978) How School Leavers See Their Future. *New Society* 46 (839) (November): 259–62.

Pahl, R. E. (1984) *Divisions of Labour.* Oxford: Blackwell.

Pahl, R. E. and Wallace, C. D. (1980) 17–19 and Unemployed on the Isle of Sheppey. Report to the Department of Employment, London: HMSO.

Pahl, R. E. and Wallace, C. D. (1985) Forms of Work and Privatisation on the Isle of Sheppey. In B. Roberts, R. Finnegan, and D. Gallie (eds.) *New Approaches to Economic Life.* Manchester: Manchester University Press.

Pahl, R. E. and Wilson, P. (1984) A Statistical Portrait of the Isle of Sheppey. Final Report to the ESRC Appendix 1. Grant No. G/00/23/0036.

Pahl, R. E. with Dennett, J. (1981) Industry and Employment on the Isle of Sheppey. Interim Report to the ESRC.

Parker, H. (1976) Boys Will Be Men: Brief Adolescence in a Down Town Neighbourhood. In G. Mungham and G. Pearson (eds.) *Working Class Youth Cultures.* London: Routledge and Kegan Paul.

Phillips, D. (1973) Young and Unemployed in a Northern City. In D. Wier (ed.) *Men and Work in Modern Britain.* London: Fontana.

Pollert, A. (1981) *Girls, Wives and Factory Lives.* London: Macmillan.

Porter, M. (1983) *Home and Work.* London: Macmillan.

Poster, C. (1971) *The School and the Community.* London: Macmillan.

Presdee, M. (1986) Agony or Ecstasy: Broken Transitions and the New Social State of Working Class Youth in Australia. BSA Conference Paper, University of Loughborough.

Raffe, D. (1984) The Transition from School to Work and the Recession: Evidence from the Scottish School Leavers Survey 1979–1983. *British Journal of the Sociology of Education.* 5, 1: 247–66.

Raffe, D. (1987) The Context of the Youth Training Scheme: An Analysis of its Strategy and Development. *British Journal of Education and Work* (forthcoming).

Roberts, K. (1968) The Entry into Employment: An Approach Towards a General Theory. Reprinted in W. M. Williams (ed.) (1974) *Occupational Choice.* London: Allen and Unwin.

Roberts, K. (1984) *School Leavers and Their Prospects.* Milton Keynes: Open University Press.

Roberts, K. (1985) ESRC Young People in Society/16–19 Initiative. A Sociological View of the Issues. Mimeo. Liverpool: University of Liverpool/ESRC.

Roberts, K., Duggan, J., and Noble, M. (1981) Unregistered Youth Unemployment and Outreach Careers Work. Department of Employment Research Paper No. 31. London: Department of Employment.

Roberts, K., Duggan, J., and Noble, M. (1982a) Youth Unemployment: An Old Problem or a New Lifestyle? *Leisure Studies* 1 (2): 71–182.

Roberts, K., Duggan, J., and Noble, M. (1982b) Out of School Youth in High Unemployment Areas: An Empirical Investigation. *British Journal of Guidance and Counselling*. 10 (1): 1–11.

Roberts, K., Duggan, J., and Noble, M. (1982c) Unregistered Youth Unemployment and Outreach Careers Work. Department of Employment Research Paper No. 32. London: Department of Employment.

Schofield, M. (1973) *The Sexual Behaviour of Young Adults*. London: Allen Lane.

Shacklady Smith, L. (1978) Sexist Assumptions and Female Delinquency. In C. Smart and B. Smart, *Women, Sexuality and Social Control*. London: Routledge and Kegan Paul.

Sharpe, S. (1976) *Just Like a Girl*. Harmondsworth: Penguin.

Sheppey School Report 1984.

Sinfield, A. (1981) *What Unemployment Means*. Oxford: Martin Robertson.

Social Trends 15 (1985) Central Statistical Office. London: HMSO.

Social Trends 16 (1986) Central Statistical Office. London: HMSO.

Solomos, J (1986) The Social and Political Context of Black Youth Unemployment: A Decade of Policy Developments and the Limits of Reform. In L. Barton and S. Walker, *Youth, Unemployment and Schooling*. Milton Keynes: Open University Press.

Spender, D. and Sarah, E. (eds.) (1980) *Learning to Lose. Sexism and Education*, London: Women's Press.

Stafford, E. (1982) The Impact of the Youth Opportunities Programme on Young People's Employment Prospects and Psychological Well-Being. *British Journal of Guidance and Counselling* 10 (1): 12–21.

Stanley, L. and Wise, S. (1983) *Breaking Out: Feminist Consciousness and Feminist Research*. London: Routledge and Kegan Paul.

Stokes, G. (1981) The Psychological and Social Consequences of Economically Precipitated Stress, PhD thesis, University of Birmingham.

The Sunday People, Sex and the Teenage Girl. Survey Report 12 and 19 May 1985.

Taylor, R. (1978) Marilyn's Friends and Rita's Customers: A Study of Party Selling as Play and as Work. *Sociological Review* 26 (3): 573–94.

Thompson, E. P. (1967) Time, Work Discipline and Industrial Capitalism. *Past and Present* 38: 56–96.

Wallace, C. D.. (1984) Informal Work in Two Sheppey Neighbourhoods. Final Report to the ESRC Appendix 11. Grant no. G/00/23/0036.

Wallace, C. D. (1985) School, Work and Unemployment. Social and Cultural Reproduction on the Isle of Sheppey. PhD thesis, University of Kent, Faculty of Social Sciences.

Wallace, C. D. (1986) From Boys and Girls to Women and Men: The Transition from School to (Un)employment. In L. Barton and S. Walker (eds.) *Youth, Unemployment, and Schooling*. Milton Keynes: Open University Press.

Wallace, C. D. (1987) From Generation to Generation: The Effects of Employment and Unemployment upon the Transition to Adulthood. In P. Brown and D. N. Ashton (eds.) *Education and Economic Life*. Lewes: Falmer.

Wallace, C. D. and Pahl, R. E. (1986) Polarisation, Unemployment and All Forms of Work. In S. Allen, K. Purcell, A. Watson, and S. Wood (eds.) *The Experience of Unemployment*. London: Macmillan (forthcoming).

Wallace, C. D. with Pahl, R. E. and Dennett, J. (1981) Housing and Residential Areas on the Isle of Sheppey. Interim Report to the ESRC.

Walsgrove, D. (1984) Policing Yourself: Youth Unemployment, Individualism and the Amplification of Normality. Paper Presented to the BSA Conference, University of Bradford.

Warr, P. (1982) A National Study of Non-Financial Employment Commitment. *Journal of Occupational Psychology* 55: 207–312.

Warr, P. (1983) Work, Jobs, and Unemployment. *Bulletin of the British Psychological Society* 36: 305–11.

Warr, P., and Jackson, P. (1984) Men Without Jobs: Some Correlation of Age and Length of Unemployment. *Journal of Ocupational Psychology* 57: 77–85.

Warr, P. and Parry, G. (1982) Paid Employment and Women's Psychological Well-Being. *Psychological Bulletin* 91 (3): 498–516.

Watts, A. G. (ed.) (1983) *Education, Employment and the Future of Work*. Milton Keynes: Open University Press.

West, M. and Newton, P. (1983) *The Transition from School to Work*. London: Croom Helm.

White Paper (1981) *A New Training Initiative*. Cmnd. 8455. London: HMSO.

Willis, P. (1977) *Learning to Labour*. Farnborough: Saxon Houuse.

Willis, P. (1981) Cultural Production Is Different From Cultural Reproduction. *Interchange* 12 (2–3): 48–77.

Willis, P. (1984a) Youth Unemployment 1. A New State. *New Society*, 29 March, pp. 475–77.

Willis, P. (1984b) Youth Unemployment 2. Ways of Living. *New Society*, 5 April, pp. 13–15.

Wilson, D. (1978) Sexual Codes and Conduct. In B. Smart and C. Smart. *Women, Sexuality and Social Control*. London: Routledge and Kegan Paul.

Youthaid (1981) *Study of the Transition from School to Working Life*. Vols. 1–3. London: Youthaid.

Youthaid. (1985) *The Fowler Review. Effects on Young People*. London: Youthaid.

Name index

Subject index